International Media Studies

Divya C. McMillin

Blackwell
Publishing

BLACKWELL PUBLISIIING
350 Main Street, Malden, MA 02148-5020, USA
9600 Garsington Road, Oxford OX4 2DQ, UK
550 Swanston Street, Carlton, Victoria 3053, Australia

First published 2007 by Blackwell Publishing Ltd

1   2007

Library of Congress Cataloging-in-Publication Data

McMillin, Divya C. (Divya Carolyn).
   International media studies / Divya C. McMillin.
      p.   cm.
   Includes bibliographical references and index.
   ISBN-13: 978-1-4051-1809-5 (hardcover : alk. paper)
   ISBN-10: 1-4051-1809-1 (hardcover : alk. paper)
   ISBN-13: 978-1-4051-1810-1 (pbk. : alk. paper)
   ISBN-10: 1-4051-1810-5 (pbk. : alk. paper)
1. Communication, International.   2. Globalization.   I. Title.

   P96.I5M359 2007
   302.2—dc22

                                        2006020374

A catalogue record for this title is available from the British Library.

Set in 10.5 on 13 pt Dante
by SNP Best-set Typesetter Ltd, Hong Kong
Printed and bound in Singapore
by Cos Printers Pte Ltd

The publisher's policy is to use permanent paper from mills that operate a sustainable forestry
policy, and which has been manufactured from pulp processed using acid-free and elementary
chlorine-free practices. Furthermore, the publisher ensures that the text paper and cover board
used have met acceptable environmental accreditation standards.

For further information on
Blackwell Publishing, visit our website:
www.blackwellpublishing.com

International Media Studies

This book is dedicated to Andy, Sitara, and Suneri

Contents

Preface

"I'm here because my job was outsourced to India," deadpanned Terry,[1] a middle-aged, Senior student in my "Global Networks, Local Identities" class on the first day of Fall quarter 2003, at the University of Washington Tacoma. A few other students sighed and nodded understandingly. My opening lecture describing some of my fieldwork examining the role of television in the lives of sweatshop laborers in transnational electronic assembly factories in Bangalore, India, sparked a variety of questions about the social conditions of the laborers, their work safety, and their medical and retirement benefits. By the end of the session, the 40-student class, more than half over the age of 35 and returning to school because they had been laid off work, were seeking promotions, or new employment, were deep in conversation about the stark realities of unemployment and less than desirable work facing them and laborers in India. No doubt the inequities in standard of living, social privilege, and structural support were vastly different between the students sitting in a brand new classroom with state-of-the-art technology and the precarious work conditions of the laborers in Bangalore (see McMillin 2003a). However, what was obvious was the interconnection and interdependency that bound them through some of the processes of globalization such as outsourcing and capitalist expansion. The media's position in facilitating these processes was apparent in both contexts.

The stark, real, and immediate social and economic implications of globalization, particularly media globalization, are felt by students and citizens around the world, but have not received sufficient attention in undergraduate text books on international communication (which refers to communication across national borders) and international media studies (which pertains to empirical analyses undertaken in the field). For my non-traditional, predominantly working-class students living in or around the blue-collar, port city of Tacoma, learning about global media networks such as BBC, CNN, and Star

TV was interesting; examining ideologies of gender, class, ethnicity, and orientation, fascinating. Yet the historicity and consequences of these structures were marginally addressed in most of their international media textbooks.

To bring to the fore the structuring of global media power and its local manifestations and implications, I embarked on this book project. Its mission is closely aligned with my teaching philosophy, which places the student as a self-learner, seeking connections between knowledge and activism. A wealth of literature exists on international communication, describing global and national media systems. These texts contribute greatly to our understanding of media giants located in the United States, Great Britain, Germany, France, Italy, and Japan. Yet, similarities and differences in media systems as they relate to colonial histories, particularly in non-western countries, are mostly absent. Studies of media content and reception are invariably housed in anthologies, understandably so because of the particularities of context. Most of these anthologies begin or end with calls for comparative analyses to draw out the cultural and media flows across and within nations. Yet comparisons themselves are difficult to assess because of the independent chapter structure of edited books.

The purpose of this book, explained further in Chapter One, is to place before the media scholar, the historicity and continuity in structures of colonialism, postcolonialism, and media globalization around the world. Obviously these are not clearly demarcated processes and colonized countries have been implicated centrally in such processes as much as their colonial masters who have been the focus of a majority of theory and research in international communication. In its linkage of case studies to interdisciplinary theory, the book draws the reader into various strains of critical dialogue in the field – a dialogue that has predominantly, and unfortunately, been the prerogative of graduate studies. The scope of case studies included then, is necessarily broad. Theoretical interpretations that connect case studies could merit individual books themselves, and are provided in this book inasmuch as they advance the narrative and contextualize the examples. Through this strategy, the book presents to the reader crucial theoretical issues in the field and demonstrates how they are grounded (or not) in reality.

The book also attempts to recharge international media research with the political energy that informed its origins, particularly in Latin America and South Asia. It identifies the significant moments in political and academic history that have fashioned international media studies, and through extensive examples, lays bare areas that require further research. Such a task is undertaken recognizing the theoretically and empirically rich writing that has gone before, and piecing together such writing to offer a comparative and ethical analysis of the field. The postcolonial framework informs this project for its direct and stunningly clear focus on the historicity of international interactions and its activist component that awards the student some direction for social justice.

To be used in an upper division or graduate class in international media, the book would do well to be situated within a framework that addresses the interconnections and interdependencies of globalization. Class lectures and accompanying readings could address comparative themes rather than nation-specific analyses. Educational videos portraying the social and cultural effects of globalization in general, and media globalization, in particular, will bring home to the student, the implications of transnational corporations and media networks. Class assignments could move beyond syntheses of theory or studies of national media systems. They could incorporate film and television analyses to draw out how community and identity are represented in such texts, and could include community-based multimedia projects that address the possibilities of activism through media. The similarities between development issues of peripheral communities within the United States and around the world can be drawn out through such projects and students will have the opportunity to make direct connections between theory and praxis. I have implemented elements of these in my classes on global media and development communication, with positive results. The book may be used in courses on international media, cultural studies, and postcolonial studies.

Acknowledgments

My debts in developing this layered book are huge. Structural support is essential for any endeavor, and the University of Washington has been a steadying hand in this regard. Through a UW President's Faculty Development Fellowship, Royalty Research Fund, 2005–06 research sabbatical, and consecutive UW-Tacoma Founder's Endowment Grants spanning 1998 to 2006, I have been able to conduct extensive fieldwork explorations in India and examine processes of media globalization from various dimensions of production and consumption. Students in my global media, development communication, and cultural studies classes kept me sensitive to the needs of my target readers. In particular, Lisa Kuruvilla provided a fresh perspective to the opening arguments of the book.

Ethnographic fieldwork among urban, semi-urban, and rural teenagers and families, sweatshop workers, and call center employees, has allowed me to address questions of audience agency and subjectivity through a complex and interdisciplinary framework. I am thankful to all my respondents who candidly discussed their lives and media habits with me, trusting me to represent their stories fairly. Further, although a separate project, funding from the Internationales Zentralinstitut für das Jugend- und Bildungsfernsehen (IZI), Bayerischer Rundfunk, Munich (2004–6), expanded my research to pre-teens and teenagers, adding depth in terms of theory and methodology to my approach to the book.

At Blackwell Publishers, Jayne Fargnoli, who approached me to write this book, provided feedback on the proposal and, through nuanced questions and advice, did much to help refine the proposal. Ken Provencher steadily supported the book's progress, Susan Dunsmore provided close copy-editing, and Linda Auld ably managed the book's production. I am grateful to the anonymous reviewers of the proposal and book manuscript. Their detailed suggestions for improvement demonstrated a close reading of the text and resulted

11

in a manuscript that is all the better for their scrutiny. The thoroughness of their review conveyed a sense of collegiality and reinforced to me our primary role as educators: to make our teaching and writing as accessible and critical as we can to our communities of learners and co-educators.

Apart from money and time, personal and emotional support are crucial. I thank my mother, friend, and colleague, Susheela, for advising me on post-colonial literature, assisting me with fieldwork, and cooking my favorite dishes when I craved them most. Her guidance, professionally and personally, has sustained me for as long as I can remember. My father David's strong advice to live in the present (a challenge for someone intrigued by colonial pasts) kept me grounded through the highs and lows of research and fieldwork. I have drawn great strength from the bond I share with my sisters. My eldest sister Arathi was instrumental in locating key respondents and facilitating interviews for several stages of my fieldwork. Her home, family, and nurturance will always have a special place in my academic career. My sister Pavithra, with her encouraging emails and phone calls, niece Koel and nephews Shaurya, Roshin and Kirin, sister Harsha, with regular accounts of her family life, reminded me that there was more to life than just academia. My brothers-in-law, Vikram, Paul, and Tony, kept my spirits up with their endless supply of jokes and inane observations.

My husband Andy's faith in my writing has helped me, through this and other research projects. Our vibrant 4-year-old, Sitara, continues to flit, carefree, through her world of ladybugs, spiders, and birds, because of Andy's tender shoulder-to-shoulder parenting, even through his own demanding work. I thank both of them for their patience and support. Our newborn Suneri, who grew to term with this book, endured long hours in front of the computer and I thank her for adding so much to our lives already.

Divya McMillin
August 2006

Chapter One

Introduction

Suddenly the world seems wobbly. The still centers of power, be they ex-colonizers like Great Britain or contemporary economic and military giants like the United States, are teetering just a bit, looking to communities on the periphery to balance their ever increasing need for human and material resources. China and India are the new hot spots and American media conservatives theorize that the outsourcing of particularly high and low tech jobs to these nations means that we are finally witnessing the birth of a flat world where equal economic opportunities await the qualified urbanite (Friedman 2005). India in particular is the latest object of capitalist desire with US President George W. Bush standing in line with France's Jacques Chirac, Saudi Arabia's King Abdullah, and Australian Prime Minister John Howard to assess its further potential as a labor and R&D base (Zakaria 2006). Such transactions and interdependencies between countries are touted as sure evidence of globalization where national boundaries are submerged in transnational flows of labor and capital. Global media networks facilitate such flows and provide a common image and language currency for transnational actors to draw from. Declarations of an even playing field are heady no doubt, but are ideological constructs of entrenched structures of difference, as we shall explore in this book.

Liberalization reforms in the 1980s that swept across many countries in the tri continent,[1] that is, Africa, Asia, and Latin America, and media globalization, beginning arguably with the advent of satellite television in the early 1990s, have provided exciting new ground for research in international communication. Hybrid media products that showcase elements of global, national, and local, and the greater variety of consumer choices in local markets around the world, have led to theoretical speculations that most tri continent nations now stand on the firm grounds of modernity. Globalization is seen as a consequence of modernity (Mudibme-Boyi 2002), and has been labeled as an era of cultural convergence and of universal imperatives driven by a global market logic (Mattelart 2003). The globalization of media has been regarded as a homogenizing force, promoting integration and hindering cultural resistance. It has been described as a regionalizing force as well, where regional media giants such as movie industries in India, Egypt, and Latin America, distribute their products to audiences in their respective subcontinents, and, to a limited extent, compete with the global media giants situated in the industrialized[2] world (Thussu 1998). These regional geolinguistic markets have undercut the dominance of global media corporations and global-local[3] alliances have created new structures of production and consumption. Audience studies highlight the possibilities of agency and resistance because of the sheer diversity of choices available to consumers hitherto limited by state-controlled media and markets.

This book assesses the trajectories research in international communication have taken, and historicizes contemporary processes of media globalization. Beginning with an overview of the dominant paradigms of the field, it shifts focus from national media systems and the fixity of nation-states to transnational media phenomena that reveal nodes of interconnectivity and interdependence. Numerous examples are used throughout in discussions of media systems and rituals of media consumption to illustrate these interconnections. Using a postcolonial theoretical framework that is critical, interdisciplinary, international, historical, and multicultural, the book delves into contemporary media phenomenon from around the world to posit that theories of media globalization have to carve out a space that is distinct from Eurocentric, political economy-biased theories of international communication. It does not address the wealth of research that exists on diasporic communities, to maintain its focus on tri continent production and consumption contexts. The book, although drawing in descriptions of the function of print media (for the most part a privatized elite medium in many tri continent countries), will necessarily highlight the role of television, and to a certain extent radio, as an important tool in the construction of the postcolonial nation. This is because television was positioned at the apex of modernity in the 1950s and 1960s in the west (Ang 1996) and logically followed this positioning in postcolonial governments of the tri continent, themselves heavily influenced by colonial traditions as well as the dominant paradigm of mass communication research in the same era.

The postcolonial framework is one that is continuously engaged in the location of power. It recognizes the continuity of structures of domination through precolonial, colonial, and postcolonial eras (Pieterse and Parekh 1995), and interrogates the causes and consequences of enduring hierarchies of power. Use of this framework in this project is informed by the work of such scholars as Spivak (1988a, b), Guha (1994), Prakash (1990), Mukherjee (1996), Vijaykumar (1996) and Trivedi (1996), to name but a few engaged in the debate of such terms. The intent of the book is not merely to engage in the work of the negative (to borrow from Spivak), but to point to ways in which scholars of global media processes can advance their own empirical research and build theory, particularly in the neglected area of television production and reception in Africa, Asia, and Latin America. In doing so, it does not blandly deconstruct only western structures of imperialism but critiques those of the non-western as well, keeping in mind Chow's admonition that:

> [U]ntil and unless we grant non-Western authors and texts – be these texts of fiction, theory, film, popular music, or criticism – the same kind of verbal, psychical, theoretical density and complexity that we have copiously endowed upon Western authors and texts, we will never be able to extricate our readings from the kind of idealism in which the East–West divide... is currently mired. (1998, p. xxi)

Postcolonial studies are comparative and as explained in various parts of the book, they refer to the texts and practices of formerly colonized countries, to the historical processes of colonization they experienced, and to the psychological impact of the experience. Postcolonial theory is an academic endeavor that seeks to investigate the Enlightenment claims of universality and the "originality" of European legal and social practices. To work with a postcolonial framework means to understand the "nation" as a heterogeneous space, one with uneven development, always under construction, and never complete. Rather than merely addressing the interrelatedness of north–south and center–periphery dichotomies, a critical postcolonial position is engaged "with the underlying problem of opening up critical spaces for new narratives of becoming and emancipation" (Venn 2006, p. 1). Yet, as Young (2003, p. 7) points out, the term "postcolonial" is an unpopular one because it unsettles existing hierarchies and threatens privilege. Its radical stance rejects the assumed superiority of Western cultures and instead, demands equality and well-being across the world. The radical agenda is useful for the premise of this book in its intent to connect theory to avenues of activism in the field. In particular, it problematizes the romanticization of consumer agency in media globalization.

To explain, the diversity of media and other consumer products in the local marketplace is often equated with freedom and autonomy of the consumer. Liberal market logic assumes that consumers make informed choices and that government interference by way of regulations and policies are antithetical to the freedom of both markets and consumers (Herman and McChesney 2003).

In an age of media globalization, the implications of this logic in developing societies have to be assessed critically before we raise the flag on a borderless world of limitless choice and democratic participation. The following example illustrates this point.

In August 2003, newspapers in the Indian subcontinent broke the scandalous allegation that at least 12 soft drinks marketed by Coca-Cola and PepsiCo contained dangerously high levels of pesticides. Touting this as yet another example of ruthless US domination, newspaper editorials and political conservatives across the nation called for a boycott of the drinks and for more stringent quality controls in Indian manufacturing plants. The Delhi-based Centre for Science and Environment (CSE), collected samples randomly from various soft drinks including Coca-Cola, Pepsi, and Mountain Dew, and, using a US Environment Protection Agency protocol, found that 87 percent of the samples contained high levels of toxic pesticides such as DDT and its metabolites, lindane, chlorphyrifos, and malathion (agents that could induce cancer, fetal malformations, and genetic changes, respectively) at levels 14 to 36 times higher than the standard (*The Deccan Herald*, Aug. 6, 2003, p. 1). With consumption of over 6.5 billion bottles per year, the soft drinks market is a big-money sector in India. The Indian parliament in Delhi stopped the supply of soft drinks at its sessions (*The Deccan Herald*, Aug. 7, 2003, p. 1) and Opposition members in Karnataka demanded a boycott of soft drinks in the state (*The Deccan Herald*, Aug. 7, 2003, p. 4).

Yet within cities, people continued their soft drink consumption, for the most part, unconcerned by the controversy. For example, consumers interviewed around Bangalore city by the *Deccan Herald* newspaper during the week of the breaking story were nonchalant about the furor. "I don't get the taste of pesticide in my Pepsi," Mamta, a student of fashion designing was reported to have said. Another, an engineering student claimed, "I don't think it's that big a deal." Finally, a mother was reported as saying, "I am not totally convinced about this. This is a transnational product and I haven't asked my children to stop drinking Pepsi." Her children were used to Pepsi and had not faced any health problems, she said. Soft drink sales around the city remained brisk (*The Deccan Herald*, Aug. 7, 2003, p. B). Pepsi sponsorship of popular television programs such as the long-running, call-in music video show, *Pepsi Ungal Choice* (Pepsi (is) Your Choice) on the private, Tamil-language Sun TV network, and Coke's co-branding with McDonald's ensured the soft drinks stayed in India's urban imaginary as advocates of people's choices and their freedom to choose from a diversified and liberalized market. The nonchalant response of soft drink consumers around the city cannot be interpreted as mere individual ignorance or a lack of concern for personal and familial health that would be unacceptable in Western contexts. Such responses can be understood as symbols of the consumers' idealistic faith in the foreign product, assuming that it has been subjected to rigorous health and safety standards that local products may not receive. These responses are emblematic of the residual yet potent ordering of the ex-colonized and colonizer structure where the Western product (despite the fact that it is produced on local soil) is seen as superior and therefore, of good quality. The responses also convey a cultural acceptance of daily rituals as part of a larger flow of life where it seems unnecessary to make a big fuss over mundane routines. They should be regarded as representative of a complex cultural fabric rather than an autonomous consumer agency.

Despite political opposition and the stark reality of possibly toxic consumer products on the local market, the "so what?" consumption of the vilified soft drinks is triumphantly held up as evidence of the people's freedom to choose. With lax safety regulations by the nation-state and the lack of awareness-raising campaigns on the dangers of ingesting the tainted products, the fetishization of consumer agency becomes easy. Such an environment provides rich ground for profit for transnational media networks that see themselves as having a finger on the pulse of local audiences and consumers in a way no government can. The retreat of the nation-state in an era of globalization that is accompanied by aggressive capitalist expansion in societies that have unevenly developed infrastructures to support such expansion, translates into a field of opportunities for foreign investors. To be able to understand what people want to see on television and deliver it to them in formats that are aesthetically pleasing and progressive, bracketed within advertisements for products that can extend program identities to the viewer is truly the winning strategy global media networks hope to achieve.

The issue of people's choices in the global market was precisely the reasoning used by top executives of such networks as the BBC and Animal Planet to debunk the myth of cultural imperialism at a November 9, 2004, symposium entitled "Television and Globalization: An East–West Symposium on the Cultural Marketplace," at the Boston University School of Management. The senior vice-president and general manager of Animal Planet International stated that the networks' co-productions with local media companies in China and India, its use of local talent behind and in front of the camera, and its focus on what he called "local stickiness," that is, the appeal factor of content for local audiences, all proved that local audiences and consumers were integral components of the program production process; they were not mere recipients of foreign programming and products as is the primary accusation of cultural imperialism.

If we are to follow this liberal pluralist market logic, we can find ample evidence of people's choices vs. government mandates across the world. To continue with the Indian example, while the national government decries, at various historic moments, the pollution of Indian culture through foreign products in the Indian marketplace (*The Times of India*, Aug. 14, 1997, pp. 7, 11) or through aggressively commercial-oriented television programming (McMillin 2001), audience consumption of products and programs remains high and the labor supply for various transnational corporations (TNCs) – be they call centers, sweat shops, ancillary factories, or even pyramid marketing schemes – stays plentiful. For low-skilled sweat-shop workers, semi-skilled call center employees, or even highly skilled doctors and information technology (IT) professionals, TNCs provide a wide variety of job opportunities simply unavailable before the nation's economic liberalization policy in 1991.

Media globalization brings to the fore the tension between boundary maintenance and economic liberalization; it shows the adaptation and opportunism of the people, primarily because these are the best options available. But the focus only on people's choices as an indicator of the presence, or not, of culturally imperialistic processes, is misguided. It negates the power of structure by diverting attention solely to cultural rituals and romanticizing the agency of consumers. The equation of audience choices with audience freedom and autonomy in a capitalist environment, presumes that the audience is a coherent and contained unit. The logics of democratic capitalism, be they liberalist pluralist or market, converge and audiences are seen as clearly demarcated demographic and psychographic segments (Ang 1996).

In particular, globalization keenly affects women and women's issues around the world. With the global expansion of transnational production units to tri continent countries, women are drawn into the labor force in ways that reinforce their subjective positioning within a patriarchal structure. If we are to study media globalization in any real sense, we have to scrutinize the interconnections and interdependencies among countries, between state and transnational structure and popular and local cultures, and understand how historical processes such as colonization and imperialism translate into contemporary social, political, and economic power differentials.

In a networked world, the question of media power becomes a central one. It is *"an emergent form of social power* in complex societies whose basic infrastructure depends increasingly on the fast circulation of information and images" (Couldry and Curran 2003, p. 4, emphasis in original). The damning legacy of the Eurocentric conceptualization of the modern nation and the corresponding positivist paradigm of development communication in international media studies has led to a construction of a world of dichotomies: North–South, East–West, First World–Third World, Occident–Orient, and so on. Yet some centers contain peripheries within them as in the slums of inner cities of the

United States, and some peripheries have become financial and industrial centers such as Singapore, South Korea, and Hong Kong. Despite the complex flows of people, media, finances, ideologies, and technologies across the world (Appadurai 1992), the field of international communication is still dominated by analyses that perpetuate these dichotomies.

The position that the opening up of people's choices in various markets of the world signifies the demise of cultural imperialism, is to completely sidestep the issue of power. The social effects of such choices, the uneven development, and short-term benefits that accrue from these choices, all in the face of huge economic profits for transnational media giants, have to be identified and assessed before we can celebrate the emergence of a border-less world where cultural imperialism exists only in theory, not in reality. The liberalist view that a free market encourages diversity and limits government control must be tempered by the fact that in such an environment, diversity of discourses is quelled and corporate ideology upheld (Ma 2000; McMillin 2003a).

The challenges of comparative study are significant – colonial histories differ markedly from region to region and between countries from the same region. Development experiences vary between one country and its neighbor based on political and social structures, and entrenched traditions, religions, and languages. The book conducts a comparative analysis nevertheless, focusing on countries of the tri continent to bring to the fore the experiences of areas normally excluded or marginalized in discussions of global media. At the same time, careful attention is paid to exceptions, so as not to fall into the trap of the postcolonial generalist, lumping all ex-colonies under one umbrella of experience (Chow 1996). Appadurai (1996, p. 11) points out that in analyses of transnational processes, we need to remember that each similarity may hide real differences so that "the last turtle is always a matter of method-ological convenience or stamina." The challenge to the scholar of international processes is to understand that cultural landscapes are fluid and open and provide the site for transactions and flows, all tempered by structures of power. The essential task then is to examine cultural rituals of populations taking into account the power component as well (Trouillot 2002).

In its attention to non-Western television production and consumption, this book addresses the challenges of a postcolonial framework: it attempts to reconstruct historical structures of knowledge production, privilege alternate methodologies, and point to activist interventions in combating imperialistic forces of global consumerism (see Shome and Hegde 2002; Schwarz 2000). The following sections describe some basic terms used in the book before mapping its layout.

7

From International Communication to Media Globalization

International communication has been defined, quite simply, as the "communication that occurs across international borders, that is over the borders of nation states" (Fortner 1993, p. 6). More recently, McPhail defines international communication as, "The cultural, economic, political, social, and technical analysis of communication patterns and effects across and between nation states" (2002, p. 2). According to Mohammadi (1997), international communication is a subfield of communication and media studies where research may be divided according to three categories. The first focuses on issues of culture and commodification. The second includes the study of how information is distributed by media conglomerates around the world. The third engages in the inquiry of the challenges faced by developing countries in such processes.

A seminal text in the field, *Four Theories of the Press* by Siebert, Peterson and Schramm (1956), used to be a foundational feature in undergraduate classes and served as a starting point for understanding the political philosophies of nations and their influence in the ordering of press systems across the globe. These authors proposed three demarcations: (1) liberal democracies (deriving from libertarian and social responsibility models); (2) Soviet totalitarianism; and (3) authoritarianism (which includes most of the developing world, fascist countries, and the colonial west). Drawing from Siebert et al.'s divisions, Stevenson (1994) focuses on global communication to address the cultural influence of global media networks around the world. In doing so, he highlights *Anglo American dominance* in the spread of the English language, Western popular culture, technology, and news biases; resurgence of *cultural conflict*, emergence of a *global culture* as disseminated by Disney, for example, and the emergence of development *grassroots journalism*. Stevenson organizes the study of the world according to political systems such as authoritarian, libertarian, communist, and social responsibility; and according to Western (combining libertarian and social responsibility), development (drawing from authoritarianism and communist theories), and revolutionary concepts. Further, Fortner (1993) identifies six characteristics of international communication: *internationality* which pertains to the purpose of transmission as in the propagandic mission of the Voice of America or Radio Russia; *channels* which refers to ownership in terms of private or public; *distribution technologies* such as radio waves, film, audio, or video; *content forms* such as news or entertainment; *cultural consequences* which translate into the impact of transnational flows on local audiences; and the *political nature* of such communication.

Scholarship on international communication, therefore, is primarily concerned with exchanges between national governments; scholarship on globalization focuses on exchanges between transnational corporations and consumers around the world (Thussu 2000). Although useful starting points for an understanding of international media processes, Curran and Park (2000) assert that these neat categorizations set up a tradition of generalizations that provide a false sense of competence of the various ways in which media is consumed and produced around the world.

This book contends that *international media studies*, which refers to empirical analyses of international media,[4] may be broadly divided into descriptive analyses where scholars describe the origins and history of international communication; critical political economy analyses where researchers, informed primarily by the Marxist tradition of the Frankfurt School document the phenomenal power and reach of global media empires; textual analyses where empiricists, using a variety of methods such as content, semiotic, and ideological analysis, examine the volume and content of media flows and assess their ideological implications for audiences; and finally, audience analyses where researchers employ such methods as surveys and ethnography to evaluate consumer responses to media texts.

Tehranian and Tehranian (1997) identify four major strains of international theory. The first is *realism* where the primary focus is the geopolitical struggle of power taking the nation as the unit of analysis. The second is *liberalism* where international interdependency and free trade are regarded as necessary paths to global harmony. The third pertains to *Marxism and neo-Marxism* where class conflict between and within central and peripheral nations of the world system is regarded as a persistent process through eras of imperialism, colonialism, and neo-colonialism. Neo-colonialism refers to the continued control of formerly colonized regions through indirect means such as trade and financial policies rather than direct military or political control. The fourth is *communitarianism*, which focuses on the centrality of institutions, culture, and community in international politics.

Various anthologies address media systems in non-Western countries. However, these anthologies include chapters that, for the most part, stand alone with little comparative analysis. Reception studies invariably focus on native responses to North American media (Downing 1996). A fairly recent survey of international media research pointedly focuses on Europe and North America with a brief chapter on Latin America (see Corner et al. 1997). The generalization of US and UK experiences to the rest of the world is a growing source of embarrassment among scholars of international media (Curran and Park 2000; Downing 1996, 2003) who have identified the sore need for comparative studies (Schudson 1996; Sparks 1998), particularly with the globalization of media.

   Globalization is a process that goes beyond communication across borders. It is a process that seeks to establish a global interconnected and interdependent economic, political, and cultural system (Moran 2004). It is crucial to examine nodes of interconnectivity and interdependence rather than conduct mere nation-based analyses. International media studies can no longer afford its heavy bias toward Western theories, media structures, and media audiences (Thussu 1998), where "It has become routine for universalistic observations about the media to be advanced in English-language books on the basis of evidence derived from a handful of countries" (Curran and Park 2000, p. 3). Strong criticisms of the Eurocentric bias of international communication, although drawing attention to issues of cultural globalization and geolin-guistic markets, continue to study these processes in relation to "nation" as a product of European modernity. Media dynamics are then mapped on to the political economy structure where the nation is considered centrally important, as influential in shaping media in the country, and as a marker of difference from other countries (Curran and Park 2000; Wilkin 2001). This approach reifies a Eurocentric understanding of nation and its ideological assumptions of coherence in language, cultural tradition, history, political system, and so on.

   Globalization is a hybrid theoretical perspective drawing from theories on Americanization, capitalism, Westernization, and postmodernity, each textured by varying approaches such as social science, political science, and cultural and critical studies to name but a few. Globalization refers to the global reach of transnational corporations (TNCs) and the interconnectedness of local economies. The cultural convergence of global corporations is evident in the transnational nature of software and hardware of such media productions as film, video, television, magazines, and CDs (Boyd-Barrett 1997). Globalization means the availability of global and local products on the marketplace, providing simultaneous spaces for the expression of individual identities and class domination (Bauman 1998). Quite simply, it thrives on the logic of capitalism and is facilitated by the new technologies and consumer ideologies that drive the marketplace (Jameson and Miyoshi 1998). In a globalized world economy, a new system of centers and peripheries has emerged, propelled by advances in science, technology, productivity, consumption, and creativity. Geographic location is no longer the organizing criteria behind the development of centers and peripheries (Tehranian and Tehranian 1997).

   Trouillot (2002) gives us two images of globalization. The first, commonly held by political economists of mass media, posits that globalization results in cultural homogeneity across the globe as more and more people have access to the same cultural images and products (see also Hamelink 1983; Mattelart 1983; Schiller 1969, 1976, 1989). These scholars are concerned with the phenomenal concentration of economic power of mixed media and non-media corporations that are responsible for the global production and distribution of media hardware and software, and that are in partnership with local media conglomerates (Boyd-Barrett 1997). In the political economy view, "global" is often considered synonymous for a "site of cultural erosion and destruction, and the 'local' as the site of pristine cultural 'authenticity'" (Ang 1996, p. 153). The second view, held by cultural theorists, is a little more nuanced, and regards globalization as including processes of cultural appropriation where people take what is relevant to their own contexts and orient or adapt it to their local needs (see also Appadurai 1996; Featherstone 1995). The tension between these two images is suppressed in globalization studies because the media, particularly advertising, spins the limited range of expression in a globalized world, into unlimited, individual choices in local contexts.

Media globalization, a phase arguably marked in developing countries by the arrival of satellite television in the early 1990s, is a phase where the discourse of localism, specificity, and heterogeneity in such theoretical frameworks as poststructuralism and postcolonialism has come of age. What this means is that audience-viewing rituals and local program production practices across the world, particularly in countries of the tri continent (which have been variously termed as peripheral, non-Western, developing, underdeveloped, or southern, depending on the academic convention of the time), have to be drawn into the central discourse of global media theory for us to understand, holistically, the nature of international communication. According to Stevenson (1994), the use of "global" instead of "international" signifies a trend in international communication, to focus on the role of culture in the production and consumption of media messages. Yet scholarly attention on media globalization has focused on the industry, whether it is surveys of global media empires (McChesney 1998; McPhail 2002) or an assessment of the ideological function of media capitalism (Featherstone 1995; Mattelart 1994; Schiller 1998).

The assumption in theories of globalization is that the nation-state is on its way out as a modern, central, political, and economic authority (Appadurai 1996), and its goals have been overthrown by the imperatives of transnational corporations (Aksoy and Robins 1992), most of which are anchored in the United States, Great Britain, and Japan (Morley and Robins 1995), leading to a disorganized capitalism (Lash and Urry 1987). Although opponents of the "demise-of-the-nation-state" view highlight the continued central role of the nation-state as a policy-maker and boundary enforcer (Burton 2003; Hirst and Thompson 1995), the debate from both sides continues at the level of macro institutions, be they national governments or transnational corporations. The term "global" is usually conflated with core, industrialized nations such as the United States, Great Britain, Germany, and France, with specific attention to North American media flows (Herman and McChesney 2003). The common contention in these debates written with varying critical perspectives, is that global media corporations, which are all based in core nations, depend heavily on foreign customers and merge or diversify to sustain their global corporate ideology of maximizing profits for owners and shareholders. Because of the overriding motive for profit, media content is embedded in formats that have proved lucrative across national boundaries (such as the soap opera, game show, variety show, and anchored music countdowns), leading to a general homogenizing or modernizing trend across the world (ibid.). The dynamics of local media production and consumption in these countries are increasingly overshadowed in the attention to global and transnational structures of media flow.

The general conclusion then, is that in the late twentieth century and early twenty-first century, media ownership continues to be dominated by Western countries headed by the United States, leading to an Americanization of cultures within nations too economically weak to resist the onslaught of inexpensive programming (Thussu 2000). Reviewing the role of global communication in the past half century, Schiller (2000) makes three observations for the twenty-first century: First, the US is thriving and will continue to thrive as a capitalist economy; second, existing structural relations such as that between labor and capital will continue despite scholarly assertions to the contrary; and third, the political economy framework is crucial to understand the developments in global communication far more than a focus on culture. He maintains that:

> The ever popular proposition that the cultural/media sector can be regarded as autonomous and free-standing has been believed by material conditions that have generated a configuration of cultural production that simply cannot be explained without recourse to political economy. (ibid., p. 50)

Scholars who lay much importance on the presence of global media conglomerates talk about global citizenship, global social justice, a global civil society, and the role of global communication in these processes (Wilkin 2001). Global connectivity is theorized to propel global consciousness. A simple question surfaces in this assertion above: global consciousness for whom? It is clear that scholars of the political economy of media are conflating "global" with the technology-rich countries and the technology elite in poorer countries. Global consciousness, if facilitated by global media, is a privilege to those who have access to such media and those whose realities allow the time and energy to develop a global consciousness. Moran (2004) comments on political economy generalizations stating that the assumption of cultural homogeneity based on the evidence of global networks of film, television programs, and music distribution is to deny the important differences between marketing strategies and the social and cultural effects of such strategies.

Despite its cultural implications, globalization is still studied as a primarily economic phenomenon (Robertson 1990; Tehranian 1999; Wallerstein 1990a) and as the spread of modernity (Giddens 1990), reviving broad political economy analyses that make assumptions on culture and reception. Consequently, media globalization is theorized to follow the imperatives of the market with expansion into new nations and regions to establish the informational and ideological context necessary to legitimize the political, economic, and moral bases for a capitalist environment.

No doubt political economy analyses are crucial for a structural understanding of media processes; however, such a focus closes off a holistic understanding of media globalization through an examination of effects. It distracts from a more critical assessment of the enduring power of colonial and imperial histories of most countries across the world, particularly those of the tri continent, which texture and shape their current media environments. It also sidesteps the dynamics of the ground, of lived experiences that may wrestle with, accommodate, ignore, or even subvert structure.

Postcolonial discourse, associated with a specific moment in a nation's history as it shrugged off the shackles of colonial rule, offers an invigorating and meticulous framework by which to analyze media production and consumption. It represents a framework for studying the continuing ideological effects of colonialism and the very real economic, cultural, and social effects of neo-colonialism. What is more relevant in the understanding of the power of international media and local audiences is a discussion of how such issues of race, gender, class, and ethnicity have been transformed. Empirical textual, audience, and political economy analyses using such a framework are frequently relegated to the margins of scholarly inquiry (Shome and Hegde 2002), indicating an academic nervousness to engage in anything that does not first proceed from the center, that does not first acknowledge the power of global media capitals and transnational media flows before addressing local reception processes that may include resistance. Trouillot (2002) calls the real and theoretical dominance of the west over the past 500 years, the "North Atlantic hegemony," and contends that important questions to address are how and why such a hegemony developed, why it is so widespread, and why it is so convincing. He writes that the "historicization of the west – its practices, concepts, assumptions, claims, and genealogies – is a central theoretical challenge of our times" (ibid., p. 16).

"Post" theories such as poststructuralism, postmodernism, and postcolonialism offer a critical theoretical framework to examine the enduring dynamics of colonialism in a global era, and question such phenomena as resistance and hybridity. In particular, and relevant to this book, *"postcolonial* refers not to a simple periodization but rather to a methodological revisionism which enables a wholesale critique of western structures of knowledge and power, particularly those of the post-Enlightenment period" (Mongia 1996, p. 2, emphasis added). Guha (1994) points to the importance of moving away from statist historiographies of culture and society because such constructions perpetuate hierarchies of power, leaving subaltern voices unheard. He writes, "[O]ur critique of statist discourse cannot by itself produce an alternative historiography. For that to happen the critique must move beyond conceptualization into the next stage – that is, the practice of re-writing history" ibid., (p. 11). Using Guha's admonition, this book goes beyond a description of structures of media power and adds to the growing scholarship on rituals of media consumption. Its focus on media production and consumption in Asia, Africa, and Latin America, will allow the examination of television reception not just by urban middle-class and upper-class audiences, but by subaltern[5] groups such as women, lower castes, and lower classes as well.

In twenty-first-century international media studies, crucial questions arise: in an era of globalization, how do local media networks and audiences accommodate competing and overlapping narratives of global, national, and local identities? And, what are the implications of national strategies of control on global and transnational flows of television and on its consumption by national and subnational communities? The postcolonial critique charts a new direction for international media studies "in which the 'lower end' of the colonial difference would no longer be the place of shame and ignorance but of epistemic potential" (Mignolo and Schiwy 2002, p. 251). It reminds readers that time and again, they have to ask the question, "Where is power located?" before they can make any conclusions about global, national, or local media production and consumption.

Mapping the Book

This first chapter, *Introduction*, has set up the problematic, that is, the scant attention to media studies, particularly rituals of consumption, in tri continent countries that may reconfigure our understanding of global, national, and local media production, flow, and consumption.

Chapter Two, *The Fixity of Nation in International Media Studies*, contains a critique of the field of international media studies. Beginning with a description of the theoretical conceptualizations of the "modern" nation, it demonstrates how this conceptualisation has fashioned the study of international communication, with particular attention to development communication. The endurance of the idea of the modern European nation as *the* model for developing countries to aspire to, the chapter illustrates, has led to limited models of research in international media studies that place great priority on macro structures of communication and development and not the micro level of lived experiences. The chapter highlights critical theories such as world system, dependency, and cultural and media imperialism theories to argue that although more nuanced in their approach to the imbalances in global development, predominantly focus on the structural power of the media. This leads to vast gaps in media reception analyses in general and of non-Western audience studies in particular. The chapter describes briefly the New World Information and Communication Order and New World Economic Order debates of the 1970s that emerged in this climate of critical academic research.

Chapter Three, *Connecting Structure and Culture*, describes contributions of cultural studies and critical theory to the study of media institutions, content, and audiences. It highlights the interventions of feminist scholars in shifting the epistemological standpoint of conventional international media scholarship from the male to that of the female consumer. The significant contributions of postcolonial theory are described, which draws issues of feminism into its analysis and subverts the Eurocentric hegemony of the field. Postcolonial criticisms of the "nation as modern" premise are addressed, and the postcolonial framework is explained, foregrounding its South Asian roots, its political and interventionist stances, and its deconstructionist trappings that continuously demand a de-anchoring of epistemology from centers of knowledge production, usually the imperial centers themselves located in the western world.

Chapter Four, *Reviving the Pure Nation: Media as Postcolonial Savior*, describes the role of the media in facilitating cultural continuity between colonial and postcolonial structures of power. Television and radio, in particular, were used as builders of the postcolonial nation, along, for the most part, the Enlightenment presumptions of the modern nation. Using case studies from tri continent countries, the chapter examines the ideological function of broadcast media in particular in arranging and sustaining hierarchies. Special attention is paid to the *telenovela*, a popular international soap/drama television format that incorporates themes of entertainment and education. Although widely successful among particularly Latin American, African, and South Asian audiences for the alternative they provide to the news shows and documentaries that monopolize prime-time, state-sponsored television, these shows also perpetuate stereotypes of women as caregivers and nurturers in the domestic sphere, subservient and deferent to men in the public sphere. The chapter ends with examples of media representations of women in India and China to illustrate the heightened controls on women's freedoms just as these nations are opening up to foreign investment and influence through sweeping reforms in the economy.

Chapter Five, *Competing Networks, Hybrid Identities*, addresses the challenges of globalization posed to the nation-state's ideological control of centralized television networks, in the form of hybrid programming. Using extensive examples from Asia, the chapter examines the profitability of cloned, copied, and plagiarized game shows, talk shows, and music programs. Again, the postcolonial framework urges the question of the interrelationship between culture and power. The chapter concludes with a discussion of the cultural implications of the power play between global and local programming.

Chapter Six, *Grounding Theory: Audiences and Subjective Agency*, highlights non-Western audience reception of global and local media. The chapter provides a description of the contributions of literary studies, British cultural studies, and anthropology to the study of media reception. The trend toward romanticizing reception is critiqued and, using postcolonial theory, the concepts of limited agency and subjectivity are discussed. Through the description of ethnographic case studies, the chapter points to processes of audience adaptation, subversion, and even dismissal of global and local ideologies. The attention to audience responses to media content and the role and function of media in their daily lives leads to a discussion of the correspondence between processes of production and consumption, both embedded within the same cultural context.

Chapter Seven, *Reconfiguring the Global in International Media Studies*, draws from the preceding chapters in its assessment of how attention to the local transforms the way we understand and study international media networks and their reception. Through a careful delineation of the differences between Western and non-Western viewing contexts, the chapter identifies several areas where theory and empiricism in international media need to be developed. It urges attention to non-"hot spots" of the world, particularly rural areas of tri continent countries, to provide a holistic understanding of how media around the world are consumed. In addition, it addresses the need for the linkage of research to activism and identifies several avenues for such effort.

As the conclusion of the book, Chapter Eight, *The Politics of International Media Research*, draws the work of the previous chapters together to provide the reader with a sense of the continuity among academic positions, biases in research, and representation or under-representation of themes. It addresses challenges to conducting critical ethnographies and to the representation of results within an academic environment that stipulates specific criteria for research recognition and reward. The chapter ends with a critical discussion of the viability of the nation-state.

Chapter Two

The Fixity of Nation in International Media Studies

The terms *inter national communication* flag postmodern privilege where the nation has not only achieved modernity through its political and economic coherence, but has achieved a certain level of technological competence to communicate across national borders. Its people can now connect to communities across the globe and the nation can partake in global politics and economic development. Nations that have struggled under colonial regimes and that have emerged, bewildered, traumatized, and excited at their prospects in the global economy are termed postcolonial where the "post" often is easily equated with "past" implying that the possibilities of the current context are endless – the nation just has to rise to its challenges. Following the nation as modern premise, modernity is considered a phase in a nation's linear trajectory, with globalization informing or informed by modernity. Both are regarded as intertwined, making it logical to examine centralized units of information or control (such as global news agencies located in the western world) as products of this modernity and globalizing context (Boyd-Barrett and Rantanen 1998).

Such a simplistic preface to this chapter highlights a serious issue: the assumption of nation as a modern and coherent unit of analysis. The chapter provides a critical survey of international media studies using the critique of "nation as modern" as its starting point. To take up the postcolonial challenge of theoretical revisionism, it describes conceptualizations of the modern nation that form the basis of international communication and continues, in the next chapter, with a postcolonial critique of this conceptualization that deconstructs the concept's ideological assumptions. It will discuss why the modern nation as a unit of analysis in international communication is inadequate in our understanding of how media is produced and consumed by communities across the world.

By unquestioningly tethering the politically defined nation to the discourse of modernity, dominant scholarship on international communication has perpetuated a Eurocentric bias. A postcolonial critique of the field requires "a form of social criticism that bears witness to those unequal and uneven processes of representation by which the historical experience of the once-colonized Third World comes to be framed in the west" (Bhabha 1991, cited in Mongia 1996, p. 1). This means not just relegating colonialism to a certain period of history, which would fallaciously imply the present postcolonial global condition is free from inequality and power hierarchies, but a critique of conventionally held structures of knowledge and power. To undertake such a critique, the following sections describe conceptions of the modern nation and their enduring and limiting legacy for international media studies.

The Modern Nation in All its Glory

The concept of nation as modern emerged in eighteenth-century Europe with the establishment of politically defined states that possessed fairly well-ordered, centralized government, education, and communication systems. Modernity itself has been pegged to various dates and events: Gutenberg's press in 1436, the Portuguese expansion in 1492, and Descartes' *Discourse on Method* in 1637. It is associated with the rise of science in the mid-eighteenth century, the French Revolution at the end of that century, and with the emergence of Hegel's *Phenomenology of Spirit* in 1800. Modernity has also been theorized to have come about with the early nineteenth-century processes of industrialization, urbanization, and the emergence of the nation-state, and, more radically, with early twentieth-century mass media systems. Modernity is a process that privileges developments in science and technology and innovations in social, economic, political, and cultural realms that are geared toward reaching increasing levels of productivity in terms of individual income, consumption, and political participation (Tehranian and Tehranian 1997).

Whatever its origins and ideological reasons to pin it to a specific moment, modernity has been theorized and studied in contrast with an Other (such as feudalism, primitivism, underdevelopment, backwardness, and so on). Modernity may be studied as an *identity discourse* and *diffusionist project* (Pratt 2002, p. 28, emphases in original). It is an identity discourse because its key strategy is to construct and police boundaries, creating and obliterating the inferior Other while simultaneously constructing and reifying the superior Self. It is a diffusionist project because it embodies Europe's transactions with the rest of the world, the latter's locational superiority at the center, and its ability to label and classify its colonies. The important point here is that identity is

19

constructed along lines of difference and nation-building, as a process of modernity, is essentially a project of identity construction.

Discussions of imperialism, colonialism, and postcolonialism, invariably point to the rise of *global* capitalism in the late nineteenth century, when the modern European nation-state emerged (Larsen 2000). As with modernity, scholars attempt to nail globalization to a certain historic moment, be it the rapid acceleration of networks of capitalism in the 1960s or the "cargo cults" of Melanesia. Some peg it to the rise of the West five centuries ago with the conquest of the Americas, the enslavement of the New World, and the Industrial Revolution that Trouillot (2002, p. 8) calls "a first moment of globality," or an *"Atlantic moment"* (emphasis in original), resulting in the US global dominance after World War II. The Atlantic became the center of the first global empires after Europe segregated itself from territories south of the Mediterranean. More important than its historical point of origin, if there truly is one, is our understanding of the concept itself: as a process that hinges on "modern communication and transport techniques, the spread of industrial commodities, new styles of consumption and new forms of knowledge on a global scale" (van Binsbergen et al. 2004, p. 7).

The association of international communication with the birth of the modern nation in eighteenth-century Europe is a logical one because this historic period witnessed the growth of capitalism and the development of distribution systems for print media. As Anderson writes, "the convergence of capitalism and print technology on the fatal diversity of human language created the possibility of a new form of imagined community, which in its basic morphology set the stage for the modern nation" (1991, p. 46). Historians of nationalism note that state, nation, and language were terms that appeared in the Dictionary of the Royal Academy as late as 1884 (Hobsbawm 1990). European ethnology and folklore were developed in the nineteenth century with the aim of tracing the evolution of national identity and culture in folk cultures (Lofgren 1989). While it is impossible to scientifically define "nation" (Seton-Watson 1977), various theorists of nationalism attempt to describe its historical origins and cultural compositions.

Ernest Renan's (1947/1990) seminal essay, *What Is a Nation?* stresses that "nation" is a new concept in history. Although cities and tribes have existed ever since the history of mankind was documented, he believes it was the Germanic invasions from the fifth century right up to their Norman invasions in the tenth century that gave France, Burgundy, Lombardy, and Normandy their sense of identity. The invasions created a sense of commonality in that the conquerors imparted to their conquests a common name and a common religion. Simultaneously, the conquerors assimilated the customs of their conquerees, so to speak, through a process of *forgetting* where they forgot their own language and customs to a certain extent, to imbibe those of the people they had conquered. Thom's (1990) *Tribes Within Nations* critiques Renan's claims and provides a detailed genealogy of nationality as it emerges from the myths of Germanic tribes to show that a Germanist spirit existed within French nationalism. He places Renan's argument with those of Max Muller and Emile Burnouf in that all emphasize the contribution of Aryan tribes to European culture, opposing the more realistic Indo Europeanism, which acknowledges the influence of Orientalism and Indo Germanism on European culture. Bernal (1995) details the nineteenth-century Aryan model of world history where Greece was seen as racially pure and the ideal birthplace of Western civilization, a stark contrast to the African and Semitic speakers of Southwest Asia.

The sense of nationalism developed with the birth of the modern state and is considered a "pathology of modern developmental history" (Nairn 1977, p. 359). Yet the term "state" is a product of the modern era. This is because the concept was not used in its strictest meaning in classical, ancient, or medieval eras. More commonly in use were such concepts as "polis," "civitas," and "regnum." With the emergence of an institutionalized and organized society, came "state," to signify a politically defined community (see Bereciartu 1994).

The rise of nationalism as a *sentiment* has been theorized to be primordial, that is, before the emergence of the politically defined nation-state. It is also theorized to be uniquely modern and is associated specifically with the establishment of the nation as a political unit with a centralized communication system. Breuilly (1994) offers a useful demarcation of perspectives on nation and nationalism according to the following: (1) the nationalist approach; (2) the Marxist approach; (3) the psychological approach; and (4) the communications approach. These approaches are not mutually exclusive and a brief summary will help us draw out the various ways in which the nation-state has been conceptualized.

Primordial nationalism in the nationalist approach

In the *nationalist approach*, nationalism is considered to be the expression of a nation and is evident in its culture and cultural sentiments. Anthony Smith (1986), prominently associated with this approach, firmly opposes the idea that nationalism is associated with modernity. He considers the nation-as-modern view to be shallow and advocates the study of pre-modern cultural models such as myth, symbol, and historical memory to understand what constitutes

21

a nation. Nationalism begins with the *ethnie* and is developed through such indicators as a collective name, a common myth of descent, a shared history, a distinctive shared culture, an association with a specific territory, a sense of solidarity, an organized religion, and inter-territorial warfare. Smith questions the role of ethnicity and attempts to uncover the link if any, between ethnicity and nation formation. Communities eager to establish their status as a nation pledge allegiance to a coherent, progressive, political system with recognizable markers such as a national flag and national anthem, for example, and unearth ethnic roots to establish their fixity in a global context that rewards both modernity and antiquity. Smith contends that the nation cannot be regarded as a natural and primordial ordering of social life. Nor can it be considered as a modern entity, a mere product of capitalism or of an industrialized society. He traces the origins of defined communities among ancient peoples of Greece and Rome to show that the concept of "ethnie," a loosely defined primordial group, preceded the politically defined national unit. The "ethnie" was characterized by a *collective* name such as the Falashas[1] of Israel and the Muslims of Bosnia;[2] *a common myth of descent* such as Hindu theological principles[3] (see Karve 1993) where the purpose is to create "emotional and aesthetic coherence to undergird social solidarity and social self-definition" (ibid., p. 25); a *shared history* where in turn, rival histories may divide a community as evident in the clash between Orthodox priests and bourgeoisie in nineteenth-century Greece who argued for the authenticity of Byzantine and Hellenic lines, respectively; and a distinctive *shared culture* in terms of language, religion, customs, laws, folklore, food, arts, clothes, and even skin color as in the case of the African Americans in the United States. These must be considered in combination with each other because there are many cases that defy definition of *ethnie* by just language (the Maori in New Zealand, for example), or religion (the Muslims in India, Pakistan, and Bangladesh, for example); association with a particular territory even though the *ethnie* may not be in physical possession of it (the Sikh community in London, for example); and a sense of solidarity. Pre-modern *ethnie* differ from modern definitions of nations in that they lack a clear economic or legal structure or a nationalist ideology.[4] Also *ethnie* are not perennial or primordial but have emerged and disappeared and persisted right up to the present time. *Ethnies* persist through the development of local hierarchies as in the priestly and merchant classes, and localized rituals of religion, trade, and myth construction for self-preservation.

Smith identifies two strains in modernist nationalist theory: the first is a focus on the *economic foundations* of modern nations by which certain core states (Britain, France, Spain, and Holland) could impose economic and political dominance on the peripheral states of Asia, Africa, and Central and Latin

America. The second is a focus on the *political nature* of states that facilitates the universal struggle of elites for wealth and power. These strains, as seen in the work of such scholars as Gellner (1983) and Hobsbawm (1990), do not acknowledge that the "modern" characteristics of politically defined boundaries and the struggles to maintain them, were evident in pre-modern eras and in the ancient world such as the ancient Egypt conflict with Nubians and Asiatics, and the Ionian resistance to Persian expansion in 6 BC. Smith's exquisite documentation of the rise and fall of various communities across the continents from primordial to modern eras serves as a compelling argument for the existence of well-defined groups before the birth of nations in nineteenth-century Europe. Yet his is a minority view in the theory on nations and nationalism and should be reviewed with caution, bearing in mind that notions of *ethnie* have fueled regimes of power.

To explain, one criticism to the primordialist argument is that the group identity of collectivity based on kinship does not include the violence and ethnocide that also characterize primordialism. Appadurai poses a stark question (1996, p. 141): "If all societies and nations are composed of smaller units based on primordial ties, and if there are ethnic animosities buried in every national closet, why do only some explode into explicit primordial fury?" The answer can be approached of course, through comparative studies rooted in historical analysis. Appadurai contends that societies such as Western Europe and the United States have worked out primordial disorders as part of the Enlightenment project and those on this trajectory are the pro-capitalist societies of Japan, Singapore, Taiwan, Korea, Chile, Argentina, and Brazil. Those with ethnic differences such as India, the former Soviet Union, Sri Lanka, Great Britain, and Egypt are still struggling to hold together. Yet his analysis is short-sighted in that he concludes that such capitalist democracies as Germany, France, the US, and Japan seem to be free from ethnic strife. Clearly how this strife is represented in the mass media plays an important role where the Tamil-Sinhala and Indo-Pakistan wars or the ethnic conflicts in Bosnia and Somalia are sensationalized so that our sensibility of "ethnic violence" is pinned to the depraved "Third World" or unruly marginal European societies. No doubt Appadurai concedes that ethnic struggles exist in Western capitalist societies but they are not considered as devastatingly violent as those in the "global south."

The hierarchical nation in the Marxist approach

According to the *Marxist approach*, the concept of nation is associated with modernity and the rise of capitalism in eighteenth-century Europe. The consequential rise of class and class relationships is seen as instrumental in building nationhood (Breuilly 1994). Historical approaches to nationalism use the Marxist perspective and are criticized because they examine the disruptive forces of class differences as a factor in nation-formation. They focus on how certain elites establish a national consciousness for hegemonic purposes rather than on how nationalism is fostered from among the masses. Gellner (1983) may be said to take a Marxist approach to nationalism in that he evaluates its origins from within industrial social organization. He is primarily concerned with how the mass media, universal literacy, and a comprehensive system of education interact to stimulate economic growth of the nation and occupational mobility of its members. Nationalism is the imposition of cultural norms on a society by an elitist group that had hitherto functioned according to the norms of the majority of the population. Specifically, the group in power extends a high culture over the majority, which supersedes the latter's low culture. This it does through centrally controlled institutions such as schools, bureaucratic administrations, and media technologies. Such a society consists of autonomous, dispensable individuals who stay broadly, yet impersonally connected through a "shared culture" (ibid., p. 57), which is a marked change from the local, complex, and idiosyncratic micro communities they were members of before the advent of modernity.

The key phrase here is "shared culture," and this culture, Gellner asserts, is a high culture that is communicated to society through a monolithic education system. The main feature in this approach is the recognition of the hierarchical nature of the nation and the centrality of power for the maintenance of an ordering of domination and subordination, be it through government, military, education, or religious systems.

The need for identity in the psychological approach

The *psychological approach*, according to Breuilly (1994), adopts the view that people have an innate psychological need to identify with groups larger than themselves. Anderson, whose definition of nationalism is also considered a cultural one, writes that a nation is first an "imagined political community" (1991, p. 6). It is imagined because its members may never meet or know each other, yet can imagine themselves to be a part of a larger community of fellow citizens with whom they share a deep and equal connection. The nation is a limited entity because of its fixed and limited boundaries. At the same time, it is sovereign because the concept originated in the age of Enlightenment and Revolution in eighteenth-century Europe, an era when the authenticity of hierarchical and divinely sanctioned dynasties was being questioned.

While such imaginings may lead to a strong sense of nationalism, in the colonial imperialist context, they may also create what Anderson (1991) calls Anglicization where elites of a nation are western-educated, and yet are in a non-western society. They belong neither to the Western nor to their traditional society. Gellner (1983) who also addresses the psychological aspects of nationalism, notes that when change causes people to migrate to new locations, they leave behind their social roles and relations, yet identify with their groups based on the attributes they can carry with them such as language, ethnicity, and skin color. Hobsbawm calls this "proto-nationalism" (1990, p. 46) where individuals maintain allegiance to certain mythical beliefs and to political institutions even though they cross national borders and form a diasporic community. Mass media and education, as both Gellner (1983) and Hobsbawm (1990) stress, serve to sustain cultural definitions of ethnic identity.

The centrality of communication in the communications approach

In the *communications approach*, the nation is regarded as a system that has developed through internal communication among its members to forge a common identity. This approach explains how different social groups create ties that transcend differences within them and simultaneously establish links with groups outside their territorial boundaries. Also, it is through communication that nationalist movements are mobilized and sustained. Both Anderson (1991) and Gellner (1983) address the centrality of communication systems and discuss the relationship between changing communication patterns and the development of nationalism.[5]

Specifically, print-capitalism, as Anderson (1991) calls it, democratized Latin and made it accessible to the masses. The Bible was printed in vernacular languages and therefore even the lessons of religion were decentralized. He isolates three distinct ways in which print encouraged national consciousness. First, a field of exchange and communication was developed that occupied a space below Latin and above local vernaculars. In other words, print offered an intermediary plane between the elites and the masses so that there was an open channel of communication between the two, and a certain demystification of each to the other. Second, print-capitalism provided endurance to language in that the printed book was relatively permanent and could be endlessly reproduced. Nationalistic messages and historical documents could be kept and read, and this contributed to the subjective idea of the nation. Third and finally, print-capitalism created "languages-of-power" (ibid., p. 45). These were different from the earlier vernaculars used by the administration.

Hobsbawm (1990) traces the history of nationalism and organizes his research into the study of three historical phases:[6] the first stretches between the mid-eighteenth to the mid-nineteenth centuries, and is characterized by literary, cultural, and folkloric traditions. The second phase at the end of the nineteenth century is marked by a sense of political unity. National sentiment was complemented by the desire of the people to be ruled under one government. Size was an important criterion for a nation to be considered as such. Smaller nations in Europe were considered mere cultural communities because they were too small to be economically viable. During the latter part of this century, the size criterion was no longer valid since the rise of nationalists who mobilized the state caused even small states to assert themselves as nations. The third phase in the early twentieth century witnessed the rise of mass support for the ideologies of the few in power. There was a conscious sense of belonging among the masses through race, ethnicity, and religion. Hobsbawm regards language and literacy as key to the development of nationalism in these phases. He addresses the role of language in the communication between elites and peasants. A populist consciousness developed as a result of the democratization of the state and the rise of non-elitist vernacular languages. By the mid-twentieth century, he writes, language and ethnicity had become the main criteria for nationhood.

To summarize, with the exception of Smith (1986) in the nationalist approach, what is evident in scholarship on nationalism is the anchoring of a national consciousness to an eighteenth-century European industrializing context and global capitalism to the late nineteenth century. Specifically, a nation could be considered as such with the establishment of a political state, centralized communication, education, and defense systems, and a common language and culture. This relegates to pre-modern or pre-civilized status, all other nations that have not been through industrialization, that subsist primarily on agrarian economies, and that are primarily located in Central and Latin America, Asia, and Africa. Postcolonial scholars of national identity highlight the glaring exclusion of such nations in nationalism theory. We will address the postcolonial critique of nationalism theory in the next chapter.

The Legacy of the Modern Nation

As described above, the birth of the modern nation is generally associated with the emergence of printing technology (Anderson 1991), fairly well-defined central political and economic authorities (Gellner 1983), and geographical boundaries (Hobsbawm 1990) in eighteenth-century Europe. Drawing from a modernist conception of nation, grand narratives such as the *modernization theories* of Lerner (1958), Schramm (1964), Rogers (1962) and Pye (1963), placed many of the countries in Asia, Africa, and Latin America, on the periphery of global development. *World systems theory* (Wallerstein 1974) and *dependency theories* of Baran (1957), Frank (1969), and S. Amin (1974), using a critical, Marxist framework to deconstruct the assumptions of the modernization theories, also supported the center-periphery model of international communication and development. Specifically, *modernization theory* postulates that underdeveloped nations were precisely so because they had not undergone a phase of industrial revolution. However, they could "catch up" with industrialized nations through specific savings and investment schemes. More importantly, the right attitudes to development were required. To foster favorable attitudes to development, underdeveloped nations needed to subscribe to similar economic and political structures that facilitated industrialization in Western countries.

Cultural imperialism and *media imperialism* theories (Schiller 1969; Mattelart 1979) assumed the media, particularly those originating in Western countries and disseminated through efficient and sophisticated networks around the globe, had powerful effects on Third World audiences who were too weak and passive to resist. Dependency, cultural imperialism, and media imperialism theories drew from Marxist structuralism in their interrogation of imbalances in the flow of news, goods, and services between the developed core and the developing periphery (Galtung 1980; Halloran 1997). In essence, they reified the powerful effects paradigm of mass media.

The very construction of a *world system* of center and periphery, North and South, and its continuity in contemporary scholarship on transnational media flows perpetuates a dichotomic and limited understanding of the dynamic processes of globalization that may include resistance, adaptation, and appropriation. The spatial discourse of center and periphery sets up a hierarchy such that

> [T]he agency of the periphery in the creation of modernity remains systematically invisible at the center, as do the processes of diffusion from center to periphery...to be marginal or peripheral is precisely not to be disconnected from a center, but to be intimately connected in particular, highly meaningful ways that are local, not in the sense that one sees only part of the picture, but in the sense that one sees the whole picture from a particular epistemological location that is not a center. (Pratt 2002, pp. 29, 30)

The following section describes early research in international communication that used a center–periphery global configuration to assess the ideological and development potential of mass media systems.

Early Research in International Communication

The birth of international communication in the United States, Great Britain, and most European nations during the twentieth century was within a context of propaganda, national expansion, and conquest. Federal funding for communication propaganda research in the United States between World Wars I and II led to the establishment of international communication as a viable and legitimate field of study in North American universities. Communication scholars between the 1920s and 1950s, drawing heavily from sociology, economics, and political science, regarded the modern nation-state, as defined in the European context by its political, economic, and geographical coherence (as if such were indeed the realities of European nations), as the ideal for primordial communities to aspire to. They believed, as did the modernists, that "everything in agrarian societies – the nature of culture, the structure of power, the nexus of economic ties – conspired to prevent the emergence of nations" (Smith 1986, p. 69).

In 1926, Harold Lasswell examined the techniques of psychological warfare and, with Walter Lippmann, then editor of the US propaganda division, studied the effects of communication technology on the western world (Mohammadi 1997). Lippmann's *Public Opinion* (1922) and *The Phantom of the Public* (1925) advocated communication research as part of the field of social science. Both Lasswell and Lippmann promoted the "who says what to whom with what effect" formula of communication and believed the media had powerful effects on audiences. Their description of the communication process as one where a message could be conveyed to an audience to achieve the effect intended by the sender, came to be known as the magic bullet or hypodermic needle model of communication. Mass communication research truly began in the 1930s and 1940s and was primarily behaviorist and market-driven with the sender–message–medium–receiver as the dominant paradigm of audience research.

Simpson (1994) affirms that the positivist method of communication research that focused on quantifiable outcomes such as economic progress and population growth, was normalized in North American universities by the 1950s. At this time, in the Cold War context, in particularly Great Britain and the United States, the potential of the mass media for international propaganda was studied carefully. Several global events that soon followed – the collapse of the Soviet Union, the trend toward capitalism in various staunchly socialist governments around the world, most notably the Indian subcontinent, and the marginalization of those nations that persisted with authoritarian or totalitarian governments such as those in Southeast or Middle East Asia – facilitated the further rise of the United States as a formidable force in international communication.

Radio served as a powerful vehicle of propaganda. Some examples are Great Britain's BBC World Service broadcasting in Eastern bloc countries, the Middle East, Africa, and Southeast and East Asia; Germany's Deutsche Welle in the Western hemisphere, the Soviet Union's transmitters in the Cameroon, China's broadcasting in Zambia and Tanzania, Radio France Internationale in former French colonies in Africa, and most significantly, the United States Voice of America (VOA) operating from Japan, Thailand, and Sri Lanka, and Radio Marti and TV Marti in Cuba. Each broadcasting country had its specific agenda of spreading its political ideology, opening up local markets and minds, and garnering new political alliances while maintaining old ones after the retreat of colonial rule (Thussu 2000).

The US in the Cold War with the Soviet Union, attempted to cordon off the latter and its allies through the North Atlantic Treaty Organization (NATO) and the 1955 Baghdad Pact (which linked primarily Middle Eastern countries in an anti-Soviet alliance). The so-called Third World and the war-torn countries of Eastern Europe were heavily contested during the Cold War. Western Europe was relatively secured through the Marshall Plan by the United States, which was then able to concentrate its efforts in Asia and Africa by the end of the 1940s. Latin America, shielded by the Monroe Doctrine, stood apart from the Asian and African countries and in fact, provided an example of the VOA's influence in Latin America. Many Third World countries gained independence in the 1940s and 1950s, which meant they had a choice to either continue as loyal members of the Western bloc countries or explore alternative political alignments. The United States sought the former. In this context, sponsored by the Bureau of Applied Social Sciences, area studies in development communication and modernization assessed the readiness of Third World audiences for VOA propaganda. The focus of the free flow model of communication that emerged after World War II was on diminishing international barriers to trade and developing foreign markets to spread the Western way of life through capitalism and individualism. International organizations such as the World Bank, the International Monetary Fund (IMF), and more recently, the World Trade Organization (WTO), upheld the interests of the former imperial powers so that freedom from colonialism for developing economies now meant subjugation under neo-colonial forces of capitalism and globalization (Boyd-Barrett 1997).

Scholars engaging in post -World War II area studies, most notably Daniel Lerner (1958), Wilbur Schramm (1964) and Lucien Pye (1963), believed the mass media could facilitate development in Third World countries in four fundamental ways: first, mass media could break down traditional values inimical to the process of industrialization and modernization; second, they could help the developing society achieve an autonomous and integrated national identity; third, they could assist in the dissemination of specific technical skills; and fourth, they could be harnessed to spread education and improve the level of education in local schools. In traditional communication research, therefore, the nation emerged as the crucial unit of analysis ensconced in the discourse of modernity where international activity was regarded as an assertion of the nation's arrival into a modern age. The focus on national media perpetuated the myth of "nationhood," where such media were regarded as the authoritative voice of the nation, reflecting its character as potently as other icons of national power such as national anthems, flags, and state buildings (Boyd-Barrett 1997). The focus on nationalism as the locus of identity was itself a hegemonic project, subjugating in its wake other crucial nodes of identity – gender, ethnicity, class, caste, and religion, for example (Ang 1996). Drawing from a positivist, social science tradition, early development communication scholars postulated that a sequence of urbanization, literacy, extension of the mass media, and wider economic and political participation, was crucial for a society to move from traditionalism to modernity. Their functionalist approach focused on the dynamic rather than systemic qualities of developing societies and promoted mass media as a modernizing catalyst (McClelland 1966; Rogers and Shoemaker 1971; Schramm 1964). The work of these scholars is described briefly below, and provides the foundation for development communication, a significant subfield of international communication. For all the critiques that followed, it has to be given due credit for its recognition of the potential of mass media systems in developing societies. The approaches to the study of communication for national development may be divided into psychological, economic, political, and technological approaches. It should be noted that there is significant overlap in these approaches; they are not mutually exclusive.

The psychological approach to development communication

Lerner's *The Passing of Traditional Society* (1958) is a report of a 1950–51 survey of 300 individuals from six Middle Eastern countries: Turkey, Lebanon, Egypt, Syria, Jordan, and Iran, aimed at understanding why some societies transitioned from traditional to modern status while others didn't, and why some remained stable during this process while others careened toward modernization at an erratic pace involving personal anguish and social dislocation. Lerner labeled respondents "traditional" or "modern" based on their responses to two questions that asked, respectively, what the respondent would do if he[7] were president or in a position of power, and where the respondent would live if he could not live in his native village. Individuals who could not fathom being president or living anywhere but in their native village were considered traditional while those who could were classified modern. "Traditionals," according to Lerner, were characterized by their illiteracy, localism and fatalism, while the "moderns" were cosmopolitan, literate, political participants, and users of the mass media. "Transitional" individuals lay between these two extremes and possessed a psychic mobility (McClelland 1966, calls this n-Ach, for "need for achievement") to become modern, but lacked such essential components as cosmopoliteness and literacy.

The economic approach to development communication

Schramm's (1964) model of development was based on economic productivity rather than human behavior. He defined underdevelopment according to the then UNESCO's definition of a developing country as one that had less than $300 per capita income. Schramm's report was based on the findings of three major surveys of mass media in Asia, Latin America, and Africa discussed at three UNESCO meetings in Bangkok (1960), Chile (1961), and Paris (1962), respectively. He believed that the task of the mass media was to mobilize human resources to step up a country's investment in the industrial sector of society so it could stay ahead of its depletion of resources due to population growth. For this, the agricultural sector, which is the primary sector in most developing countries, should be modernized. Its lack of productivity stemmed from ancient methods of farming, scarcity of fertilizer and pesticide, high proportion of subsistence farming, and unfavorable attitudes to change. Schramm outlined individual psychological factors hindering economic progress such as fatalism and resistance to innovations. In India, for example, numerous religious holidays, degradation of manual labor, and poor media infrastructure prevented the mass media from serving as agents of change. Besides, the media were concentrated in urban centers and were accessible only to city residents. Rural areas faced such problems as washout of telephone and transmission lines during the rainy season, inadequate roads for quick repair, irregular postal service to disseminate and receive information, and lack of trained personnel to operate communication equipment. Development messages were difficult to construct because of vernacular differences among receiving populations, low literacy rates, low newspaper circulation, high costs of newsprint, low advertising incentives, and high costs of news agencies and printing presses. Legislative mechanisms and complex bureaucracies further hindered the efficient establishment of communication systems. Schramm advocated a planning commission in developing and underdeveloped societies representing both private and public sectors, to facilitate development thorough integrated education, agriculture, and health initiatives. These could be implemented through a three-step process that included taking stock of the situation, setting priorities, goals, and decisions; and reviewing the plan. He described the "new nation" as one that recognized its development problems and the need for modern administrative institutions.

The political approach to development communication

While Schramm (1964) focused on an economic model, Lucian Pye (1963), in his introduction to *Communications and Political Development*, explored the relationship between communication and political power. Pye believed that through communication, people within a society in pursuit of power were placed in relationships with one another through which social order was established. Mass communication performed an amplifying function by transforming micro individual acts to macro-level processes. The degree of development of the communication systems within a society reflected the development of society as a whole. Drawing from dominant theory on nationalism that anchored modernity to the eighteenth-century European context, Pye wrote that for people in developing countries to feel they belonged to a nation, they must possess the institutional and governmental forms that modern European states had. He asserted that for political development to occur, Enlightenment ideals of universalism such as higher levels of technology, rationality, urbanization, and industrialization, should be balanced with the relativism of the traditional societies undergoing transition. As with Lerner (1958) and Schramm's (1964) suggestions for tri continent development, Pye's universalism-relativism recommendation assumed coherence within developed countries and particularism within developing countries plagued with "traditional" values and attitudes.

The technological approach to development communication

Rogers and Svenning's *Modernisation Among Peasants* (1969), sought to study the modernization process of peasants in Colombia, India, and Kenya, through an examination of the diffusion of technological innovations to raise economic standards of living. Survey information was obtained from the male heads of households and predominantly male farming decision-makers, despite the fact that women were key contributors in these agrarian economies. The authors' theory of modernization included increasing the peasants' level of literacy,

32

mass media exposure, cosmopoliteness, empathy, achievement motivation, aspirations, innovativeness, and political knowledge, while, at the same time, lowering their sense of fatalism. To simplify to a great extent, the authors concluded that the "Web of Modernization" characterized by external communication, orientation to change, and innovative leadership was higher in "modern" villages than "traditional" villages. They based their criteria for modernization on economic productivity, as did Schramm (1964), and looked for behavioristic determinants of individual responses to innovations, as did Lerner (1958).

Rogers and Svenning (1969) described social change as a change in the *structure* (individual status) and *function* (individual roles) of a social system. New ideas are developed within a system through *innovation* and circulated by *diffusion*. *Consequence* is change occurring in the system by adoption or rejection of innovations. Social change can be *immanent* when it occurs within the system, or *contact*, when it is introduced externally. Communication can effect social change through immanence, contact, or both. The authors concluded that it was important to study peasants because they constituted the largest social group in the developing world, facilitated political stability, and posed the greatest impediment to development. Although the authors acknowledged differences existed in peasants in various parts of the world, they focused on general similarities and asserted that the subculture of the peasantry was characterized by mutual distrust in interpersonal relations, perceived limited good, dependence on and hostility to government authority, familism, lack of deferred gratification, limited spatial and temporal view of the world, and low empathy. Rogers and Shoemaker (1971) developed the idea of diffusing technological innovations to bring about social change through a five-step process: awareness, interest, evaluation, trial, and adoption. Based on their rates of adoption, people were classified as innovators, early adopters, late adopters, and laggers.

What is evident in all of these early studies of development communication is their broad categorization of Europe, the United States, and Australia as modern, and Asia, Africa, and Latin America as traditional. They failed to acknowledge that differences in race, gender, ethnicity, and socio-economic status within a developed country divided those who followed so-called "traditional" lifestyles and those who followed "modern" lifestyles within that country itself. The uncritical equation of "traditional" with "bad" or "undesirable," and "modern" with "good" or "desirable" limited the study of the dynamism and fluidity of culture as it interacted with and confronted structure. The historicity of western models of development was critiqued by scholars such as Bendix (1970) who identified the ideological and dangerous flaw in slapping on the criteria for modern nation-states as evolved from eighteenth-century Europe onto an evaluation of developing economies.

Melkote (1991) writes that these models and theories of development were problematic for their pro-innovation, pro-persuasion, pro-mass media, and pro-literacy models that assumed that the mass media, by propagating a Western, modern way of life, would trickle down to the community from innovators to laggers. Assumptions of the modernity paradigm were that positive correlations existed among major aspects of development (Hoselitz 1960), leading to covariate rates of change and irreversible and sustained development, once the society reached the take-off stage. The "take-off" factor referred to economic and social conditions of the society and most significantly, the empathy of its members.

These development studies were "lacking in theory, historical and sociological perspectives and being heavily ethnocentric, progress and development at all levels, from material resources to the industrial work ethic, were inevitably conceived in Western industrialized terms" (Boyd-Barrett 1997, p. 29). Most notably, Lerner's *The Passing of Traditional Society* was exposed for its ideological intent of creating a non-soviet body politic through an influential intellectual matrix where marketing research was used to influence communication research. The two together were used to craft strategies of psychological warfare and from this framework to influence indigenous peoples to become more susceptible to US marketing and government propaganda (Samarajiwa 1987). Inherent in such a framework was the search for objectivity and the privileging of objective knowledge for social change. Individuals in a society were treated as autonomous beings and the assumption was that people could be managed and manipulated into change, just as the data could (Trouillot 2002). The analyses of the early development scholars, although providing a wealth of information on societies around the world and noteworthy for their pioneering explorations of non-Western societies, were nonetheless ill-equipped to deal with the complex realities of a globalizing world.

The Critical Turn

In the mid-1960s, various ruptures occurred in international communication, driven by strains of critical inquiry in both the social sciences and humanities. To begin with, sociologists trained in traditional positivist methods of research as were the development communication scholars, questioned the research imperialism that followed the cultural imperialism generated by an imbalanced world system. Positivism was viewed as suspect because "knowers are detached and neutral spectators, and objects of knowledge are separate from them, inert items in knowledge-gathering processes, yielding knowledge best verified by appeals to observational data" (Code 1995, p. 17). Commenting on the early studies in development communication, Halloran (1997) writes that the overt focus on reliability (i.e., replicability) meant that oftentimes contextual differences such as socio-economic conditions, age, gender, and cultural and geographical differences were sidelined in the effort to make broad cross-cultural comparisons. Reliability sadly, then, did not directly translate to validity. True comparability could be gleaned only by taking contexts into account. The practice of drawing comparisons by subjecting different cultures in different countries to the same questions produced false conclusions of sameness and difference. He writes that not only should questions be context-specific, they should also be asked in different ways to derive the same information, if one is to make a case for reliability. Although useful in their ability to gather data from a broad range of elements, the social scientific, conventional, and non-critical method of mass communication often stumbles in its efficacy because it is used for comparative purposes where uniformity of questionnaire is privileged over specificity of context. Such privileging raises ethical questions such as, what *kind of research* is exported from the developed to developing contexts, how *suitable* these models, theories, concepts, and methods are for environments that have not experienced industrialization as have the countries of their origin, what forms of *indigenization* are necessary for the application of such frameworks to developing contexts, and, perhaps most importantly, whether *research imperialism* is following the path of political, cultural, commercial and media imperialisms. The question of research imperialism is evident in the practically one-way flow of textbooks, articles, journals, and use of "experts" in academia and international agencies from developed to developing countries across the world (Halloran 1997).[8]

In this context of critique, sociologists such as Wallerstein (1974, 1986, 1990a, 1990b), Frank (1969), and Galtung (1980) attempted to explain the system of dependency that emerged between core, developed, industrialized countries such as the United States, Great Britain, Germany, Japan, France, and the Netherlands; and peripheral, underdeveloped, and the non or partially industrialized countries of Asia, Africa, and Latin America. These scholars contributed much to the understanding of the enduring power of imperialism and colonialism in its sustenance of unequal and interdependent relations even in an age of globalization. Their work has been criticized for its overt focus on structure with inadequate attention to the role of culture and people's agency within the system. The following sections discuss world systems, cultural imperialism, and media imperialism theories before advancing to an explanation of postcolonial theory that offers avenues for examining empirically the interconnections between structure and culture.

World systems theory

World systems theory, developed by Immanuel Wallerstein (1974), is perhaps the most influential of theories that assess the organization of the global capitalist system. It states that a small group of industrialized, developed core nations expands politically and economically to semi-peripheral and peripheral nations. Core nations control the flow of technology, services, goods, and knowledge, while semi and peripheral nations provide low cost labor, raw materials, and locales for production of goods for local and core consumption.

There are six realities of the capitalist world system, according to Wallerstein (1990a). First, the capitalist world economy is constructed through an integrated and varied set of production processes. Second, the capitalist world economy ebbs and flows in cycles, originating in Europe and spreading worldwide, making it difficult to discern whether the successive expansions of the world economy results in modernization or Westernization. The modernization/Westernization dilemma is resolved through a universalist ideology that argues Western civilization is the only civilization in the world that can lead a culture from traditionalism to modernity. Third, capitalism is driven by the endless accumulation of capital, which creates a conflict in simultaneous goals of more work and less pay among workers. Universalism is again used here to motivate workers to work harder and compete with the world market. Fourth, capitalism requires movement and change; this means consistent development in the organization of production and in the sites of production as well. Development is seen as a central universalizing theme. Fifth, the capitalist system is a polarizing one that leads to progress in material goods, on the one hand, and deterioration of culture, on the other. Sixth, and finally, the capitalist system is historical and may result in global progress or damnation – either way, we can only stand by and watch. The conservative ideologies of universalism and racism–sexism identify the core nations as leaders and peripheral nations as servants and followers as the world system undergoes transition. Culture then becomes the ideological battleground of the modern world system.

Boyne (1990) critiques Wallerstein's six characteristics of the world system stating that such a conceptualization tethers culture to the vagaries of economic production. That is, culture, which can be seen as the internal *solidity* that binds a group together, and its *difference* from other groups, changes correspondingly with the changes in economic structure. Boyne concludes:

36

World system theory is like a house without glass in the windows, fuel in the fireplace, food in the cupboards, or beds upon which to sleep. Even if we grant the status of uncontestable reality to the main supports of the structure, and we should not do so lightly since we would be saying thereby that the human sciences have arrived at a shared epistemology in regard to which we can expect radical shifts, it does not follow that the understanding of culture will be exhausted by providing an account of the way that it keeps the structure from breaking apart. (1990, p. 62)

Bergeson (1990) attacks world systems theory for its assumptions that the sum of the parts equals the whole; that the parts (national economies) interact to maximize their economic power in the whole (the international system); and that the result of these interactions is necessarily some sort of international order. These faulty assumptions lead to the erroneous belief that the coherence and identity of states preceded the world order, when in reality, for most countries of the world, the international order preceded their existence. Also, the differences between core and periphery were not natural developments but specifically because of colonial subjugation after which followed a system of unequal exchange. Historical processes of conquest, political power and control, and of colonizer hegemony over colonized (specifically by the European core over its conquered empire), gave rise to real differences. These differences must be seen for what they are: political creations of global structural domination and colonialism, rather than natural occurrences. The production of raw materials by colonized countries for colonial masters was a necessity, not a free-floating response to the dynamics of supply and demand in a world market that operated on equal terms of exchange. Worsley (1990) adds that the fatal flaw in world systems theory is, again, taking the nation as the unit of analysis while ignoring the fact that most communities across the world can hardly be characterized against such a limited Eurocentric definition. These points are well taken, especially the criticism that a framework that focuses on structure submerges an analysis of individual agency. Yet, as Wallerstein (1990b) rebuts, we also have to evaluate how far this agency can truly go in a system where the economic, social, and cultural power of those who have is exponentially higher than those who do not.

Despite the important exchanges between Wallerstein and his critics, much of international media theory labors in an either/or analysis: either a focus on structure or on consumer agency. What is crucial is an examination of the flows between structure and agency, with an eye to how each transforms and is transformed by the other – a point that will be taken up in the section on postcolonial theory. Dependency theory, developed by Latin American scholars, unquestioningly uses the coherence of world systems theory to explain imbalances in the flow of goods, people, and services from core to peripheral nations.

Dependency theory

The "time-lag" in development between the center and periphery was revealed as a fallacy during the 1970s, particularly with the collapse of import substitution policies that created the debt crisis. Center–periphery relations were exposed for their support of central dominance rather than a historical circumstance where the periphery just had to catch up with the center. According to Ang:

> [T]he capitalist world-system today is not a single, undifferentiated all-encompassing whole, but a fractured one, in which forces of order and incorporation (e.g. those of globalization, unification, and "westernization") are always undercut by forces of chaos and fragmentation (e.g. localization, diversification and "indigenization")...capitalist modernity contradictorily based as it is on both fixing and unfixing meanings and identities, with the delimitation and the instrumental expansion of the social – only encourages the dominant to feverishly step up both the intensity and the range of their ordering practices. But the work will never be done; in the capitalist world-system the moment of absolute order will never come. (1996, pp. 177–8)

Dependency theory emerged as a reaction to the Eurocentric modernization theories that regarded the mass media as a means through which developing countries could become modernized, or, in essence, Westernized (Sinclair 1990). It offers a framework for the study of the political economy of international transactions.

Dependency theory refers to the imbalance in the flow of goods and services from the developed countries in the center of the world system to the developing countries on the periphery that sustains the latter in their positions of dependence on the periphery and the former in their positions of dominance at the center. Such an imbalance contributed to the formation of a world capitalist system (Hout 1993). While theories of modernization regard the individual or independent nation-state as the unit of analysis, dependency theory is concerned with the whole world system and looks at positions occupied by developed and developing countries as a reflection of the system of economic relations between them.

Much of the scholarship highlighting the role of the periphery and the fragmentation and incompleteness that exists both in the center and periphery, has come from scholars in Latin America and South Asia. A radical politicization characterizes the approach of these scholars, an edge that is mostly absent in North American cultural studies. Latin American cultural studies has its roots in the social sciences which allows it, as do the German and Nordic traditions of cultural studies (Drotner 2000a), to continuously seek the larger political ramifications of local cultural processes (Escosteguy 2001). Young notes that such politicization in particularly Latin American cultural theory is because of its subjection to US military, political, and economic domination ever since the 1823 Monroe Doctrine, resulting in "a sense of political and economic power-lessness, and corresponding lack of cultural identity" (2001, p. 194).

Four strains emerge in the Latin American critique of center–periphery politics. It is important to note that this critique was not just a theoretical reaction to imbalances in development, but specifically incorporated the Marxism of Fidel Castro and Che Guevara (Young 2002). The first addresses the contradiction where modernity in the colonial context precisely meant curtailment of individual agency, not universal freedom as promised by the center. The second attacks the myth of complementarity where diffusion, as a natural and spontaneous consequence of modernity, actually created new subordinations and transculturation as in the presence of the displaced European peasantries in the Americas to modernize, or "make white" indigenous and mestizo populations. The third critiques the centrist narrative of diffusion that assumed a bland process of assimilation and reception; yet the vocabulary developed at the periphery in response, that is, hybridity, *mestizaje*, and *créolité*, for example, signified powerful processes and identity formations as a consequence. The fourth pointed to the differentiation in the concept of progress between center and periphery. Here the distinction between modernization and modernity is crucial (Pratt 2002). Modernization is defined as the "unfolding of instrumental rationality, and modernity as the unfolding of normative rationality leading toward autonomy and self-determination" (Lechner 1990, cited in Pratt 2002, pp. 34–5). In Latin America, modernization corrodes modernity where capitalist development and western imperatives of universal modernization demolish local autonomy and agency.[9]

The dependency school of thought evolved from the integration of two intellectual camps: the neo-Marxist camp (often criticized by orthodox Marxists as incompatible with classic Marxism), and the Latin American camp that led to the formation of the ECLA or the United Nation's "Economic Commission for Latin America." The neo-Marxists are distinct from the orthodox Marxists in that they view imperialism from the periphery rather than the center, are concerned with underdevelopment rather than with development and believe the bourgeoisie are the creation and tool of imperialism and not the eventual emergence of class as a stage in the development of capitalism

(Hout 1993). Neo-Marxists such as Frank (1984) and Galtung (1980) differ from a Marxist definition of capitalism in that they regard it from the perspective of relations of exchange rather than relations of production. Frank, whose theory is based on his extensive experiences in Latin America, resists the notion that he offers an essentially Marxist interpretation of international relations. However, his famous *Theory of the Development of Underdevelopment* is based on such economic processes as capital accumulation and profit motives (Hout 1993). In essence, Frank (1984) posits that in the world system, dominant groups (such as industrialized, developed countries in the world and the wealthy bourgeoisie in the metropolis within a nation) exploit those on the periphery (such as developing, semi-agrarian countries in the world and farmers and the proletariat within a nation) and contribute to the increase in polarization between the oppressors and the oppressed. This exploitation is conducted through systematic extraction of raw materials and agricultural products from the periphery by the center in both the world system and within the nation. The profits made from this extraction are not invested in the periphery, but are used by those in the center for, invariably, luxury goods and services. Those on the periphery are denied even the minimum means of subsistence and this sometimes prevents the reproduction of labor power (Frank 1984).

Frank's notion that development and underdevelopment are necessarily simultaneous processes is evident in Galtung's (1980) *Theory of Dependency* as well. He proposes that for one to be in power, it does not merely mean that one is high in status or is innately rich in resources. It means that someone else is low in resources and power; the distribution of resources *has* to be unequal. This explains why such a stark difference exists in each society between the elite and affluent minority and the deprived majority. Galtung based his interpretation of the world system on five assumptions: (1) power and wealth are distributed unequally between the center and the periphery; (2) development is the leveling of power differentials; (3) there is a conflict of interest between the center and the periphery; (4) the center is imperialistic because it needs the periphery for capitalistic growth; and, finally, (5) exploitative center–periphery relations in the world capitalist system can never be changed. Both Frank and Galtung's models find resonance in the economic structure of colonial states.

Colonialism systematically underdeveloped the colonized state for the mobilization of resources to its imperial centre. The main effect of this strategically incomplete development of the industry of the colonized state, notes Hout (1993), was that the latter is unable to develop a capitalist system. He contends that the imperialist relationship between European colonizers and various colonies was beneficial for European countries in that they gained the capital to finance their industrialization and capital owners simultaneously found rich opportunities for investment.

Modernization, then, is an elitist, ideological strategy where essentially the liberal oligarchies of the late nineteenth and early twentieth centuries projected the illusion of well-defined states. In actuality, they themselves promoted uneven development, ignored peasant and indigenous populations and supported elite, hegemonic communities (Canclini 1995; McClintock 1995). Paralleling the intellectual ferment in the field of sociology that did much to influence the models and theories international media scholars drew from, were the battles fought at the policy level in terms of the New World Economic Order and New World Information and Communication Order debates.

New World Economic Order and New World Information and Communication Order debates

At the policy level, academics and politicians from tri continent countries denounced the stark imbalance in the flow of goods and services from developed countries, primarily the United States, Great Britain, Germany, and France, to developing countries in Asia, Latin America, and Africa. In the form of the New World Economic Order (NWEO) and the New World Information and Communication Order (NWICO) debates of the 1960s and 1970s, tri continent countries that belonged to the Movement of Non-Aligned Nations (NAM) demanded that the flow of news between the Southern and the Northern hemispheres be equalized; the dominance of the world's five largest news agencies be broken down by the development of regional and national news agencies in the tri continent; more attention be given by the media to development news rather than to violence and conflict; and government control of the media for developmental purposes be sometimes acceptable (Masmoudi 1990).[10]

The NAM countries wanted international bodies like UNESCO (United Nations Educational, Scientific, and Cultural Organization), International Telecommunication Union (ITU), and the World Bank to help strengthen the communication infrastructure in developing nations in the tri continent (see McPhail 2002, for a detailed description of the political history of these organizations). In response, UNESCO established the MacBride Commission in 1976, to investigate the nature of transnational media flows. The MacBride Report, released in 1980, supported the claims of the NWICO and identified a gross imbalance in the flow of information, goods, and services from developed to developing countries. UNESCO called for a more equitable flow and distribution of communication technologies and endorsed the use of the mass media for national development. Despite public support, the MacBride report and the UNESCO response were full of vague terms seeking the freedom of the press, balanced information, greater variety of media channels, and so on. Their support of national governments as centralized media authorities was antithetical to Western models of private media ownership (Herman and McChesney 2003). Ultimately, the effects of these debates were not far-reaching because the United States and Great Britain, which had by then secured dominance through their advanced technology in terms of ground and satellite communication systems, economic stability, and use of the dominant English language (Tunstall and Machin 1999), simply refused the demands of the developing countries. They cited the claims as oppositional to their own imperatives of market freedom and political democracy.

In 1985, the United States and Great Britain withdrew their membership of UNESCO and the tri continent countries that retained membership turned their interests to their own national development, realizing they could not alienate the two global superpowers in their own quests for progress (for further details of this debate, see Sreberny-Mohammadi 1997). It was during the 1980s that the United States, under the leadership of President Regan, and Great Britain, under Prime Minister Margaret Thatcher, moved toward aggressive capitalism and deregulation, seeking and propelling privatization of markets across the world (Herman and McChesney 2003).

Following the scathing critiques of modernization theory by primarily Latin American Marxist scholars, and the attack on the imbalance of media flows by the NWEO and NWICO debates, political economy scholars such as Mattelart (1979), Schiller (1969), and Hallin (1994) interrogated the Anglo-American dominance of global media. Such dominance was corrosive to indigenous cultures and spread American values and economic interests, they said. The work of Schiller and others gave the concepts of cultural and media imperialism wide coverage in academic circles.

Theories of cultural and media imperialism

Cultural imperialism is a central concept in international communication that refers to the political and economic domination of western countries on tri continent nations such that the latter are forced to imbibe western technology, goods and services, and the values embedded within them. *Media imperialism* is based on a similar premise and pertains to the imposition of foreign (primarily North American) media on indigenous (primarily tri continent) cultures, imposing on them cultural values that further the hegemony of the producing nation. Both cultural and media imperialism assume audiences passively accept the manipulation and control of foreign media. McPhail extends these concepts to address *electronic colonialism*, which he defines as:

> [T]he dependent relationship of LDCs (less developed countries) on the West established by the importation of communication hardware and foreign-produced software, along with engineers, technicians, and related information protocols, that establish a set of foreign norms, values, and expectations that, to varying degrees, alter domestic cultures, habits, values, and the socialization process itself. (2002, p. 14)

Cultural and media imperialism and electronic colonialism are concepts embedded in the political economy approach to mass communication that regards media industries as the site for the intersection of culture and power such that "culture" as it is defined by those in power, is disseminated to members of society. The approach draws from Marx and Engels' polemical conceptualization of ideology where they believed that human consciousness is determined by material conditions, that theoretical doctrines which regard ideas as autonomous develop through historical divisions between material and mental labor, and that the scientific study of society and history can explain and should replace theoretical doctrines. Marx and Engels' *The German Ideology* (1970) and Marx's Preface to *A Contribution to the Critique of Political Economy* (1859), drew strong connections between classes of society and methods of production and dissemination of ideas (Thompson 1990).

The political economy approach is, in essence, a revision of the structuralist view of ideology, that is, it draws connections between autonomous cultural forms and the economic forces shaping their production (Murdock and Golding 1977). Using this approach, scholars from the Frankfurt School, most notably Max Horkheimer and Theodor Adorno (1972) placed the study of the ideological role of media as central in a capitalist and patriarchal context and revived the powerful effects paradigm of communication to theorize that with few production centers and many production points, the mass media were successfully able to propagate the ideologies of the government through messages that gave audiences the illusion of democracy and variety.[11]

Horkheimer and Adorno (1972) grimly chanted the doom of society because of the culture industry. As a conduit for repetitious, standard images, they believed it gradually turned viewers into unthinking consumers of mass art. They write, "in the culture industry every element of the subject matter has its own origin in the same apparatus as that jargon whose stamp it bears" (ibid., p. 129). This subject matter reflects the social hierarchy and "consumers are the workers and employees, the farmers and the lower middle class. Capitalist production so confines them, body and soul, that they fall helpless victims to what is offered them" (ibid., p. 133).

Mainstream American behavioral science beginning in the 1940s was primarily concerned with the media's effects. Like the Frankfurt School from which it originated, the American School assumed that modern societies had become mass societies as a result of industrial capital development (Hall 1980). Lazarsfeld and Merton (1948) state that the mass media had three social roles: first, they served as tools of social control by powerful interest groups in society. Second, they created mass publics who conformed to the social and economic status quo. Finally, they deteriorated the aesthetic tastes of the audiences and imparted to them a mass debased popular culture. While the American School operated on the notion that American society was pluralist and that as a classless society, people of various ethnic origins would live together as a melting pot, the Frankfurt School was far more critical of this mass society and perceived it as composed of hierarchies of power based on socio-economic class, gender, and ethnic differences. The media, for the American intellectuals, had limited effects because they reflected the consensus of society. For the Frankfurt intellectuals, media were an ideological tool for parties in power.

Political economy scholars of international media underlined the endurance of structures and postulated that national elites facilitated the expansion of transnational corporations within their countries, often setting aside their own development goals for personal prosperity (Schiller 1976). Besides the United States and Great Britain, Japan and Brazil were accused of ruthless media expansion in regional markets (Mattelart et al. 1983) and the very presence of global media giants was considered evidence of the homogenization of culture across the globe (Mattelart 1994). These scholars asserted that deregulation and neo-liberalism in markets around the world facilitated the narcotic effects of mass media (Hills 1986; Schiller 1989). Whereas the British Empire in colonial times developed communication networks in its colonies to disseminate the imperatives of the imperial center, in the context of globalization, the United States was regarded as an aggressive manipulator of international networks to mobilize its market imperatives across the world (Schiller 1996). Among these scholars is a concern that the content of global media products is determined by the dynamics of global marketing, and that economies of scale enjoyed by the "global popular" undermine the markets for local cultural production in developing countries across the world.

The political economy approach has been critiqued for its over emphasis on ideology (Garnham 1995), and for its inadequate attention to the flows between media production and consumption (Hall 1980; Morley and Robins 1995).

Critics of this approach point out that the assumptions of cultural and media imperialism do not account for the diversity in viewing choices and historicity of viewing experiences (Boyd-Barrett 1997). In particular, Thompson (1990) critiques Horkheimer and Adorno's conception of the culture industry and the commodification of entertainment, as an attempt to tie commodification to Weber's "iron cage" of rationalization and bureaucratization with Marx and Lukács' commodification and reification to suggest that humans are entangled in historically created webs of domination. The thesis that audiences are passive recipients of mediated images and conform to the dictates of the media, has not been satisfactorily demonstrated. Thompson concludes that Horkheimer and Adorno's view of ideology is restrictive and pessimistic and regards society as integrated; it does not take into account social diversity and dissent.

Besides, in international communication, simultaneous processes of globalization and regionalization may occur where there is a displacement of national frameworks in favor of perspectives conducive to both supranational and subnational dynamics (Morley and Robins 1995). To continue with the general accusations of cultural imperialism is to assume nations are culturally coherent, audiences are passive, and lack agency. Tomlinson (2003) suggests that cultural imperialism has to be understood as a form of *domination* by one nation over another (as in the context of colonialism); as *media imperialism* (which refers to the range and reach of media institutions and their products to countries all over the world); as a *discourse on nationality* (where the availability of foreign messages is seen as a threat to local cultures); as a *critique of global capitalism* (where capitalism and consumerism lead to a homogenous body of mass consumers all over the globe and experiences are commodified); and finally, as the *critique of modernity* where tradition is romanticized. However, as Harindranath (2003) cautions, we should continue to address the differential access to media and cultural capital across the world. The mission of cultural imperialism persists today through entrenched colonial structures facilitated not just by elites in ex-colonial centers, but by center-trained elites on the periphery as well.

These criticisms point to the need for more a nuanced approach that addresses the complex correspondence between processes of media production and consumption. Various analyses followed the bulk of political economy research highlighting the Western, liberal, and pluralist biases in media studies and shifting the focus to non-Western audiences, media systems, and formats (see Curran and Park 2000; Ginsburg et al. 2002; and Moran and Keane 2004). Other studies focused on broader transnational themes such as geo-linguistic communities (see Sinclair et al. 1996), and methods of reception analysis (Murphy and Kraidy 2003). The theoretical traditions that informed these studies are briefly dealt with in the next chapter, before advancing to a description of the postcolonial approach to international media studies that critically engages in issues of media power and the flows between structure and culture.

Chapter Three

Connecting Structure and Culture in International Media Studies

While the structuralist world systems, dependency, and cultural and media imperialism theorists situated their analyses within macro structures and debated whether the mass media were tools of national development or crass capitalist expansion, new theoretical frameworks emerged such as poststructuralism, postmodernism, and postcolonialism. These called for the study of micro situations and cultural experiences to examine the role of ideology and its interweaving between structure and culture. Each of these frameworks is worthy of a chapter-length discussion; they will be highlighted in this chapter briefly as they advance our understanding of international media studies, and as they intersect with postcolonial theory.

The critical approach to media studies has come to mean more than a mere anti-positivist stance, and following a poststructuralist tradition, clearly denotes an awareness of the contexts of research and shifting epistemological positions (Ang 1996). Drawing from Marxist and poststructuralist premises, the individual is viewed as situated within a larger power structure so that agency is not absolute but limited, defined by the subject-position itself.

What is remarkable about international media studies is the political edge that charged its development in various academic institutions across the world. Appropriations of Marxist theory by Castro and Guevara informed Latin American media studies as described in the previous chapter. Similarly, British cultural studies emerged in the 1960s with the rise of the New Left in Britain as a veritable political group. The New Left actively engaged in developing a Marxist critique that denounced the orthodoxy of the British Communist Party and the Soviet Union, and equipped them with a practical approach to the analysis of lived social and economic conditions (Dahlgren 1997). Richard Hoggart's *The Uses of Literacy* (1957), Raymond Williams' *Culture and Society* (1958) and E. P. Thompson's *The Making of the English Working Class* (1963), considered founding works in the field, centrally dealt with lived culture as being intimately informed by political practices. The British qualitative tradition emerged from cultural studies, deriving from Marxist, structuralist, semiotics, and feminist frameworks (Morley 1996). The Centre for Contemporary Cultural Studies at the University of Birmingham in 1963, first under Hoggart and then under Stuart Hall, engaged in texturing Marxist theory for the study of ideology and culture, taking on varying practical applications as it was used to study issues of gender, race, class, and so on (Hall 1980). Raymond Williams' (1974) *Television: Technology and Cultural Form* suggested that television should be considered more in terms of its flow, a conceptualization that opened up awareness of how such a medium could be used for social change as well. Hall's (1981) essay on encoding and decoding and text and context provided a nuanced framework for understanding the centrality of ideology, and the polysemic nature of the text and its interpretations.

Thompson (1990) employed a "critical conception" of ideology and called it "meaning in the service of power" (ibid., p. 6), which required the study of how meaning was created and disseminated by various symbolic forms, the social contexts of those forms, and how the meaning conveyed perpetuated systems of domination and subordination. Such an investigation led to a reformulation of ideology, which allowed the scholar to abandon the notion that the stability of industrial societies depended on consensus, and to understand that meanings were circulated in society in such a way as to maintain unequal relations of power. This reformulation also facilitated an understanding that power and ideology were not merely generated and disseminated from institutions of central power, but were perpetuated at everyday sites of interaction – at home, at school, at church, and at the workplace. The contexts of mundane behavior served as sites for the examination of ideology. Cultural studies scholars drew from Louis Althusser (1971) and Italian Marxist Antonio Gramsci (1971) who argued that the efficacy of ideology lay in the negotiations of its recipients and their positions of induced consent so that they were not imposed upon, but, being embedded subjects of ideological contexts, played an active role in their own subjection.[1]

Cultural studies grew into its own as a field in the 1980s, influencing and influenced by literary and cinema studies. In the United States, it lost much of its critical edge and Marxist roots and highlighted the notion of audiences' pleasure and meaning in their negotiations with media texts (Harris 1992). Feminists and race theorists used evidence of audience pleasure to argue for the presence of resistance, romanticizing, to a certain extent, audience agency (Fiske 2001; Modleski 1982). The "powerful media effects" assertion of early functionalist mass communication research gave way to the powerful audience position among cultural studies theorists in the United States. A significant difference between the two is their conceptualization of culture.

While the former situated culture in a behaviorist and functionalist framework in that culture could be objectively studied through social scientific methods that were guided by testable hypotheses and resulted in generalizable observations, the latter deemed culture as a contradictory and open social process (Ang 1996). It examined the production and consumption of meanings that together were representative of a certain culture – a representation that was itself in flux depending on the context. Ang (ibid., p. 134) notes, "[C]ultural studies is interested in historical and particular meanings rather than in general types of behaviour, it is process-oriented rather than result-oriented, interpretive rather than explanatory." Cultural studies problematized artificial distinctions between high and low culture and evaluated popular culture as a product of capitalist commodification. Essentially, it took a "constructivist and dialectical perspective on culture, that is to say its premise is that people and institutions in specific historical circumstances produce culture, which in turn produce and reproduce society" (Dahlgren 1997, p. 53).

Cultural studies in Commonwealth countries such as Australia, Canada, and New Zealand grappled with the more politically inflected issues of post-colonialism, globalization, and national identity. As mentioned earlier, such a critical component is strongly evident in Nordic and Germanic media research as well (Drotner 2000b).

The Culturalist and Structuralist Paradigms of Cultural Studies

The culturalist and structuralist paradigms of cultural studies offered international media scholars a framework to examine how culture was articulated in a society and how it changed and was changed by its political, economic, and social structures. In brief, the culturalist paradigm regards culture as *ideas*, that is, conventions and institutions through which valued meanings are shared and made active by a community; and as *practices*, that is, culture is that which weaves itself though all social practices and is the sum of their interrelationship (Hall 1980). This definition is derived from Raymond Williams' (1958) conceptualization of culture as a dialectic between social being and social consciousness, between culture and non-culture, neither isolatable into separate entities. Culture therefore is both meanings and values of various social groups and classes as defined by their historical conditions, which they employ to negotiate with their environment. It is also the lived experiences,

traditions and practices of these groups and classes of people. Williams exposed the political function of culture and analyzed culture and power through
the concept of hegemony as introduced by Gramsci in the 1920s and 1930s.
Williams' most useful contribution to the conceptualization of culture is his
view that the underlying patterns which characterize the practices of any given
organization at any given time is a manifestation of its culture – therefore
culture may be examined through an analysis of the interrelation of social life
rather than through a reductionist framework that regards culture as the
superstructure defined by the economic base. Building on this construction of
culture, Appadurai (1996) writes that *culturalism* refers not just to the culture
or ethnicity that defines an in-group, but the cultural differences that provide
the basis for national identity politics as well. Cultural difference textures the
character of mass mediation, mobilization, and individual entitlement, and
becomes the conscious object upon which national politics are predicated.

Cultural difference is an important area of theoretical and empirical exploration in international media studies. The strategies of institutions of power,
be they media or state, provide fodder for analyses of hegemonic structures in
society. While the structuralist notion of culture was criticized for its abstract
theorization rather than concrete explication of people, institutions, or processes, it offers a framework for the study of power in a society.

Early structuralists such as Lévi-Strauss (1963) and Ferdinand de Saussure
(1966) provided the bases for semiotic and structural analyses. Lévi-Strauss
regarded culture as the categories and frameworks in thought and language
that humans organized their experience; these frameworks were produced
and transformed in the same way that language itself was produced and
transformed. Hall (1980) notes that the structural approach views meaning as
not a practice, but a social production through language and symbolization.
A dominant meaning is produced through the regular marginalizing and
de-legitimizing of alternative constructions and the regular legitimizing of
dominant meaning.

Poststructuralists interrogated the integrity of the relationship between
sign and signifier and introduced the notion of multiple positions occupied by
both. Chow (2002) outlines three significant contributions of poststructuralism: (1) unlocking the fixed relationship between signifier and signified so that
difference, rather than sameness is how identity is conceptualized; (2) reconfiguring identity so that it is seen as mobile, indeterminable, and protean; and,
finally, (3) positioning culture such that it is fluid, a dynamic playing field in
which identities are foregrounded. As dealt with in greater depth in the concluding chapter in this book, the poststructuralist notion of fluid identities and
culture is a provocative concept in international media studies particularly in

processes of globalization marked by transnational flows of people and media products. Hybridity becomes a key concept in addressing the various combinations of global, national, and local media content, and media ethnographers urge us to think of audience communities and their media consumption in terms of their fluidity and flexibility, not rooted to specific times and spaces (Couldry 2003; Massey 1997; Murphy 2003). Important to inject at this point is Chow's (2002) critique of the poststructuralist approach to international phenomena. She notes that such an approach is damaging because the connotation of culture as a value-free zone blanketing differences and housing diversity, is just not concurrent with reality. She argues:

> In other words, once transposed into sociocultural and/or apolitical terrains, the poststructuralist specialization in difference, a revolution on its own terms, appears quite inadequate in accounting for how the purportedly liberating movements of difference and hybridity can and do become hierarchically organized as signs of minoritization and inferiority in various contemporary world situations. (ibid., p. 134)

The problematizing of hybridity and fluidity is taken up in later sections of this book and the key point to remember here is that such freedom of "flow" is a privilege of an elite few in urban centers around the world.

Feminist Theory and Cultural Studies

With the important reconceptualizations of culture and the centrality of ideology highlighted by the Birmingham School of Cultural Studies, feminist interventions in media studies gained currency in the 1980s. Feminist scholars questioned the naturalization of masculinity and masculine discourse in media studies and argued for the "feminine" as a new epistemological standpoint. Female subjectivity was the focus of subsequent audience studies (see Brundson 1981; McRobbie 1982; Modleski 1982; and Radway 1984, for example) and women's viewing and reading pleasure were highlighted with somewhat loose connections to their larger social contexts, despite the efforts of the founders of cultural studies, particularly Raymond Williams, to establish that culture was not a value-free term (Bird 2003).

Strongly influenced by theories of poststructuralism, feminist scholars interrogated the hegemonic unity of subject and culture. The term "postmodern" became a catchword in the humanities. Poststructural and postmodern theory largely produced by such French theorists as Foucault (1980), Derrida

51

(1976), Baudrillard (1983), and Lyotard (1984), placed at the center of their analyses, the ideas of difference and cultural heterogeneity. Essentially used to signify diversity and complexity (Hebdige 1988), the postmodern is sometimes, quite myopically, constructed itself as the linear next-step in the modernity trajectory. Although various descriptions of the postmodern abound (see Lyotard 1984; McRobbie 1994; and Smart 1993, for example), perhaps the most accessible is provided by Ang (1996, p. 2):

> If the Enlightenment project of modernity was based on a belief in the modernity of a world singularly organized around the principles of universal reason, rationality and truth, then postmodernity signals not so much a radical end of the modern era, its wholesale supersession and negation by an alternative set of beliefs, but rather an awareness and recognition of the political and epistemological *limits* of those principles – which Lyotard (1984) has called the loss of master narratives.

The dominant paradigm of international communication simply failed to account for the decentralization, transnationalism, and commercialization of media, particularly television, through which culture had become a commodifying opportunity for consumption. Featherstone (1990) adds that postmodernism represents a key turn in conceptualizations of global culture. Global culture is no longer viewed as a process of homogenization or cultural imperialism that follows the path of European colonialism. It is regarded as a process that involves immense complexity and diversity in its flows among local discourses and cultural rituals that may resist and subvert entrenched systems of order.

Despite the poststructuralist dismantling of the ideological coherence of structures of power, feminist scholars also exposed the impracticality of deconstructionist theories contending that they had limited results for marginalized groups. Specifically, the exposure of ideology does little to empower those most bound by it, usually gender, ethnic, religious, and sexual minorities around the world. For example, Hartsock (1987/1990) critiqued Foucault for his bland assertion that the oppressed should resist power, without actually delineating how this could be done. Hartsock argued for the transformation of power relations through a revised and reconstructed theory involving five steps: first, women have to recognize themselves as makers of history, not just as nonbeings, but as through whom the male self is constructed; second, their work should be developed on an epistemological base to show that systematic knowledge of the world of the marginalized is possible; third, a theory is needed that acknowledges that within women's daily activities is embedded an understanding of the world; fourth, women should understand the difficulty of creating alternatives; and finally, women need an engaged vision where they actively participate in altering power relations.

Van Zoonen (1994) adds that power is not a monolithic entity that some groups possess while others do not. To translate feminist theory into practice, van Zoonen seeks a radical politicization in the feminist research process, both internally by questioning power relations inherent in doing research, and externally by striving to produce results that are relevant to the feminist endeavor. She offers a critique of conventional audience analyses that focus on the male/female distinction without taking into account such intersecting variables as race, ethnicity, and sexuality, to name a few. She writes that gender should be regarded as an "ongoing process by which subjects are constituted often in paradoxical ways. The identity that emerges is therefore fragmented and dynamic; gender does not determine or exhaust identity" (ibid., p. 33).

Critical feminist scholars in development communication also called for a shift from the positivist to structuralist approach, from a formalist to substantive perspective, from an ethnocentric to polycentric understanding, from the dichotomic endogenism vs. exogenism to the globalism framework, from economic to interdisciplinary approaches, and from holistic to problem-oriented approaches. They offered an alternative to the functionalist development paradigm through a critical, participatory grassroots framework. Steeves (1993) explains that the dominant paradigm did not address the experiences of women although they played an important economic role in development. She notes three major critical approaches that developed as a reaction to the dominant paradigm: women in development (WID), grass-roots critique of development, and the political economy of communication approaches, respectively. The basic principles shared by scholars of these areas of critique are that development communication must liberate, should proceed from the perspective of women that must be understood through dialogue (which engages many levels of power), and should be placed within its context.

Riaño (1994) adds that feminist communication positions women as producers of meaning and goes beyond development communication, which regards women as subjects of information, as participants, and as subjects of change respectively. Goals of feminist communication are to name oppressions of race, gender, sexual orientation and disability; negotiate fair representation and equality of access, construct individual and collective identities, and produce alternate meanings. Feminist communication is closely linked to action to achieve ownership, inclusion, and accountability for women in the development process. It does not focus just on creating consciousness of subordination, influencing public policies, or encouraging support for development campaigns as do alternative, participatory,[2] and development communication respectively. Messages are horizontal and circulate through exchange and networks of meaning to create empowerment. Most importantly, writes Riaño (1994), feminist communication questions the public/ private dichotomy which limits women and their concerns to the private sphere, rarely acknowledging their problems and issues in the public sphere of discussion and policy-making. Such a framework critiques the validity of the dominant metaphor of "women's silence," which is associated with passivity. This perpetuates their marginalization in development discourse instead of opening up new avenues for communicative and social action – avenues that may be possible through an understanding that silence itself is multidimensional and representative of varied experiences. Gender issues are central to postcolonial theory as well – its attention to subaltern politics intimately draws in feminist concerns.

Vickers and Dhruvarajan (2002) point to an emerging paradigm for the study of women particularly in an era of media globalization. This paradigm consists of three strains: the recognition of the voices of minority and marginalized women as authentic; the expansion of scholarship to non-Western women; and the increase in numbers of non-Western women in the Western world, blurring the lines between archaic dichotomies such as North and South and First and Third Worlds. This new paradigm then is keenly aware of difference and locality of the subject and marks a departure from earlier paradigms of (particularly western) feminism that generalized the experiences of women across the world. The authors note that Western feminist theory positions women in general as oppressed and victims, when obviously vast differences exist in patterns of oppression and victimization. They seek a one-world feminist approach where the effectiveness and validity of women's movements are considered within a global context, as opposed to the "one-sisterhood" approach of WID feminists who tended more to speak for their tri continent counterparts (Goetz 1988) than allow the latter to speak for themselves.

The Postcolonial Approach to International Media Studies

As indicated in the previous sections, while the structuralists directed attention to structures in society through the study of structures in language, it was the poststructuralists who focused on power and its presence in micro relationships as well as macro institutions. The strength of postcolonial theory lies in its critique of Orientalism (Said 1979), investigation of subaltern identities (Spivak 1988a), discussion of minority discourse (JanMohamed and Lloyd

54

1990), and its formulation of hybridity as part of culture (Bhabha 1990). Post-colonial scholars, like the poststructuralists, are interested in the interrogation of the ideologies that sustain various regimes in power and share the political edge of Latin American media studies and British cultural studies. Anti-colonial movements in Asia, Africa, and Central and South America, co-opted the tenets of Marxism to formulate their unique resistances.[3] Whereas nationalism was context-specific and subjected to local politics, Marxism was translatable across national borders and provided the common, anti-colonial, political language through which activist leaders from very different political climates could communicate and empathize with one another.[4] According to Young (2001), tricontinental Marxism provided the basis for postcolonial theory. Resistance to twentieth-century capitalism through staunch adherence to Marxist principles is evident in the 1917 Bolshevik Revolution in Russia and anti-colonial independence movements in Asia, Southeast Asia, Africa, and the Caribbean; although these gradually disintegrated into socialist failure, they transformed capitalism itself in their socialist appropriations as seen in many tri continent countries today.

The overriding concern of postcolonial scholars is to establish the contemporary nature of colonialism. They protest against Western paradigms of media effects through which tri continent societies are studied. They emphasize that textual and audience analyses have to be conducted with a keen awareness of the multiplicity of actor and audience identities, experiences, and social, cultural, and political realities (Guha 1994; Spivak 1996).

The historical anchoring of postcolonial theory

The relevance of a postcolonial framework for international media studies lies in its focus on national liberation movements around the world (beginning in 1947 with India's liberation from British rule), ending the political supremacy of Europe. By World War I, most of the world was dominated by imperial powers and Britain controlled one-fifth of the world in area and one quarter in population. After the Great War, Germany, through its fascist ideology of *Lebensraum*, tried to colonize Europe itself. Italy lost its colonies, and Japan lost its South Asian territories to colonial powers of Europe and the United States. The seven primary colonial powers (Britain, France, the Netherlands, Belgium, Denmark, Australia, and New Zealand) gave up imperial control of their colonies from 1945 onwards. The colonies of fascist Spain and Portugal, the fascist apartheid regime of South Africa, and the territories under the Soviet Union and the United States remained politically unchanged at this time. Young (2001) writes that although the United States could technically claim postcolonial status, it is a veritable colonial power having annexed territories (for example, Hawaii in 1898), conquering them through wars (for example, California, Texas, Nevada, Utah, Puerto Rico, and Guam), or buying them from other imperial powers (for example, Louisiana from France in 1803, Florida from Spain in 1819, and Alaska from the Russian Imperial Government in 1867).

In the postcolonial era, wars and conflicts in various countries are characterized mostly by anti-colonial struggles. Some examples are East Timor's long struggle for independence from Indonesia which invaded it when a Portuguese colony, Tibet and Taiwan's resistance from China, Kashmir's from India, Palestine and the West Bank's from Israel, and the First Nations' reprisals in Canada, Ethiopia, New Zealand, and the United States. Struggles for independence by indigenous peoples such as the Kurds in Afghanistan and Tamils in Sri Lanka who seek protection by joining other decolonized groups (for example, the Catholics in Northern Ireland who seek to join Ireland); by diasporic communities who cannot return to their native land (for example, the Koreans in Japan); by the low caste and tribal communities in India, Bangladesh and Japan; and by ethnic and poor minorities across the world, also texture the political and social terrain in the postcolonial era.[5] All these struggles continue at the same time that Europe and decolonized countries are contending with the devastating violence of colonialism, a process that symbolically started in 1492. Such violence encompassed slavery and enforced migration of such peoples as Africans, Americans, Arabs, Asians, and Europeans, with the intent to destroy some cultures and privilege others. Postcolonial cultural critique demands renewed scrutiny of the history of colonialism especially from those who have not been heard and who have endured its effects. More importantly, it requires an examination of colonialism's contemporary imprint on social and cultural life (Young 2001).

The global landscape has obviously undergone significant political and economic changes since the eighteenth, nineteenth and early twentieth centuries. Nation-states acknowledged that to establish a space and place for themselves in the global market, allegiance with a larger regional entity was necessary. This allegiance was based on economic and political agendas and created a struggle within the members of the nation-state to maintain their unique cultural identities, and at the same time, subscribe to the identity of the larger region. With the 1955 Bandung Conference on non-alignment, the "Third World" emerged as a political unit and in this historical and political context, "postcolonial" refers to the struggle by oppressed states against European colonialists. Twenty-nine African and Asian countries participated and its significance is in its formation of an alliance of postcolonial countries calling for an end to all forms of colonization and the establishment of human rights standards. It set up the basis for the Movement of Non-Aligned countries in 1961 that sought to create a power bloc of the "Third World." However, post-Cold War power structures made non-alignment virtually impossible and the "Third World" coalition was structurally weakened by internal conflicts. The Havana Conference of 1966 resulted in the tricontinental alliance of Asia, Africa, and Central and South America and a formal recognition of the globalization of anti-colonial resistance (Young 2001). By 1987, 160 nation-states had registered autonomous status with the United Nations and many more followed with the disintegration of the Soviet Union in 1989.

Appiah (1996) writes that the "post" in both postcolonialism and postmodernity refers to the clearing space after colonialism and modernity (if the latter can be characterized as a distinct era) and a site for processes of transnational commodification. The "post" in both terms challenges earlier restrictive narratives of colonialism and modernity. Yet postcolonialism is intimately and crucially informed by the conditions of colonialism experienced by countries across the world. Chow (1998) disagrees with Appiah and underscores the importance of studying postcolonial cultures in their contexts instead of erasing particularities in a bland effort to universalize or generalize where postcolonialism is seen as the same as postmodernism, and where the connecting word "post" signifies "after" and not much more. Schwarz asserts:

> Postcolonial studies alerts us that the very forms through which we study the world, the academic disciplines, are implicitly structured by Europe's imperial dominance of the world since 1500...Postcolonial studies...is the radical philosophy that interrogates both the past history and ongoing legacies of European colonialism in order to undo them. (2000, p. 4)

Besides its historical definition, therefore, postcolonial studies has an activist and ethical component in that it questions the violence that occurs in imperial domination and a rethinking of peoples and cultures by the experiences that bind them, not just by ethnicity or nationality.

Academic contexts of postcolonial theory

Postcolonial studies grew as a subfield of English literature, History, and Philosophy in academic institutions around the world, varying in its focus and politics based on its geographic location. Scholars in settler societies such as Australia, New Zealand, and Canada (the OZCAN school), united by their history of British domination and generally peaceful liberation to enjoy privileged trade and migration sanctions, engaged in Commonwealth literature as

57

the literary expression of English speakers in former British colonies. By the 1960s, however, in the post-Bandung Conference context, newly independent nations in Africa, the Caribbean, and even Latin America banded together as the "Third World" where they asserted that the common colonial English language that bound them together was itself most oppressive, a language of the oppressor.

The word "postcolonial" has therefore been used to refer to historical demarcation, academic tradition, and theoretical revisionism. To explain, first, "postcolonial" has been studied as an historical signifier of a nation's independence from colonial rule. Second, as an academic tradition, the term has been used to describe "Third World" or "Commonwealth literature" taught in English Departments primarily in postcolonial or Commonwealth countries, which seeks "to describe colonial discourse analysis, to detail the situation of migrant groups within First World States, and to specify oppositional reading practices" (Mongia 1996, p. 2). Finally, in terms of theoretical revisionism, the postcolonial framework attempts to rethink how knowledge has been constructed. That is, it "[problematizes] the nation-state and its ideologies and [reveals] the difficulty in conceiving the nation even as an 'imagined community'" – an imagination or a call to imagination rooted in Enlightenment notions of freedom, democracy, and modernity. Such notions have proved disastrous for subaltern communities of class, gender, ethnicity, religions and sexuality, showing that, "[O]ld narratives of progress and reason are inadequate for addressing contemporary realities and the numerous fractures that attend them" (ibid., p. 5).

The early beginnings of postcolonial theory as an academic field are credited to Edward Said's foundational work, *Orientalism*[6] (1978) where he asserted that Orientalism should be understood "as a discourse...by which European culture was able to manage – and even produce – the Orient politically, sociologically, militarily, ideologically, scientifically, and imaginatively, during the post-Enlightenment period" (ibid., p. 23). Writing about the trend in Western nations after World War II to engage in area studies, Said states that the intent was not altruistic but malevolent, to encourage uneven development of the colonies such that it would enhance the prosperity of the imperial center. In this context, Orientalism emerged as an important area of study for Western scholars and non-Western elites, to map out the Orient, categorize its features and discipline its peoples and territories for Western consumption.

Said explains the concept of Orientalism in three distinct ways: first, as a label for those who conduct scholarship and pedagogy about the Orient not as an apolitical exercise but with the real intention of domination and for intimate understanding and control; second, a term based on the ontological and epistemological difference between Orient and Occident (where methodologically, the Orient was strategically placed external to the west and examined for its stylistic, linguistic, and cultural differences, not for accuracy of representation in itself); and third, a referent to the institutionalized domination and subjugation of the East by the West, beginning approximately in the late eighteenth century. Understanding the term should include a recognition of its conceptual consistency among scholars and statesmen of the West and East, of the relationship of power and domination between West and East, and, finally, and perhaps most important, the hegemonic context in the Gramscian sense, that has persisted through centuries, providing a consensual and flexible superiority, "which puts the Westerner in a whole series of possible relationships with the Orient without ever losing him the relative upperhand" (ibid., p. 25).

Following *Orientalism*, various analyses of literary texts from Commonwealth countries emerged that drew critical connections between the text and its social and political structures. Important to highlight here are the significant contributions of postcolonial scholars from the Indian subcontinent. As a response to the elite nationalism promulgated by the Indian National Congress and its enduring power after the nation's independence from British rule in 1947, Indian historians and intellectuals used Marxist structuralism to develop postcolonial theory that reverted focus onto the peasantry away from the bourgeois elite.[7] Notable among these scholars, also considered founding proponents of postcolonial theory, are Aijaz Ahmad (1992), Homi K. Bhabha (1990), Ranajit Guha (1994), Dipesh Chakrabarty (1989), Gayatri Spivak (1988a, b), and Rajeswari Sunder Rajan (1993). Spivak and Bhabha's presentations at two symposia in Essex in 1982 and 1984 were published in the *Europe and its Others* volumes. These presentations addressed the relegation of peasants and women in the Indian independence struggle to a specific place and task, which they saw as an elitist, patriarchal construction of these subaltern populations.

Around the same time, in 1982, the Centre for the Contemporary Cultural Studies in Birmingham published *The Empire Strikes Back*[8] and the first volume of *Subaltern Studies: Writings on South Asian History and Society* appeared in New Delhi. As Mongia reflects, "one witnessed a fundamental reassessment of modes of knowledge production in a whole range of academic disciplines such as anthropology, history, literary studies, and sociology" (1996, p. 14). The task of postcolonial scholars was to question Western-derived narratives such as "modernity as progress" and "freedom and democracy as universal desirables."

Theorizing the subaltern

Indian postcolonial theory is intimately informed by Gramsci whose essays addressed the internal colonization of the agricultural south by the industrial north in Italy, a process that foreshadowed similar ones in many parts of the globe. It was in Gramsci's *The Modern Prince* (1957) that the term "subaltern" emerged, synonymous with subordinate. This concept was reworked by Indian theorists to mean, "the general attribute of subordination in South Asian society whether this is expressed in terms of class, caste, age, gender, and office or in any other way" (Guha 1982, cited in Young 2001, p. 354). The definition was extended later to focus particularly on women (Spivak 1988a).

Young summarizes that "the subaltern has become a synonym for any marginalized or disempowered minority group, particularly on the grounds of gender and ethnicity" (2001, p. 354). The concept of the subaltern allowed tricontinental scholars to critique and theorize extensively the failure of independence movements to bring about real social transformation. What happened in reality was the continued privileging of elite groups who, like their colonial predecessors, fueled capitalist endeavors.

The notion of victimization in the case of the subaltern is a much debated one. Postcolonial feminists argue that the epistemological positioning of the subaltern woman as victim relegates to her the position of an object, to be spoken for and about, not a speaking agent herself (Mohanty 2003). Sunder Rajan comments:

> While I am sympathetic to a feminist politics that seeks to resist intervention, I am also anxious, like many feminists in this part of the globe, to discover what might make intervention possible. If "victim" and "agent" are adopted as exclusive and excluding labels for the female subject, and if, further, victimhood is equated with helplessness and agency with self-sufficiency, all feminist politics will be rendered either inauthentic or unnecessary. (1993, p. 313)

What these scholars are attempting to do is point to the blurring lines between victimization and agency and to the importance of addressing context when making interpretations of these positions. To take up the postcolonial challenge of theoretical revisionism, the following sections describe the postcolonial critique of "nation" and "nationalism" as it is constructed by European scholarship and present a few questions about theory and method raised by postcolonial scholars.

Postcolonial critiques of nationalism

Postcolonial theorists critique European scholarship on nationalism in three important ways. First, they do not regard the emergence of nationalism as coincidental with modernity as is seen in the work of Anderson (1991), Gellner (1983), and Hobsbawm (1990). Chatterjee (1993) objects to Anderson's (1991) idea that Europe provided "modular" forms for the rest of the world from which the latter imagined their communities. This, the author states, relegates the rest of the world to the position of mere consumers of modernity and does not account for anti-colonial nationalism where identity was based on *difference* from the western modular forms. He writes:

> Europe and the Americas, the only true subjects of history, have thought out on our behalf not only the script of colonial enlightenment and exploitation, but also that of our anticolonial resistance and postcolonial misery. Even our imaginations must remain forever colonized. (1993, p. 5)

Chatterjee argues further that Anderson's notion of a common language facilitated by print-capitalism as essential to the imagination of a nation, is also inadequate. In colonized states, the technologies of print capitalism – the printing press and rudimentary mass media systems, all were effective in circulating the English language as one of administrative power. Yet nationalist elites fought for the authenticity of vernacular languages as well. Van der Veer (1997), like Smith (1986), critiques the tendency to view nationalism as opposed to traditionalism and parochialism, and writes that the larger frameworks of nationalism existed before the colonial era and are built upon and modified through religious nationalism. In his examination of religious nationalism in India, Van der Veer writes "we need both an analysis of 'tradition' that is not prejudiced by the discourse of modernity and a theory of the impact of colonialism and orientalism that does not deny agency to colonial subjects" (1997, p. x).

   Second, postcolonial scholars question the character of nationalism itself and posit that nationalism (particularly in such a country as India) is not uniform in character (as presumed by Anderson (1991) and Gellner (1983)), but composed of anti-colonial and religious nationalisms as well. Rajagopal (1996) writes that Anderson's (1991) conflation of national consciousness with modernity is problematic because he applies the term "modern" equally to them and does not account for contradictory and uneven development characteristic of developing countries. Van der Veer (1997) critiques Gellner's (1983) overarching modernization theory and comments that the basic flaw in this theory as well as in those of many Marxist analyses of capitalist expansion, is the assumption that a social system may be integrated only through the sharing of a common culture dependent on a moral consensus. He argues that nationalism also "creates other nationalisms – religious, ethnic, linguistic, secular – but not a common culture. The modernization paradigm makes too much of homogenization, while it overlooks 'antagonization' and 'heterogenization.' The forging of identity always creates diversity" (1997, p. 15).

Third, postcolonial scholars contest the definitions of state and nation as either denying the role of state (Anderson 1991), or awarding too much agency to it (Gellner 1983). Rajagopal (1996) critiques Anderson's cultural definition of national identity in that the latter underplays the role of the state and romanticizes the liberal democratic nation as if it is a mere social condition. The assumption that the nation is created and sustained in the imagination may lead to a conceptualization of it as an idea insulated from reality, safe from the ravages of state. However, this is misleading because society is held together not just by shared values, but through the "coercive and constraining power of social institutions, and the sedimented practices operating across these institutions" (1996, p. 445). He recognizes the importance of governing structures that organize popular imagination of the nation. Similarly, he critiques Gellner (1983) and Hobsbawm (1990) for awarding too much agency to the state and its institutions such as education and defense, for the development of the nation.

The postcolonial attention to difference

As indicated earlier in this chapter, postcolonial scholars caution against the tendency to either equate postcolonial studies with ethnic studies (Schwarz 2000) or lump all postcolonial countries under one umbrella of experience (Chow 1998). Some societies, such as those of Canada, Australia, and New Zealand, are considered settler societies where colonialism is still a dominant force and therefore cannot be considered postcolonial (Vickers and Dhruvarajan 2002). Schwarz (2000) discusses postcolonial studies in North America and asserts that the differences in colonial policies and strategies of integration between European white settlers in America and those in other parts of the world creates a different sort of postcoloniality in the United States. Postcolonial studies in the United States is distinct from ethnic studies because of American exceptionalism which presumes that the histories of America and Europe are different; academic plurality where the work of non-US scholars on colonial history did not fit well with those engaging in ethnic studies; and legal developments where changes in immigration laws in the 1960s provided entry to a significant number of academic professionals who proceeded to carve a space for their studies on postcolonial countries.

Chow (2000) reminds us that the study of East Asian countries such as China, Japan, Korea, and Taiwan as postcolonial is problematic. Although they share some of the similarities with other Asian countries such as India, Bangladesh, Vietnam, Malaysia, and the Philippines, to name a few, they (with the exception of Taiwan) were not territorially dominated by old European colonial powers for long periods of time. When occupied, they maintained primary use of their language and in the contemporary context, cannot, especially in the case of Taiwan, Hong Kong, and Singapore, be termed "Third World" because of their economic development. Also, some of these countries were imperialized by East Asian cultures themselves as we see in the example of China's use of imperialist force on Mongolia, Taiwan, Tibet, and Xinjiang. The British and Portuguese colonies until 1997, of Hong Kong and Macau, respectively, are prime examples of newly postcolonial countries that are marginalized in postcolonial analyses and discourse. In her discussion of Hong Kong, Chow poses a few intriguing questions:

> [H]ow do we talk about a postcoloniality that is a forced return (without the consent of the country's residents) to a "mother country," itself as imperialistic as the previous colonizer? Is Hong Kong then simply an anomaly in the history of colonialism? Or does it not, in its obligatory "restoration" to China in fact recrystallize and highlight the problem of "origins" that has often been suppressed in other postcolonial cultures because of ethnic pride? (2000, p. 151)

Hong Kong's repossession of its precolonial state is actually China's possession of Hong Kong in a neocolonialist sense. Hong Kong's "authentic language" is then not English, nor standard Chinese, but a daily, lived, practiced mix of Cantonese, English, and written Chinese. In this manner, the postcoloniality of India and Hong Kong cannot be equated even though they are both former British colonies because while the former can attempt to uncover Indian native historiography underneath colonial appropriations, for the latter, the task is twofold in moving past British and also Chinese historiographic manipulations. Besides dissimilarities in colonial experiences, some nations were born of fragmentation, not so-called coherence. For example, Indonesia was created by Dutch, Japanese, and Javanese colonialists, and Palestine meanders across Israel-controlled territories (Young 2003).

Apart from the careful attention to differing postcolonial experiences, the postcolonial framework calls for an awareness of difference among its subjects as well – be they dominant elites or subalterns. Such a call emerged as a reaction to mainstream Western feminism that tended to focus mainly on gender struggles (to the marginalization of caste, class, religious, ethnic, and other issues) and generalize this focus to non-Western women as well (Mohanty 2003; Vickers and Dhruvarajan 2002). In situating postcolonial subjects along lines of difference, engagement with such a framework demands that the postcolonial scholar think of herself or himself in terms of difference as well, and how this difference translates into inclusion or exclusion with dominant groups (Vickers and Dhruvarajan 2002; Young 2003).

The *attention to difference* itself, however, could also lead to a glorification of that difference in terms of diversity and multiculturalism that distracts from the material inequities that produce such a difference. This crucial point is taken up in the concluding chapter of the book. The primary point here is that differences are considered as epistemological points of enquiry, rather than sameness, as was the tendency in dominant frames of analysis from a variety of fields (Zinn et al. 2000).

Therefore, rather than dismiss the idea of nation entirely, we must understand it as a divided and conflicted entity and examine its various collisions with global capital. While the discourse on postcolonialism has remained rigorous because of the dialogue about terms and interpretation among its scholars, what has emerged is a broad concern that postcolonialism should not become a bland label for the work done by tri continent intellectuals in the Western world, or those merely influenced by postmodernism and poststructuralism. This would only create yet another area of study that would gain identity in its relation to Western theory. What is required is a constant alertness to new intellectual productions and the ways in which they interrogate entrenched Western norms of intellect, modernity, and nationalism.

In the following chapters, the various facets of media production, representation, and consumption in tri continent countries will be addressed. Included in the tri continent are countries of the Far East even though they have not been under conventional European domination like those of South Asia or Africa; these will be placed within their historical and political contexts. This is to address the criticism of postcolonial studies that it tends to deploy its framework as a "universal structuring formation" (Mongia 1996, p. 6), lumping together diverse postcolonial experience under unifying labels. The postcolonial framework will inform the analysis, keeping us alert to the cultural implications of structural manipulations of media across the tri continent. Burton leaves us with important questions to consider in this endeavor:

> How do we resist the seduction of national narratives and make sense of the violences they enact under the guise of patriotism, imperial and otherwise? How do we convince students that this is a valuable project, connected to the

development of civic participation in the twenty-first century in transformative and enduring ways? What does that maneuver lead away from, exactly? What does it turn us toward, precisely? Do we, as inheritors of post-Enlightenment, post imperial thinking ourselves, even have the tools for undertaking such an enterprise? If Eurocentrism and "the planetary" together characterize modernity, [how] do new imperial histories rupture that binary? What do accelerated discourses of globalization in institutions of higher education mean for the study of nation and empire? (2003, pp. 13–14)

Keeping these questions in mind, we turn to the next chapter, which focuses on political and media institutions of tri continent countries to address the flows and influences of globalization. The postcolonial framework reminds us to look for interconnections among various media systems, allowing us to examine such phenomena as hybrid programming, and cloning and collaging of formats as representations of the dynamic flux in national media systems responding to a globalizing media environment. Postcolonial theory further opens up the field of international media research in its attention to the various power differentials that undergird structure and culture and more importantly, in its historicization of current processes within their colonial and imperial contexts.

Chapter Four

Reviving the Pure Nation
Media as Postcolonial Savior

Modernity's premises, to recap briefly from Chapter Two, were that religious traditions would give way to a greater belief in science, increase in rationality, and structured leisure. Mass media, in such conditions, would (as pointed out by the Frankfurt School critics of mass culture) reduce the masses to cogs in an industrial wheel, using their minimal earnings to consume fetishized products in the marketplace to regain lost connections in a futile attempt to heal their fragmented selves.

Yet, evidence of just the opposite is widely available. In Egypt, India, Nigeria, and Lebanon, for example, sophisticated, "modern" mass media systems use religion precisely to advance notions of the modern, progressive system and simultaneously admonish those who do not belong (either by caste or religion) in the dominant narrative, or those who transgress patriarchal notions of gender and nationhood. Also, far from sedating the masses, as we shall see in Chapter Six, decentralized media, particularly with the presence of satellite and private cable networks, facilitate agency, selectivity, and even resistance at various levels.

This chapter argues that media systems serve as sites for the reproduction of patriarchal and colonial structures. The postcolonial theoretical framework allows us to critique the perdurability of constructions of nation, citizen, and community, themselves repositories of residual ideologies of colonialism. The objective in this chapter is not to create an oppositional discourse to conventional, descriptive (as opposed to truly critical) international media studies, but to uncover those hidden spaces in theory that have been submerged in the trend to highlight global media giants anchored in the leading industrialized nations of the world.

The call to move away from binaries in the study of globalization is not new. The damning limitations of the positivist paradigm of development communication and early international scholarship have been extensively critiqued.

No doubt the strong US and British alliance through imperial, world wars, Cold War, and deregulation eras led to their combined domination over time. Similar press freedoms, political philosophies, and coincidence of deregulation in the United States and privatization in Great Britain in the 1980s facilitated their combined growth with the United States leading in international news, movies, book publishing, advertising, and music industries, and Great Britain a close second. Rupert Murdoch's BskyB and Star TV led in British domestic and international entertainment, respectively, and a significant portion of the programming was imported from US media (Tunstall and Machin 1999). The technological and economic advantage of industrialized core countries and their status as former imperial powers also mean they are leaders in global media through such corporate giants as AOL-Time Warner, CNN, Viacom, and Disney in the United States; Sony in Japan; Bertelsmann in Germany; British Sky Broadcasting and Pearson in Great Britain; and Vivendi Universal, Matra Hachette, Canal Plus, and Pathé in France, to name but a few (McPhail 2002).

Yet the very presence of foreign, primarily US programming in various parts of the world continues to revive the closed arguments of cultural and media imperialism without adequate explanation of exactly how these programs are accommodated, hybridized, or even resisted at the level of consumption. Globalization does not automatically mean an undermining of the sovereignty of nation-states, nor a homogenization of Third World cultures as a response to the presence of global media products in their markets (Featherstone 1990). The strong influence of sociology on the field of international communication has led to an overt focus on the European modern state as a model for society (Arnason 1990; Mennell 1990; B. Turner 1990), submerging the relationship between culture and agency (Archer 1990).

The demarcation of the world into a three-world (center, semi-periphery, and periphery) political and economic system (Wallerstein 1990a), does not address the role culture plays (Worsley 1990), nor does it interrogate adequately the power relations that drive such a system (Bergeson 1990). While the goal of industrialized nations since the 1880s was a unified "borderless" global nation-state for the sake of economic progress (Robertson 1990), and the media have been used extensively to facilitate the lowering of political boundaries (Canclini 1995; Morley and Robins 1995; Price 1995), we need to draw attention back to the history and structures that make those interconnections possible and examine the correspondence among media production, representation, and consumption. Analyses of global media content and networks provide strong evidence that media flow and reception across the world are textured by a variety of local factors.

First, the majority of the world's population does not receive programming from transnational "imperialist" networks such as Star TV, CNN, and BBC (Harindranath 2003). Regional giants such as Televisa in Mexico and Globo in Brazil dominate geolinguistic areas (Fox 1997). To cite a couple of examples, only around 10 percent of households in Egypt and around 13 percent in India receive satellite television (see Abu-Lughod 2005 and McMillin 2001, respectively). Foreign programming, in many non-media centric societies, may comprise a small percentage of the viewer's total media experience, yet forms an extension of neocolonial processes facilitated by institutions already entrenched since colonial times such as educational, legal, and administrative systems. Second, within nations, access to media is differentiated by caste, class, ethnic, economic, and geographic differentiations (Ferguson 1993). Third, among populations receiving transnational media, most prefer domestic, vernacular language programming since production and reception quality of local programming, particularly beginning in the 1990s, are almost as good as or better than foreign programming (De la Garde 1994; Ferguson 1993; McMillin 2001, 2002b; Straubhaar 1991; Waterman and Rogers 1994). Even subtitled foreign programming does not rate as highly (Dupagne and Waterman 1999) as locally produced programs (Wang 1993). Finally, the booming format industry particularly in Asian countries has facilitated the production of highly popular cloned, copied, unlicensed, and licensed hybrid programs, reducing the popularity of foreign programs considerably (Moran and Keane 2004).

An overt focus on the structure of global media networks located in the Western hemisphere, leads to assumptions on how they are accommodated all over the world. Rising urbanization and cosmopolitanism in countries across the world, leading to a growing middle class exposed to transnational media networks such as the BBC, CNN, and MTV; global icons such as Michael Jackson and Tom Cruise, and shows such as Fox's *American Idol* and ABC's *Who Wants to Be a Millionaire* (duly cloned for local contexts) lead to bland assumptions of a shared global culture partaken of equally by consumers everywhere. No doubt the United States dominates the program production industry, yet such centers in Brazil and Japan, for example (the latter itself a strong colonial master of East Asia), dominate geolingual regions (Sinclair et al. 1996). By keeping media industries in the tri continent on the margins of academic discourse, we fail to understand the incredible impact of colonialism on the development of their media systems, the regional influence of these systems, and the unique character they take on as they assert their postcolonial identities and meet the challenges of globalization.

To examine the dynamics of media production in tri continent countries, the following sections will address the following broad themes in the role of mass media: as an extension of colonial power, as a builder of the postcolonial state, and subsequently as a patriarchal vehicle for the restoration of the chaste, female nation.

Defining the Third World

Although the term tri continent is used to refer to Asia, Latin America, and Africa in this book, a section on the political baggage associated with the term "Third World" will be useful here. Scholars of international communication have attempted to define the First, Second, and Third Worlds (see McPhail 2002). While lists of countries in these categories may be easy to obtain, accompanied by the caution that demarcations are not hard and fast with members slipping among categories based on their political and economic contexts, what is more important is to recognize the diversity in these categories. The Third World has been used to refer to newly independent nations of the global South, also collectively called the non-aligned nations that did not form alliances with the superpowers of the then Soviet Union or the United States in the Cold War. Shohat and Stam (1994) discuss the complexities of Third World nomenclature. For example, the countries in this strata are not generally poor in resources as is evidenced by the oil-rich Venezuela and Iraq; they are not non-white as seen in the examples of Argentina and Ireland; they are not primarily agrarian, as is evident in the highly industrialized economies of Brazil, Argentina, and India; and they are far from culturally backward as demonstrated by internationally recognized artists and writers from these regions. Turkey and Iran were never directly colonized, although they have been indirectly subjected to European domination.

In particular, primary knowledge of the Middle East in international communication was derived from functionalist, positivist, linear development communication studies, particularly Daniel Lerner's (1958) *Passing of Traditional Society* focusing on Turkey, Syria, Iraq, and Iran. The "Middle East," itself a post-World War I European label, shares the legacy of the Ottoman Empire and colonial rule, yet is marked by differences in its regions, confounding the Eurocentric notions of state and nation. The unified construction of the Middle East is ironically taken up by native scholars themselves. Hamid Mowlana's model of "Islamic communication" has been critiqued for its assumptions of a monolithic Islamic culture and Muslim world. Khiabany (2003) argues that there are around 1.2 billion Muslims in the world, 55 member states in the Organization of Islamic Countries (OIC) and great variations in how Islam is practiced in countries with the largest Muslim populations:

Indonesia, Pakistan, Bangladesh, India, Turkey, Iran, Egypt, Nigeria, and China. The complexities are numerous: Arabic is widely spoken, but Turkish, Persian, and Hebrew are also dominant languages. Islam, differentiated between Shiiite and Sunni, is a dominant religion; other important ones in the region are Christianity and Judaism. The 1905 Iranian Constitutional Reform and Atatürk's modernization of Turkey introduced Western political and economic models, yet most nations continue as autocratic and monarchic republics (Sreberny 2000).

Among Middle Eastern countries, the United Arab Emirates, Kuwait, and Israel are among the countries with the highest GNP in the world, while Yemen is among the lowest. Democracy is not progressive, but uneven, with some states holding multiparty elections (as in Algeria, Tunisia, Egypt, Morocco, Jordan, and Yemen), some with consultative councils (Bahrain, Oman, and Saudi Arabia), and some battling political violence and civil unrest erupting with the election of liberal presidents (Iran in 1997, for example). Sreberny (2000) asserts that the Middle East cannot be essentialized as one coherent unit. It is a complex region with strong differences in historical and contemporary political, cultural, and social contexts. A similar position is taken up by Canclini (1995) regarding the complexity of Latin American countries.

Shohat and Stam attempt to classify Third World countries by their colonial experiences, defining colonialism itself "as the process by which European powers reached positions of economic, military, political and cultural hegemony in much of Asia, Africa, and the Americas" (1994, p. 15). It follows then, that the Third World comprises "the colonized, neocolonized, or decolonized nations and 'minorities' whose structural disadvantages have been shaped by the colonial process and by the unequal division of labor" (ibid., p. 25). As pointed out in Chapter Three, even this definition is faulty because it fails to take into account the political histories of East Asian countries such as China, Taiwan, Korea, and Japan, that were not colonized by Europe for as long durations as were the countries in South Asia, Africa, and the Americas (Chow 2000). In the case of China, Young (2001) notes that it was not formally dominated by the Europeans or North Americans and only partially colonized by Japan. Mao's revolution was anti-imperialist against the armies of Imperial Japan and the bourgeois nationalists supported by Great Britain and the United States.

The sections below identify broad patterns in the development of media systems in postcolonial countries of the tri continent. Attention is provided to variations in these patterns and care is taken to address examples of divergence.

Mass Media as Extensions of Colonial Administrative Power

The purpose of beginning this section with a discussion of mass media in colonial regimes is to point to the cultural continuity in structures of control between colonial and postcolonial governments. Specifically, colonialism and postcolonialism cannot be regarded as dichotomous phases where postcolonialism marks a rupture from colonialism or marks the point at which national consciousness emerged; colonialism does not mark a break from pre-colonial traditions. Colonial rulers were primarily concerned with creating and maintaining the basic conditions of their rule, which they did by reorganizing existing hierarchical structures. As Young puts it:

> As long as the power structure is there, you can put anything into it that you like (such as the variable constituent elements of nationalism)...The colonial power may have been relatively coherent before the first gin and tonic at least, but anti-colonial opposition was typically fragmented and various, and came from different quarters and classes that were in turn often competing with or opposed to each other. (2001, p. 173)

Values and institutions had to be grafted onto existing traditional society to be followed, a strategy continued by postcolonial governments (Pieterse and Parekh 1995).

The focus of mass media systems during colonial regimes was on furthering administrative efficiency. The private vernacular press played a significant role in independence struggles as did community radio. In countries plagued with poverty and illiteracy, which characterizes much of the colonized countries of the tri continent, the private press was also an elite one, and mobilized those who had the economic and intellectual means to lead the freedom struggle.

Representations of colonized countries in the media, with cinema being the most significant popular mass medium of the time, were an integral part of the narrative of *Orientalism,* which placed European colonies in the position of the needy subject, requiring discipline and punishment. Orientalism, according to Said (1978), could be considered a corporate institution for specifically French and British colonizers in dealing with the Orient. It was, in essence, a Western style of dominating and restructuring the Orient by studying it as an object, describing it, teaching it, making authoritative conclusions about it, and ruling it. This system of dominance was taken on by the United States over British and French ex-colonies, after World War II.

Ahluwahlia (2003) uses Said's central points about the project of Orientalism in his discussion of Africanism as a discourse that facilitated the

Enlightenment rationale of domination of lesser races and that justified slavery and colonialism. Whether it was the Portuguese, English, French, Dutch, Spaniards, or North Americans, from 1492 to around 1870, thousands of slaves were removed from their lands to live or die in the service of their masters. Ahluwahlia cites Hegel's construction of Africa in his 1830–31 Jena lectures where he states:

> The Negro exhibits the natural man in his wild and untamed state. We must lay aside all thought of reverence and morality – all that we call feeling – if we would rightly comprehend him; there is nothing harmonious with humanity to be found in this type of character. (2003, p. 30)

Hegel reflected the tradition of the Enlightenment, as did Marx, and evolution was regarded as a linear trajectory, leaving developed countries with the task of showing less developed countries how to achieve development. In this vein, Eze (2002) shows how Africa is constructed as a mirror of the modern West and critiques Lévy-Bruhl's *La Mentalité Primitive* (Primitive Mentality, 1923), which asserted that African knowledge was based on mysticism, not rationality. The demands of human labor with the development of plantations in Europe and the Americas corresponded to a shift in "European anthropological, literary, artistic, and philosophical characterizations of 'the African' or 'the Negro'" (2002, p. 56). As the relationship between Europe and Africa shifted from mined labor to actual occupation, the theory on the pre-rational, subhuman character of Africans began to sit as reality. Early mass media systems played a significant role in circulating this "reality."

In particular, cinema in various colonies served as a powerful ideological agent of colonial power. The cinema narrative provided the linguistic and ideological structures to legitimize various discourses of imperial power. Cinema technology reached various parts of the world from London and New York to Mexico City and Shanghai with the 1890s Lumières' *cinématographe*, leading to the beginnings of the Brazilian film industry as early as 1908. Despite burgeoning indigenous film industries in various colonies,[1] the leading imperialist countries, Great Britain, France, the United States, and Germany, dominated film production and distribution, propagating the "positional superiority" (Said 1979, p. 25) of the Westerner and the racial inferiority of the colonized.

Shohat and Stam (1994) list five ways in which colonial racism played out: first, by projecting a lack in the colonized population in terms of a lack of order, propriety, modesty, material resources, and history; second, by projecting a hierarchy in placing, for example, Europeans over non-Europeans and modernism over traditionalism; third, by blaming the victim; fourth, by refusing empathy in placing the protagonist at a skeptical distance from colonial struggles; and finally, a systematic devalorization of native life where murder and genocide of the same were casually authorized.

Colonialist fiction of Rudyard Kipling (on India) and H. Rider Haggard, Edgar Wallace, and Edgar Rice Burroughs (on Africa) provided fodder for film narratives. Imperial ideology was transnationalized in that tales of the bravery of French Foreign Legion and of the British Raj, for example, provided a space for racial solidarity among Europeans and forced colonized spectators to identify with their colonial masters, leading to ambivalence and self-loathing in the latter, who were otherized in the cinematic narrative.

Imperial colonial discourse was disseminated through such films as *Le Musulman Rigolo* (The Funny Muslim, 1902), and *Ali Brouffe à Huile* (Ali Eats with Oil, 1902) that caricatured Arabs. While the Production Code of the Motion Picture Producers and Directors of America, Inc. thought it fit to modify Jane's two-piece outfit into one piece in the *Tarzan* series, African women were naked in the background. Films such as *The Dance of Fatima* (1903) and *Bird of Paradise* (1932) showed the dancing rituals of non-white women, exoticizing them and fetishizing their "primitive" and uninhibited religious expressions. Other examples are *Rastus in Zululand* (1910), a Sigmund Lubin comedy; *Fighting Blood* (1911), and *Last of the Mohicans* (1920), which portrayed Native American savagery. George Stevens' *Gunga Din* (1939) showed the British conquering savage Punjabis in India and the famous Shirley Temple film *Wee Willie Winkie* (1937), represented the backwardness of India. W.S. Van Dyke's *Stanley and Livingstone* (1939) glamorized British colonialism in Africa and *Khartoum* (1966) depicted an English-American allegiance facilitating an "historical in-betweenness of the US itself, as at once an anticolonial revolutionary power in relation to Europe, and a colonizing, hegemonic power in relation to Native American and African peoples" (Shohat and Stam, 1994, p. 113). British imperialist epics such as *Lives of a Bengal Lancer* (1938), *Four Men and a Prayer* (1938), and *Gunga Din* (1939) were remade as the US Westerns *Geronimo* (1940), *Fury at Furnace Creek* (1940) and *Soldiers Three* (1951), respectively, demonstrating the translatability of the conquest trope for differing imperial authorities. The Western movie itself became a paradigm for glamorizing American border conquests.[2]

Colonizers also monopolized indigenous film production and distribution systems in their colonies. Monopoly of local cinema meant that British (in Southeast Asia and Africa) and French colonizers (in Egypt and parts of Africa) could mandate that a positive image of the empire be projected in indigenous films. For example, Shohat and Stam explain, in Trinidad, "scenes intended to ridicule or criticize unfairly British social life" were forbidden (1994, p. 112). White men could not be degraded, shown as violent towards natives such as Chinese, Negroes, and Indians, and portrayal of equality between *"men* of one race and *girls* of another race" was taboo (ibid., p. 112, emphases added). Hong Kong cinema in the 1920s could not portray armed conflict between whites and Chinese nor show white women immodestly dressed. The French attempted to quell the growing Egyptian national cinema by establishing a production center in Morocco for the sole purpose of opposing Egyptian cinema. While there is a wealth of film theory delineating the ideological power of representation, Fiske (2003) provides a succinct way for us to conceptualize the lasting impact of representation. He argues that miniature samples of "reality" may be taken as true representations of the whole, imposing the superiority of the First World and establishing that the Third World is the site for the exercise of First World power. Specifically, the imperializing knowledge produced by the First World is a First World product itself. The Third World therefore cannot be represented on its own terms because it is not the author of such a representation. He writes that, "The power to control place is the power to control people. Power is never exerted only through technological control, but always through discursive control as well: the power to do and the power to know are inseparable" (ibid., p. 279).

Representation, therefore, is control, and what emerged from these films was the clear message that peoples of the Orient were backward, effeminate, and also malleable, making them prime targets for Western attention and salvation. By slapping on "second-order Darwinism" (Shohat and Stam 1994, p. 35), the backward Oriental-African and the advanced European-Aryan could be clearly demarcated, legitimizing the subjugation of the former by the latter because of "biologically determined" incompetencies.

Although Said (1978) has been critiqued for his dichotomized delineation of Orient and Occident, his description of the pervasive power of Orientalist discourse – be it through images, the written word, administrative policies, or academic endeavors – is an important contribution to our understanding of how the world and its peoples came to be arranged and regarded in popular media and imaginations. A crucial point here is that many of these images were co-opted by the colonized themselves, depicting minorities and women in subservient and childlike subject positions, with ethnic elites taking on the role of imperial masters. We shall address this point later in the chapter.

Imperialists in South and Far East Asia also seized control of the mass media to further colonial imperatives. In Malay countries (that is, Malaysia, Indonesia, Singapore, and Brunei that use Malay as their national language), successive colonial regimes[3] developed centralized communication systems to boost colonial rule and trade. Although the Dutch pushed for consolidation over the archipelago called the Netherlands East Indies, the British, through the British East India Company maintained their foothold in Southeast Asia for 150 years. The company's influence was pervasive in local governance, jurisprudence, business practices, language, lifestyle, and mass communication. Radio arrived in these areas beginning with Dutch radio programs in the Netherland East Indies in 1925 and the Empire Service of the BBC in South and Southeast Asia in 1932. Radio networks established by colonial governments (such as the Nederlands Indische Radio Omroep Maatschappij or NIROM in Java) followed the BBC public service model with limited advertising for licenses and receivers. Early programs were broadcast directly from the Netherlands or Britain and were popular for their good quality and reliability of programming, even though they initially kept to the hours of the countries from where they originated. Short-wave stations were set up in the British colonial empire in South and Southeast Asia under the Empire Broadcasting Network in 1931 through negotiations between the BBC and the Colonial Office.

With the Japanese occupation of the area beginning in 1941, five centuries of European domination came to an end. Japanese occupation meant control over the local radio station, ZHJ, to broadcast news of British surrender and the strength of Japanese forces. As it served in facilitating Dutch or British colonial imperatives, Malayan radio was used to propagate Japanese language, ideology, and Nippon military supremacy, to establish a "Greater East-Asia Co-Prosperity Sphere" free of European colonialism. Lack of well-developed mass communication systems in Singapore, Indonesia, and Malaya meant that Japanese broadcasts monopolized the airwaves, and those caught listening to foreign broadcasts were severely punished. Sets were altered such that coils for shortwave bands were removed and seals put on knobs to ensure they stayed on the occupation station (Chu 1984, cited in McDaniel 1994).

The Japanese surrender at Pearl Harbor in 1945 meant the resumption of British rule in Singapore, and Malaya and British Military Administration (BMA) control over broadcasts on Radio Malaya, to narrate the Allied side of the war. The BMA in Malaya in 1946 continued to clamp down on radio operations, using it for propaganda regarding the allied forces' mission and music from local organizations. In the 1950s, Radio Malaya was split between the Federation (South Thailand Peninsula) and Singapore – this split later facilitated the transition of Singapore to an independent state (McDaniel 1994). Similar examples of colonial control over media may be found in Mexico, under the Soviet Communist Party until the 1920s (Hallin 2000), in the countries of South America under French, Italian, and Spanish control since the 1800s (Waisbord 2000) and in Zimbabwe (Rønning and Kupe 2000).

The systematic suppression of indigenous media and the encoding of a positive colonial image into early media law and policy in the colonies, ensured that media systems were limited in their development and provided a specific ordering, a symbolic structure where the colonizer had the upper hand and the colonized was the menial slave. Colonial administrators also treated vastly disparate territories as unified entities. For example, in the Malay countries, various consortia of governance by the early nineteenth century such as the Straits Settlements consisting of Singapore, Malacca, Penang, Province Wellesley and other small territories; the Federated States of Malaysia (FMS), consisting of Negeri Sembilan, Selangor, and Pahang; and the Unfederated Malay States (UMS) consisting of the four northern states of Malaysia and Johore, although culturally diverse, were treated as unified trading units and identified as backward areas for development through mass media in the context of the 1960s development studies (McDaniel 1994). Similarly, Canclini (1995) notes that in the case of Latin America, all countries in the region were classified as backward even though hybrid variations of modernity and traditionalism existed, where, for example, influences of the indigenous traditions of the Meso-American and Andean areas and colonial Catholic Hispanism intermingled with the educated, modern lifestyles of urban Santiago, Lima, Bogota, or Mexico City. The irony is that anti-colonial nationalists, in striving to assert their need for independence and recognition of cultural diversity, themselves resorted to national unification strategies, privileging the elite, intellectual classes.

The colonial state may have been successful in its domination of the external, material sphere but was starkly aware of its failure to intervene in the inner spiritual sphere especially when it came to the rights of women and children. Colonial and national social reformers faced staunch resistance from nationalist elites who defended religious and secular traditions that defined women's moral character, their legal rights and their familial and social duties. The backwardness of women in colonial societies, then, was blamed on the traditionalism of the native culture. Colonized nationalists asserted that although European power could be imposed on the external material sphere, such imposition had no effect on the essential identity of the East. The inner spiritual sphere remained untainted and it was here that the East was sovereign, shaper of its own destiny (Chatterjee 1993).

The struggle over representation in the material and spiritual spheres continues to this day and is integral to the nationalist project. After independence, the task of the postcolonial media system was to forge a new identity for the nation that had been "purified" of the colonial experience. The battle over what emerged becomes a fascinating study of the role of state-owned and private media in constructing identities that resonate with local cultural bases and that are mobile and lucrative in the marketplace. As mentioned earlier, the strategy of newly elected postcolonial governments often imitated that of the colonizers themselves where the nation was constructed as a monolithic entity, with women, lower castes, and ethnic minorities identified as projects to be rescued, legitimizing political policies that were oftentimes just as elitist and hegemonic as those of the colonial rulers.[4] Although colonizers could be kept out of the inner spiritual sphere as nationalists claimed, it also meant that the latter exerted a hegemonic control over this sphere, privileging a "national culture" and an "essential tradition" (Chatterjee 1993, p. 134) structured within domination and exclusion. The heady rhetoric of freedom, equality, and cultural integrity was accompanied by stark dichotomies that segregated the elite few who could partake of the benefits of the new, liberated state from the vast masses who couldn't. The masses were co-opted into important narratives and real struggles for freedom, but could not be culturally integrated with those who led them.

In India, for example, women were subjected to another system of patriarchy. Nationalists awarded upper-class Hindu women a prestigious intellectual place in society with limited freedom, of course, while lower-class women were restricted in a variety of ways and portrayed as brash, vulgar, and coarse subjects, to be readily available for male desire – a representation that persists in Indian popular media today. The next section examines examples showing that the character of national broadcast media is integrally connected to its relationship with the national government.

Mass Media as Nation Builders and Postcolonial Saviors

The use of centralized media systems, particularly broadcasting, for hegemonic control and as an ideological tool by national elites to propagate a sense of national and regional identity, has been well documented (Featherstone 1995; Morley and Robins 1995; Rajagopal 1996). National media systems serve as vehicles for the dissemination of ideologies of power to establish and maintain relations of domination (Thompson 1990; Price 1995), and radio and television act as co-conspirators in establishing and sustaining the "dominant codes" of nation (Hall 1980). National capitalist and state patriarchies carried on the dominant structures of transnational Western capitalist and colonial patriarchies (M. Yang 1999) and Canclini refers to such state intervention as "cultural patrimony" (1995, p. 108). Sreberny (2000) contends that centrist, patriarchal policies construct the national citizenry as passive and childlike, incapable of making viable choices and therefore necessarily subjected to political influence and control for its own protection.

Electronic media are grafted onto large nation-building projects to recover a glorious, pure, utopian past from the ravages of colonial and other invasions, as we see in the broadcast of Hindu nationalist epics in India (Mankekar 1999) and Chinese operas and musicals in Hong Kong (Ang 1996), to create an "official national cultural identity" (Hamilton 2002, p. 153). Nostalgia becomes an ideological construction, represented by a longing for a utopian and golden past, denying its real history and origins and hoping for a recreation of such a past in its future (Stewart 1993). Modern mass media therefore, become central state projects of modernity and cosmopolitanism and play an integral role in constructing a transnational imaginary (M. Yang 2002) and a national locality. Appadurai (1996) identifies three points of interactive struggle in the production of locality: the efforts of the nation-state to draw local contexts and neighborhoods into its allegiance, the increasing ruptures among territory, subjectivity, and collective social movement; and, finally, the gradual disappearance between virtual and real contexts, due to mass media.

In re-creating a utopian past and a pure local present, cultural patrimony reinstates structures of social differences between different social groups who have differentiated access to production and distribution of products. It follows then, that "the symbolic capital of the subaltern groups has a place, but one that is subordinate, secondary, or on the margins of hegemonic institutions and apparatuses" (Canclini 1995, p. 136). Although products produced by subalterns have high creative and aesthetic value, they by themselves cannot achieve any great market value if they are not co-opted into a patrimonial private structure that banks on resources of production and distribution expertise.

The following paragraphs address examples of mass media as vehicles of nation-building. It should be pointed out at the outset that although patterns of centralized control are apparent across various countries, particularly socialist democracies such as India and Malaysia, this control is textured by the political and economic environment in each country. Strong patron–client relationships exist between government and private media entrepreneurs in the case of military powers of Taiwan and North Korea. Government-supervised private investment exists in the case of China while government-sponsored development media dominate in the socialist democracies of South Asia and Africa.

In various postcolonial countries, television was introduced after independence in the 1950s and 1960s (for example, in the 1950s in Egypt and Kuwait,

1956 in Algeria, 1959 in India and Lebanon, 1960 in Senegal, 1962 in Morocco, 1965 in Saudi Arabia, 1968 in Jordan, 1969 in the emirates of Abu Dhabi and Dubai, and as recently as 1992 in Tunisia, 1999 in Malawi, and 2000 in Botswana, to name but a few examples). Early development of media systems in these areas was facilitated by former colonial masters (either by the ex-colonial government directly or private entrepreneurs in the country) or by other dominant nations seeking new alliances after the retreat of colonialism. Financial donations from supranational agencies (UNESCO in the case of Senegal, Bolivia, Chile, and Peru, and the UN in the case of India, for example), ensured that television was used as a tool for development and a voice for the government, both resonating with the goals of newly elected governments in these countries. Broadcast structures were set up that imitated that of the public service model of the colonial country (examples are the Office de Radiodiffusion-Télévision Sénégalaise, or ORTS, of Senegal modeled on the French ORTF; and Hong Kong's Radio and Television Hong Kong or RTHK and India's Doordarshan on the BBC).

Linear developmentalist objectives were successful because they had staunch proponents in developing countries themselves. Early broadcasts were about farming, health, nutrition, sanitation, entrepreneurial skills, women's literacy, and other such development themes, driven, to a large extent by the well-funded area development studies described in Chapter Two. Many of these were sponsored or directly created by ex-colonialists. Contemporary examples are pro-social dramas such as *The Archers* in Afghanistan, produced and broadcast by BBC Radio 4 (Skuse 2002), and *Crossroads* in Kazakhstan, produced by the Portobello Media company in London and sponsored by the British Know-How Fund aimed at community development.

Programs were broadcast in either the language of the former colonial power (for example, French in Senegal and English in India) or the national language (for example, Wolof in Senegal and Hindi in India), to establish language supremacy in very diverse multilingual societies. Television, in particular, was also used in varying degrees and with differing outcomes, to promote religious supremacy in such countries as Egypt, Iran, India, and Lebanon, for example (see Abrahamian 1999; Abu-Lughod 2002; Mankekar 1999; Kraidy 2003). While Western development scholars believed deeply entrenched religions of developing countries were instrumental in keeping them from development because of their accompanying fatalism and belief in the magical, these countries used religion as an integral part of the postcolonial state's modernizing project. Print media continued in the language of the colonizer, and sustained its elevated position as the lingua franca of the nation. Goals were invariably education, information, and entertainment.

The patron–client relationship

The political and economic environments of postcolonial countries play a crucial and obvious role in determining the exact process by which centralized mass media systems have developed. In authoritarian countries that are under military dictatorships (such as North Korea) or still largely under Communist regimes (such as China and Cuba) strong patron–client relationships exist between the government and media. Dictatorships characterized most of the countries in 1970s Latin America (Argentina, Bolivia, Brazil, Chile, Ecuador, Paraguay, Peru, Uruguay and, apart from Costa Rica, all the countries of Central America); it was in the 1980s and 1990s that these countries made the transition to democratic societies and in the process, encouraged strong and steady growth in their media industries (Fox 1997). Economic liberalization and aggressive capitalism became an integral part of strategies for national development.

To begin with a few examples from East Asia, Taiwan adopted the Japanese commercial television model in the 1960s, itself patterned after that of the United States. Taiwan's policy of state capitalism (as in Korea) meant that television under its three channels (Taiwan Television Enterprise or TTV established in 1962, China Television Company or CTV in 1968, and Chinese Television System or CTS in 1971), did not have to compete in the free market, broadcasting in Mandarin rather than local dialects (Formosa Television or FTV was established much later in 1997). In Korea, the KMT party under Chiang Kai-Shek and his son Chiang Ching-Kuo from 1949 till 1987, exercised tight control over the media to maintain its identity as Taiwan passed from Japan to China in 1945 and as the KMT subsequently retreated to Taiwan from mainland China after its defeat in 1949. In this context,

> Constitutional rights, including freedom of speech and the press, were suspended on the grounds that political stability was a prerequisite to economic growth and anti communism required unified leadership. The media not only accepted authoritarian rule, but also helped rationalize it. (C-C. Lee 2000, p. 125)

Through *guanxi* (personal ties) and informal arrangements, the state maintained its close relationship with an elite press, forbidding association with labor unions or social activist groups. The *United Daily News* and *China Times* beginning in the 1950s rose to prominence in the 1970s full of sensational crime stories, enjoying two-thirds of Taiwan's subscriptions and advertising. Alternative voices in the form of the *Free China* newspaper in the 1950s and others in the 1970s and 1980s supported the *Dangwai* (oppositional movement) and advocated a free and anti-communist press. These were strongly influenced by the US-style watchdog adversary journalism (C-C. Lee 2000). The successive Park and Chun governments of the 1960s-1980s resulted in the merging of newspaper broadcasting companies with only one newspaper per province (except Seoul). Journalists critical of the government were forced to resign and intelligence officials closely monitored reporters and presses to ensure conformity with the Media Policy Office of the Ministry of Culture and Information. This meant only those reporters and media companies that supported the government thrived, with tax cuts and bribes in ample supply, in return for favorable press coverage. The practice of electing media officials from the same region as the president ensured loyalty and allegiance between press and political power. Taiwan now has a combination of commercial and public television stations. The Taiwanese government abolished martial law in 1987, relaxed bans on newspapers in 1988 and established the Cable Television Law in 1993 to regulate the television industry (Liu and Chen 2004).

Television in Korea began in 1956 with the sale of RCA television monitors by a private investor, and as part of the government's efforts at modernization. Its regulation began in the 1960s and in 1961, the national broadcasting system KBS-TV was established by the military regime. As in Japan, early programs in Korea were primarily American due to poorly developed production facilities and high cost of indigenous programs (Choe and Kang 2001). KBS-TV's competitor was the commercial TBC (Tongyang Broadcasting Company) joined by another commercial one in the 1970s. With the gradual decrease in cost of television sets and consequent rise in its sales, viewer demand for indigenous programming grew and that for foreign programs diminished considerably, relegating them to late night and other unpopular time slots. Satellite television and further diversification of private channels in the 1990s and early 2000s further increased the appetite for local programming. The Korean television industry (now expanded to the public systems KBS and MBC and commercial Seoul Broadcasting System (SBS) and TBC), resorts to large-scale copying of Japanese formats despite the Korean Broadcasting Law, which prohibits plagiarism.

The patron–client relationship evident in the above examples is characteristic of similar political systems in Latin American countries. Primary structural changes in Latin America between the 1950s and 1970s were first, diversification of economic development, urban expansion, local market expansion because of increase in literacy, emergence of new communication technologies (most notably television and home appliances), and new political movements that embraced technology (Canclini 1995). Media in Latin

American countries stand as stark examples of critical dependency theory in their representation of the unequal flow of programs and products from core to periphery (Fox 1997). In Bolivia, Chile, and Peru, television was developed for its educational potential, according to UNESCO guidelines (notable exceptions in Latin America are Argentina where television was introduced as a propaganda vehicle of Perón, and Colombia, where television was introduced to further the Rojas Pinilla dictatorship). In South America, the liberal Anglo-Saxon press model, gaining popularity after World War II, clashed with political philosophies of the region. Far from the free-market revolution experienced by US newspapers at the turn of the nineteenth century, the South American press stayed under government control. This led to self-censorship and "cooperation rather than adversarialism, [and] mutual advantages rather than complete autonomy" (Waisbord 2000, p. 51). The relationship between media and state is a strong one; the media, particularly print, practice self-censorship and partisan politics. Military dictatorships in South American countries in the 1970s (except for Colombia and Venezuela) meant that the media were strictly controlled (for example, Chile's *El Mercurio* openly supported Pinochet, and Brazil's Globo network was a blatant voice for the government). Such control often led to fragmentary media systems, where, for example, in Argentina in the early 1970s, programming was centrally produced and disseminated to local independent stations. In Brazil, from 1964 till 1985, the government centralized the media system and developed communication networks for its political propaganda. In Peru, from 1968 till 1980, the government limited private and foreign capital to focus on social and educational goals of the poor and rural population (Waisbord 2000).

Mexico, ruled by the Communist Party of the Soviet Union until the 1920s, was subsequently under the Partido Revolucionario Institutional (PRI) until the 2000s. The media were a hegemonic weapon of the PRI. Televisa (owned by Emilio Azcárraga Jr. until his death in 1997), Mexico's dominant television company produced the *telenovela* and marked the nation as an innovator in the entertainment-education format (Singhal and Rogers 1999) and as an entertainment giant in the country and in Latin America. The PRI has been termed the "perfect dictatorship" without blatant authoritarianism, yet enjoying "clientilist" relationships with small businesses, workers, and farmers who serve the PRI for material benefits and favors (Hallin 2000, p. 98). A wealth of research is available to show that most political stories in the newspapers or on television are favorable to the PRI (see Adler 1993; Miller and Darling 1997).

In the Middle East, countries such as Algeria, Egypt, Iraq, Syria, Libya, Yemen, and Sudan have broadcast systems that are under strict government control, were introduced by revolutionary regimes, have high propaganda content, and promote revolutionary leaders (which H. Amin 1996, calls the Mobilization Broadcast Model). Countries such as Morocco, Kuwait, Tunisia, Jordan, Qatar, Bahrain, and Oman, and emirates such as Abu Dhabi and Dubai are under less government control, were introduced by the government and private individuals, contain predominantly religious and entertainment programs and target Arab expatriates (H. Amin 1996, calls this the Governmental Model). An exception is Israel where television was reluctantly introduced in the late 1960s after much speculation of its inherent value for a conservative public (Katz et al. 1997).

With the establishment of the Administration for Information and Publication in 1951, the Permanent Committee for Arab Media in 1960, and the Council of Arab Information Ministers in 1964, ARABSAT was launched in 1967 to provide public service for the nations under its league. Its satellites 1A and 1B were inaugurated in 1985 and provided news, education, and emergency announcements. Broadcasts were technologically sophisticated, yet were highly controlled to avoid propaganda by individual countries (H. Amin 1996). The suppression of broadcasting development by state governments propelled the video market in the 1990s. Many Arab television systems were developed to tap into the expatriate economy as, for example, the Space Network in Dubai (1992), TV7 in Tunisia (1992), the 2M international channel in Morocco (1989), and the Kuwait Space Network in Kuwait (1992). For postcolonial governments, diversity was celebrated inasmuch as it could be part of the national development project and could provide avenues for economic profitability.

Government-supervised private investment

China provides an example of strict state control over the media in tandem with encouragement of privatization. M. Yang (2002) makes a distinction between nation and state in the case of China where the twentieth-century Chinese state apparatus sought to impose itself on a nation struggling to elude the state. Western and Japanese culture were available in China during the early part of the twentieth century, reminding people that China's poverty and "backwardness" stood as a stark contrast to the West and Japan, even as these were vilified as imperialists in the Chinese press. China sealed itself from the rest of the world for 30 years after the Communist Revolution in 1949, to develop its own brand of nationalism after the intrusions of Western imperialists during the mid-nineteenth-century Opium Wars and Treaty Port systems, and the Japanese take-over of Shandong in 1914, annexation of Manchuria, and invasion of Eastern China in 1937 (ibid.). Foreign interactions were limited to

Soviet bloc and non-aligned Third World countries. Foreign contacts by the people, whether it was with popular culture or even family abroad, were punished. With the establishment of the Central People's Broadcasting System in 1949, all print, film, and broadcast media came under the government, propagating a homogenous national culture, with little or no space for regional identities.

Television began in China in 1958 with Beijing Television (renamed China Central Television or CCTV in 1976) and controlled by the Chinese Propaganda Department. In post-Mao China, pluralization and diversity characterized the media environment, with influence from Taiwanese and Hong Kong popular culture evident in the new Eastern Broadcast (radio) Station established in Shanghai in 1993. Increase in diversity of media technologies (DVDs, VCDs, CDs, VHS tapes, cell phones, etc.) and decentralization of earlier state-controlled technologies such as telephones allowed the Chinese population to interact with the outside world in a way not possible during Mao's regime.

During the mid-1980s and early 1990s, the number of television sets increased phenomenally. Imported programs from Taiwan, Hong Kong, the United States, Japan, Russia, and Europe through satellite, were far more popular than those on the state-owned network. Deregulation came about in the mid-1980s and cable television began in the 1990s through a wiring system initially set up in the 1950s for loudspeaker propaganda networks. Chinese media had to conform to the conservative, bureaucratic structure of other state-controlled organizations to ensure transmissions were in line with Party messages. Historic costume dramas increased in the 1980s in an attempt to meet audience needs, and in contrast to the staid news and education programs, were highly successful. The decentralization reforms of Deng Xiaoping, which Keane calls "a commodity economy with socialist characteristics" (2004b, p. 88), and later Jiang Zemin, have led to numerous semi-commercial stations as opposed to the central propaganda media machine under Mao. With the 1994 Chinese Propaganda Department's media policy of "Six Nos": "no private media ownership; no shareholding of media organizations; no discussion of a press law; no discussion of the commodity nature of news; no joint ventures with foreign companies; and no openness for foreign satellite television" (Chadha and Kavoori 2000, p. 419), foreign television programming was severely curtailed.

Currently media at the national level are monitored closely, yet provincial and local media networks, highly dependent on advertising revenue, are somewhat autonomous. Print media are far more restricted than television. Local papers receive less scrutiny than party papers at national, provincial, and municipal levels. The Chinese government takes a strong stand against imperialism and criticizes transnational media corporations, yet from the mid 1990s, the government has allowed conglomerates and encourages media mergers to quell the rise of minority and independent papers (Ma 2000). Uniform pay scales for journalists shifted to "paid journalism" (Chen and Chan 1998), where journalists can receive incentives and pay from government and private organizations above their regular salaries, to promote stories. The media, as non-profit organizations (as opposed to administrative organizations which receive government funding, and profitable enterprises which depend on private profits), are increasingly dependent on advertising revenues. Hong Kong's liberal media continues relatively autonomously and avoids conflict with the Chinese government through its depoliticized and self-censored programming.

Hong Kong has always evidenced openness to foreign cultural products from Japan, New York, and London, with its 150 years of British colonial rule. The high cost of local programs leads to program translation (in the form of dubbing or subtitling which Fung also terms "minimal localization" (2004, p. 75). Hong Kongers enjoy a wide variety of programming, from Western programs on English language channels to Japanese and Chinese programs from Japan and mainland China or Taiwan, respectively. With its return to Chinese sovereignty in 1997, Hong Kong's capitalism became China's new ideology driving its market liberalization policy[5] (Ma 2000).

Government-sponsored development media

In countries under socialist democracies, governments exercise authoritarian control over media systems, yet recognize the importance of privatization to step up the national economy. Privatization of media is uneven and government control over major networks translates into sluggish development and below average production quality of programs. As Nyamnjoh (2004) notes in the case of many countries in Africa, a strong connection exists between global consumer capitalism and authoritative African governments who seize centralized control of states to facilitate elite and foreign investor capitalist interests. The World Bank and the International Monetary Fund (IMF) impose goals of liberal democracy and civil society on Africa rather than understand the reality of democratic structures that are already in place. Implementing such neoliberal ideals through Structural Adjustment Programs (SAPs) by enlisting the support of local governments, these institutions have been successful in constructing violent regimes of exclusion and inclusion as is seen in the case of the "state-condoned violence among the Ogonic minority in relation to the entitlements over the oil in the Niger Delta of Nigeria."

Globalization, therefore, does not lead to the homogenization of cultures but to "an intensification of hierarchies and inequalities among individuals, groups and cultures" (ibid., p. 64).

A case in point is South Africa,[6] struggling with the residual devastating effects of apartheid after 300 years of racial oppression. In the 1990s, as much as 60 percent of the country's black population was poor as opposed to 1 percent of the white population. The top income bracket contained 65 percent of white and 45 percent of Indian households while only 17 percent coloreds (an official census category) and 10 percent Africans were in the top 20 percent (Jacobs 2003). Unemployment was as high as 40 percent and crime rates are among the highest in the world. South Africa is a prominent media center in Africa and its 1999 Broadcasting Act stipulates that the media be used for education, nation-building, and community development. The African National Congress deregulated the media in 1996, leading to a surge in radio stations (most of them community radio). The South African Broadcasting Corporation (SABC) runs the three national television networks, two pay-TV channels and Bop TV (showing music videos and programs). TV Africa, although based in the country, does not broadcast within it but externally (in English and French) to around 26 countries in the African continent. A commercial network, etv, competes with SABC and carries US and British programs. The SABC also operates 20 regional and national radio services in 11 languages. Zegeye and Harris (2003, p. 8) state:

> Identities of the Apartheid represented by such labels as "black," "white," "African," "Indian," "Malay," "European" and others were emptied out, refilled, reconfigured and stabilized…There is a new ideology of South Africanism based on a form of anti-racism that consciously seeks to recognize, work with, and take into account what postcolonialists have called "differences"…This perspective disavows fixity and singularity in the expression of identity.

In South Africa then, the role of the media becomes one that has to incorporate, in its policy, strategies such as President Thabo Mbeki's "African Renaissance" to revive and construct an image of Africa that is far removed from Western stereotypes of the bushland beggar (Ahluwahlia 2003).

In Zimbabwe, the defeat of Ian Smith's Rhodesian Front government led to independence in 1980 under the Unilateral Declaration of Independence (UDI). While other Southern African countries such as Zambia, Tanzania, and Mozambique ideologically supported their new nationalist governments, in Zimbabwe, conflict between authoritarianism and democracy was obvious. The Zimbabwe Mass Media Trust (ZMMT) was established by the government in 1981 to help the transition of the public print media from white minority control to serving the needs of a broader section of society. As a non-governmental, non-partisan body, the Trust encouraged business partnerships with private Zimbabwean investors. It gained control over the national news agency ZIANA (a new school of journalism) and the Kingston national book distributors and established the Community Newspapers group. It is therefore legally bound to the government, yet it is not owned by the government and therefore can change its legal autonomy when desired. It is also not a solely private enterprise but is an important shareholder of media interests under the loose supervision of a Board of Directors. With the ZBC (Zimbabwe Broadcasting Corporation) it is the ZANU (PF)'s symbol of decolonization and democratization of the media. Although broadcasting corporations changed policies and personnel after colonialism, they continued the organizational structures and operations established under colonialism (Rønning and Kupe 2000).

As is the case in many postcolonial countries (India, Malaysia, and other countries in Africa), Zimbabwe's broadcasting network is under a national broadcaster, the ZBC, is controlled by the government, and is based in the nation's capital. It broadcasts programs on national integration (such as patriotic songs, regional dances, patriotic poems and legends), education, health, and sanitation, through four national channels. Rønning and Kupe (2000) write that quality is poor, content is boring and rural populations are largely ignored because of low transmission quality and inaccessibility to television sets. Radio is far more pervasive, dominated by music and educational programs. Under the Rhodesian Broadcasting Act of 1957, the ZBC has monopoly status and is accountable to the Minister of Information, Posts and Telecommunication. The government bias and control are obvious in broadcasts of the ZBC. An assessment by the BBC of the ZBC in 1980 when the nation won independence resulted in the recommendation that the ZBC diversify into a round-the-clock FM music station, an FM educational station, and community radio with a view to capital and technical expansion. By 1997, a further assessment revealed the corporation was bankrupt and inefficient due to its bureaucratic, state-sponsored structure. The only solution was aggressive commercialism. The uneasy correspondence between commercialism and state control is not yet resolved and the majority of broadcasts still contain a strong government bias. In such an environment, investigative reports are rare, but provide an important function in monolithic party systems that do not have political opposition (examples of courageous critical independent papers are *Zimbabwe Independent* and *Daily Gazette*, and magazines such as *Parade* and *Horizon*).

As in African countries, television in South Asian countries was introduced to foster goals of national development. In Malaysia,[7] television (Talivishen Malaysia) was introduced in 1963 under state control (the Department of

Broadcasting – RTM – under the supervision of the Ministry of Information). Programs focused on development and education and were produced in rudimentary, makeshift studios. A second channel was established in 1969 and the two channels are referred to as TV1 and TV2. In 1984, TV3, a commercial television station was launched.[8] Television arrived in Singapore in 1963 as well, with 52 community viewing centers already in place. Remarkably, even before the first telecast, one in 12 homes owned a television set in anticipation of the broadcast. The focus of early telecasts was to further the government's projects in the areas of employment, social services, education, and health. Examples of early programs are *The New Adventures of Charlie Chan*, *Huckleberry Hound*, *Rampaian Malaysia* (a variety show), and *TV Looks at Singapore* (Lim 2004).[9]

Tight government control over national television is evident in India as well. The task of the Indian government after independence from British rule in 1947, was to foster economic growth by developing the shaky industrial sector, cut down the country's large population, develop such areas as transport, agriculture, health, education, sanitation, water and electric supply; and most importantly, to sustain the national sentiment of the people that they were free agents of a single, sovereign, secular nation, not slaves to a colonial master (Kust 1964). Mass media rose in importance as a vehicle for unification; television, under the state-owned national network Doordarshan, was projected, ever since the first rudimentary telecast in 1959, as a symbol of the nation's modernity, progress, and freedom (Doordarshan, 1996). Doordarshan used Hindi in its national programming for serials and news shows during prime time, as a strategy for nation building through language unification, despite the fact that India is a country of 25 states, each with its own official language and dialects.

Development rhetoric was strong in UN and UNESCO conferences and the role of television for rural development was studied in depth in India. The Satellite Instructional Television Experiment (SITE) project, an experiment in satellite technology, was launched in the 1970s through the joint efforts of the Indian Space Research Centre (ISRO), NASA (USA), Doordarshan, and various state governments in the country. Using the Application Technology Satellite (ATS-6), programs were beamed to 2,400 villages in six states (Chatterji 1991), to educate people in rural areas on agriculture, health, and sanitation, and to provide supplementary lessons for primary school students. A second objective was to foster national unity among various linguistic, religious, and political groups (Rao 1987). Besides the obvious function of Doordarshan for economic and social development, centralized control of this national network was an important political strategy for various ruling parties in the nation. Structures of power in the government overlapped with those in the media with politicians and media personnel moving back and forth between government and media jobs (Mitra 1993). Under the Prasar Bharati (Media Autonomy) Bill introduced in 1980 and finally passed in 1997, Doordarshan and All India Radio became "autonomous" bodies no longer under government sponsorship, but under its advisory care.

What these examples show is that colonial legislative and media systems stayed more or less intact in postcolonial times, only the nature of the guard changed (see also McDaniel 2002). Media policies in these countries, particularly in South and Southeast Asia, carry to this day the strong influence of colonial media policies. Centralized control of media systems, even when accompanied by private investment, also meant centralized control over content. Programs generated within patriarchal, conservative contexts squarely placed the responsibility of family, community, and national development on women. Beginning most notably with the *telenovela* in Mexico, serialized fiction and documentaries prescribed a variety of roles for women both in the domestic and public sphere where they enjoyed a certain empowerment and agency, were simultaneously keepers of local religious and cultural traditions, spoke up to male miscreants, and yet deferred to strong males in their social contexts. Mexican *telenovelas* are popular in markets as far away as Poland, China, and Russia (Fox 1997). The following section describes early *telenovelas* briefly before moving on to examples of some of the representations of women in national media. The postcolonial framework urges us to evaluate how media content represents the character of the postcolonial nation. As a reflector of the patriarchal conservatism of its elite controllers, postcolonial television in particular relied on existing gender, class, and caste hierarchies to produce discourses of progress, technology, and innovation. These hierarchies placed gender and ethnic minorities as objects of ridicule and rescue, identifying urban upper-class males as the progenitors of the new nation.

The *Telenovela* for National Development

While postcolonial governments were struggling to establish centralized media systems and define the parameters of their programming for community and economic development, Latin American television producers developed the *telenovela* format that embedded goals of both. A pioneer in the entertainment-education genre, the *telenovela* embodied the idea that mass media have guarded powerful effects and if used effectively, can serve as tools for development. Brown and Singhal (1990) write that education for the viewing masses may be conveyed through pro-social television, which combines entertainment television with educational television. The authors define

89

entertainment television as a set of "televised performances intended to capture the interest or attention of individuals, giving them pleasure and/or amusement." On the other hand, "Educational television refers to a televised program of instruction and training intended to develop an individual's mental, moral or physical skills to achieve a particular end" (ibid., p. 260).

Beginning with Miguel Sabido's *telenovelas* based on the rags-to-riches story of *Simplemente Maria*, soaps, serials, and short films bearing development themes were produced in various developing countries. *Hum Log* in India, *In a Lighter Time* in Nigeria, *Twende na Wakati* in Tanzania, and *Neria* and *More Time* in Zimbabwe are a few examples. The structure of entertainment-education programs is based on Bandura's Social Learning theory, Bentley's Dramatic Theory, and Jung's Archetypal Theory. Primary among these is Bandura's Social Learning Theory, which postulates that an individual's behavior is learned from his or her social environment. Songs, sitcoms, and films were structured so that they incorporated themes of sexual responsibility (as in Mexico's *Cuando Estemos Junto*) and widows' legal rights (as in Zimbabwe's *Neria*) (Brown and Singhal 1990).

The success of these programs lies in the strong correspondence between production and consumption. Skuse's (2002) study of BBC World Service's 15-minute social realist radio soap, *Khana-e-nau, Zindagi-e-nau* (*New Home, New Life*) in Dari (Afghan Persian) or *Naway Kor, Naway J'wand* in the Pashtu language, set in a mountainous region of Afghanistan, and broadcast three times weekly, based on the BBC Radio 4's *The Archers*, provides a good example of the entertainment-education format. The settings of the program (such as a shady spring where women collected water and exchanged opinions and gossip), characters, use of local languages, and the temperate climate of the region, which corresponded with the broad seasons of the soap, all lent the program a realism that audiences could relate to. Although listeners critiqued the soap in that its characters were more affluent, did not face the realities of war, and generally lived comfortable lives compared to the listeners' own realities of scanty water and electric supply and social conflict, the program performed a crucial educative function in that:

> [It] remind[s] farmers through its more didactic storylines [of] when and what to plant, what techniques to follow, how to preserve soil quality, how to tend livestock, identify disease in livestock or care for animals during the cold winter months, and so on. (ibid., p. 418)

Women listeners took to selling eggs and chickens for their own economic independence following the example of the older female characters in the soap.

So real were some of the soap narratives that listeners would hold meetings to mourn the passing of a favorite character or celebrate the marriage or birth of another.

The advantages of these shows are that they reach a wide audience through the mass media, are entertaining, are far more effective in attracting and retaining audiences than programs based solely on education and information, and are relatively inexpensive to produce since the cost of production is limited to first copy costs. Because they are produced by educators and trained personnel, the program itself is generally of good quality.

Restoring the Female Nation

As national elites extolled the geographical glory of the newly independent nation and created national anthems describing the value of fertile lands, beauteous mountains, life-giving rivers, and enduring traditions and cultures, they also constructed the nation as a chaste and virtuous female. Chatterjee (1993), as mentioned earlier in this chapter explains how these elites were able to subjugate women through colonial and postcolonial eras through an ideological divide between the material and spiritual spheres. To explain, the anticolonial nationalism of Asian and African countries provides ample evidence of distinct divisions between the external material sphere and internal spiritual sphere where the spiritual sphere was chalked out as an area of nationalist hegemony, with control over traditions and customs. The colonial state intervened, dominated, and controlled the external material sphere taking care not to tread into the spiritual sphere, where, in essence the nation was imagined. In this latter sphere, the traditions of family were guarded against colonial intervention. What this meant was that social evils (as, for example, *sati* or widow immolation and child marriage in India) continued and were protected by national elites as a terrain only they could arbitrate on. The Indian woman's modernity was carefully defined on their terms where she could be educated and refined in the arts, yet had to maintain her traditional role to be distinct from the brazen "Western" woman.

M. Yang provides a similar analysis of such ideological demarcations in the case of late imperial China where the " 'inner' (*nei*) household space for women and 'outer' (*wai*) space for men" (1996, p. 18) were clearly demarcated. Women were charged with the responsibility of patrilineal continuity in their domestic spaces while the state and empire stood firmly entrenched in the public domain as symbols of the patriarchal family stamped with the paternal authority and authenticity of the emperor and his officials.

As we shall see later in the case of cinema in India, in China as well, 1920s and 1930s films portrayed the woman as an individual who needed to be controlled either for her sexual freedom or social corruption. In the 1930s nationalistic war years, she embodied the raped nation, a Motherland to be rescued, while in the Maoist era of the 1960s and 1970s, she symbolized the gratitude of the masses for its liberation by the socialist party. The woman in Taiwan and Hong Kong, on the other hand, became a symbol of capitalist desire, a consuming subject in the burgeoning bourgeois family.

For macho-nationalists, the domestic sphere stood as the best safeguard of traditional culture and values, neatly separated from the mechanisms of construction of the new state, which was itself modeled on the European state (Young 2003). Women and modernity, therefore, occupied opposing realms. Progress in the public realm signifying greater economic opportunities for men as leaders in a patriarchal system, meant subjugation of women in the private realm since the latter were keepers of sacred tradition. The "motherland" appears all too frequently in nationalist rhetoric of tri continent countries, a hegemonic strategy that neatly excludes the woman from active participation in building the nation or becoming its beneficiary. Like the land, the woman is an object for cultivation, curtailment, and discipline. Donadey comments:

> [W]hen women are equated to the land, there is no discursive space for them as citizens. When woman stands in for nation; it becomes difficult to present the women of nation as agents in that nation's constitution because their body image is being activated as the object for which to fight. (2001, p. XXX).

Ironically, entertainment-education programs, while depicting a variety of roles for women and outlining various avenues for empowerment and action, also re-created a patriarchal structure that identified women as objects, not agents, of change. The project of women's development in many socialist countries became synonymous with national development. Women, framed as victims of social backwardness, became symbols of modernity as well, because efforts to educate women and make them self-reliant were integrated with efforts at modernity. In the modern state where mass media functioned as centralized ideological apparatuses and as privatized mechanisms of consumption, women continued as objects of representation and were denied agency in the production of discourse. Early reformers in the Middle East and South Asia directed nationalist efforts toward achieving modernity. In doing so, women were privileged because their progress was seen as a key to modernity. Yet this privilege was regulated by the patriarchal society so that they were modern in the public sphere in terms of work and education, yet conservative in the private sphere, at home (Kandiyoti 1994). Zutshi (1993) writes that the conflation of nation and woman set the latter up as the terrain upon which ideological battles were fought. Control of the nation as the body politic was integrated with control of the female body.

In many tricontinental liberation movements, feminism was tolerated as a way to include women in the freedom struggle but was not supported in any real or material sense through or after the independence movement. Women, therefore, had to fight the double patriarchy and colonization by colonialists *and* indigenous domination. Movements of resistance took on unique cultural forms, quite distinct from Western feminism (Young 2001). As various historians have documented, violence against women such as *sati* in India and female circumcision in 1920s East Africa and Kenya, were used as projects for reformation by the British colonialists *and* as symbols of cultural integrity by local nationalists. Once again women and children were spoken for, and a battle for and against their rights was fought on the site of their bodies, with their minds excluded from the discourse. In many countries (Algeria, Zimbabwe, Iran, and Guinea-Bissau, for example), women found themselves subject to stringent controls after independence even though they had achieved some importance during the freedom struggle. Here again, it is important to identify the cultural continuity in the construction of the woman as an object to be rescued, through colonial and postcolonial times. Striking examples emerge from India and China.

Rescuing the Brown Woman

In the case of India, historian Yousouf Ali writes, "With us, the daughter is not a daughter all the days of her life. She is only a daughter until she is a wife. Then she enters into a new circle and new relationships, and she literally worships a new set of gods" (cited in Devendra 1994, p. 2). Chakravarti (1989), in her fascinating historiography of the emergence of the image of Indian womanhood in the nineteenth century, comments that this image constituted the Aryan woman who was upheld as a Vedic superwoman (which refers to the archetypal Indian woman such as the goddess Parvati the Nurturer, and her manifestation, Durga, the Destroyer). Spivak (1988a, p. 613) critiques Orientalist constructions of the Indian woman as an entity requiring protection and writes that the abolition of *sati* by the British was generally interpreted as:

"white men saving brown women from brown men" ... Against this is the Indian nativist argument, a parody of the nostalgia for lost origins: "The women actually wanted to die." The two sentences go a long way to legitimize each other. One never encounters the testimony of the women's voice-consciousness.

Indian nationalist writings were similar to Orientalist ones in that they also described India as a unified female body. Women's movements and writing of this period internalized the ideal of Aryan womanhood and its role in nationalism. Sangari and Vaid (1989, p. 10) contend that efforts to recover the ideologically pure tradition in the nationalist period were synonymous with those to restore the "traditional" woman. The "eternal" past had to be retrieved to meet the needs of the present. Ancient scriptures and religious canons were used to construct a nation as distinct from the colonial state and simultaneously, as inherently non-egalitarian. Socially constructed roles for women embodied these nation-building strategies in their limited social and economic value.

For all Mahatma Gandhi's efforts to empower women, his strategies were ultimately limiting to them. For example, he rejected those parts of the Hindu scriptures that denigrated women and urged them to participate in the *swadeshi* (self-reliance) movement where they would spin and wear *khadi* (home-spun) clothes. By drawing upon mythological women like Sita, Savitri, and Draupadi (all of whom, to simplify greatly, received divine intervention in the midst of crises because of their faith and virtue) and adorning them in *khadi*, Gandhi framed the female body as a symbol for national liberation. His feminization of self in spinning his own cloth and helping with household chores further reinforced the value of women in the private sphere, as guardians of tradition and resistors of foreign influence (Devendra 1994; Forbes 1996; R. Kumar 1993). Gandhi's fear of women's sexuality and the overt rituals of celibacy he imposed on himself and his followers, projected women as "dangerous, even if unwittingly so, for their very being constituted a sexual threat" (R. Kumar 1993, p. 85). Such framing curtailed women's participation in the public sphere of nationalist resistance and, although providing impetus for important reformations in women's education, further entrenched the patriarchal vision of the passive, long-suffering female in the domestic sphere (Katrak 1992; McMillin 2002b).

The carefully controlled freedom of the "modern woman" in India is evident in extensive textual analyses of pre-liberalized television (Dhanraj 1994; Krishnan and Dighe 1990) and post-liberalized television as well. McMillin (2002b) writes that the representation of women in the 1990s was not very different from that of the 1980s. In sitcoms, documentaries, dramas, and film-based variety shows, women were portrayed as creators of such social problems as AIDS, prostitution, bad parenting, and stressful marriages. They were rarely initiators of solutions and were projected as lively, yet subservient housewives who sacrificed their passions to submit to the pressures of society. The quintessential chaste, honorable, and passive Aryan woman served as the desirable norm on contemporary television. Her weakness and sexuality served as sites of male and female viewing pleasure in a cultural context in which both text and audience were embedded, drawing from the same codes of ideological realism.

In Indian cinema, pre-independence movies included many action films featuring "Fearless Nadia," a Bombay stuntwoman with a Greek mother and Welsh father, who masqueraded as a male action hero (examples are *Toofan Mail*, 1932; *Flying Ranee*, 1939; and *Son of Toofan Mail*, 1947). Providing a sense of power and courage, these action films soon gave way to overtly nationalistic films as the nation moved towards heightened struggles for independence. Such movies upheld the poor farmer (e.g. *Do Bigha Zameen, Mother Earth*) and the poor urban resident (e.g. *Footpath*, 1953; *Pyasa*, 1957). Realist cinema reflected the ethos of the age and portrayed ideal village and community life, the corruption of wealth, and a unified national identity. In the post-independence period, cinema depicted again and again, women-centered narratives revolving around the courtesan and/or prostitute role. Famous actresses portrayed the tragic lives of various fictional and quasi-fictional heroines who remained pure and strong in character yet were exploited by men, and eventually died when their true identities were revealed (e.g. *Adalat*, 1957), or were rejected by their families even though they had been kidnapped into prostitution at a young age (e.g. *Pakeezah*, 1971; *Umrao Jaan*, 1981). Chakravarty (1993) writes that the heroines of such films were the classic subalterns – they were economically productive, yet their money, as were their bodies, was tainted, making suspect women who could be economically independent in real life. Tragic heroines could be pure in heart and mind and be rescued or left to their fates, depending on the whim of the men in their lives. The liberation of the nation was accompanied by the imprisonment of women and their bodies in the media.

Disciplining the Peasant and the Prostitute

Similarly in China, D-H. Lee (2004) explains the Confucianist "Thrice Following" principle of a woman's social position: as a follower of her father when young, her husband when married, and her son when old. Despite some freedoms exercised by women in ancient China (Mann and Cheng 2001) and their positions as rulers (To 1995, cited in D-H. Lee 2004), for the most part, women were relegated to the private sphere and even their role as rulers was invariably to carry on the legacy of their dead husbands and maintain the operations of the patrilineal family. An important point to be made here is that struggles for representation in China were with state socialism, not Western colonialism – a possibility not entertained in mainstream postcolonial theory (Spivak 1988b) where the tri continent is constituted primarily in relation to colonial violence (see Rofel 1999). In Maoist (mainland) China, women were encouraged to enter the public labor sphere through state-sponsored education, women's rights and employment programs, yet they were denied participation in state discourse.

In Taiwan as well, the KMT facilitated women's development as a labor force, yet took great pains to maintain Confucian norms for women's roles. Martial law (1948–87) that curtailed content of newspapers and banned public gatherings and demonstrations, strongly opposed the women's movement because feminism was considered tantamount to promiscuity, immorality, and group marriage (M. Yang 1999). Yet the post-martial law period (1987 onwards) also saw an increase in small and medium-sized businesses and factories requiring a larger labor force and encouraging activist consumer, women, student, labor, and human rights groups to oppose state restrictions through the mass media (Hsiao 1992, cited in M. Yang 1999).

Feminism in China emerged from a "state feminism" sponsored by the Chinese Communist Party (CCP) as it emerged in Scandinavia and Egypt in the 1960s, and refers to the organization of state resources and strategies to ensure women's equality, reproductive rights, and employment opportunities. Similar state feminism projects were implemented in Eastern Europe and the former Soviet Union (Meyer 1985), and arguably resulted not in women's emancipation, but a shift in power from micro domestic patriarchy to macro state interventionist patriarchy (Verdery 1994). M. Yang (1999) poignantly points out that the male–female binary is not emphasized in socialist state feminism. The removal of "woman" as a category antithetical to "man" makes it difficult for Chinese women to establish their independence from a patriarchal, male state.

Therefore in the case of China, even with the Great Leap Forward (1958–61) when women entered waged labor, and the "Memorial Requesting a Ban on the Binding of Women's Feet" in the Maoist Era, women's freedoms were subjugated in favor of nation-building projects. The Cultural Revolution desexualized women, enforcing short hair and army clothes so that females and males were indistinguishable from behind. In the 1950s and 1960s, magazines portrayed women as plainly dressed, and engaged in agricultural and mechanical labor. By carefully managing women's representations in the public sphere, the state made invisible women's dual loads as primary workers in and out of the home *and* the sexual division of labor where men continued in high-ranking positions of power. The state then not only managed gender and sexuality but was gendered itself, a masculinizing project that was undertaken by both its male and female inhabitants (Enloe 1989; Peterson 1992; C. Sutton 1995).

In 1980s China, films provided a space for the unfolding conflict between traditional Chinese and progressive western ideals. Recurrent themes were father–son conflicts with sons inevitably being killed by their fathers, a symbol of the oppression of tradition and of political persecution. Women were annihilated both in terms of their absence from such conflict and in their acceptance of a male-dominated culture in that women's voices in these films were legitimated only when they dressed up as men, or acquired the persona of a man. Pop culture in the same decade exemplified male elite culture, especially with television historical dramas situated in the late Qing dynasty with the Manchus who had conquered the Han, as the Other, with powerful "man-impersonating" women such as the Empress Dowager Ci Xi (Yehenala) personifying evil and corruption. Thus Chinese popular culture rewrote its women at a time when its borders were opening up to new logics of women's subjectivity. In the early 1980s, women were represented as the fecund Mother Earth and in the late 1980s as sinister and mysterious, contaminating bloodlines through connivance and promiscuity. They were conjured as hindrances to men's rightful place in history (an example is *Red Sorghum*, 1987, where a woman's ultimate defeat is a man's victory). China's first television soap, *Yearning* (1990), firmly placed the female protagonist in a traditional and submissive role, frustrating women's groups such as the Women's Federation, yet distracting and appeasing a conflicted public who had just witnessed open dissent in the Tiananmen Square tragedy just the year before.

In the late 1980s and early 1990s, film, novel, and television narratives shifted the space of failure from the terrain (as in Su Tong's *My Hometown of Maples and Poplars*) to the domestic space, whether a house (in Zhang Yimou's *Ju Dou*) or haunted mansion (in Su Tong's *Wives and Concubines* and Zhang Yimou's *Raise the Red Lantern*), to set up the domestic space as an exotic Other for Western eyes and to signify a space that imprisons women (Jinhua 1999). Women's failure in these narratives stemmed not only from their failure to please men but also in their bickering and policing of each other, and as keepers and glorifiers of the very patriarchal structure that bound them. Women had to bear the double burden of the "historical unconscious and the historical task of castration" (ibid., p. 198). The woman was simultaneously the arbitrator of sacrificial ceremonies and the victim of the sacrifice. She was drawn into the writing of the very history that subjugated her and offered her up for exploitation.

In the early 1990s, confronted with the increasing influx of images and political policies from the West, Chinese filmmakers turned to effeminize the male *vis-à-vis* the Western male and female (see for example, Wang Anyi's *My Uncle's Story*, 1991, which tells the tale of the gradual subjugation of a Chinese man by a Western woman) or exoticize the woman for Western consumption (as in Zhang Yimou's *Raise the Red Lantern* and Chen Kaige's *Farewell My Concubine*, 1993, both nominated for Academy Awards) Jinhua comments:

> [T]he project to subvert and change the social status quo becomes an effort to perpetuate the gender order, and reflections on the political and historical fate of the nation become the presentation of the male subject's individual suffering. In this way, the male narrator brings about the pardoning of men at the expense of women's exile. Women's attempts at representing diverse voices and biographies are appropriated by a dominant male culture and packaged for male-voyeuristic gaze. (1999, p. 202)

Serials such as *Foreign Women in Beijing* (1995) portrayed white American women in Beijing and their positions as objects of desire to Chinese males. This strategy was crucial for China to pursue its position as a world leader with or superior to Western nations. The nation as a feminized state had to make way for a masculinized persona that was legitimized by and in the West. Although in reality it is far more common for Chinese women to marry foreign men overseas, the portrayal of White women and Chinese men in primary roles to the almost entire exclusion of Chinese women symbolically constructs Chinese manhood as the embodiment of both quintessential Chineseness and transnational modernity (Erwin 1999).

M. Yang (1996) summarizes that images of women in 1990s China were of the virtuous, raped, battered, brutalized, or career woman, invariably a failure in family life, or the immoral, sexy, action woman who transgressed female boundaries, yet was capable of audience empathy. Young women as male consorts were most common in television commercials (Notar 1994). In this new order, "male subjectivity and its power are made invisible as in the Maoist gender order, but this invisibility is not based on an erasure or blurring of genders but depends on the *hypervisibility* of the female image" (M. Yang 1996, p. 50, emphasis added).

In Hong Kong and Taiwan as well, mainland Chinese women were an integral part of nation-building in television narratives. They entered television storylines as prostitutes, conniving career women, or all-giving mothers and grandmothers, and performed a crucial function as paradigmatic oppositions to the larger narrative of national progress and modernity represented by Hong Kong and Taiwanese primary characters. For example, Taiwanese media in the mid-1990s had ample representations of the *dalumei* (mainland sister), who is literally a prostitute able to make money by performing a variety of roles, reflecting the reality of the migration of women from mainland China to Taiwan to serve as mistresses, prostitutes, and even surrogate mothers for Taiwanese businessmen. Shih writes: "[T]he dalumei, a gendered embodiment of dalu (mainland), incarnates for the readership the economic threats of usurping and exhausting Taiwan capital through her seductiveness and the political threat of migration, infiltration, and invasion" (1999, p. 290).

Similarly, in Hong Kong, mainland immigrants were considered backward and depraved and the *dalumei* prostitutes of Taiwan served the same function in Hong Kong. Hong Kong films, especially in the early 1990s, represented their contrast and difference from China to establish their own identity, portraying the *biaojie* (older female cousin characterized for her backwardness, lack of culture and modern sensibility, and inclination for corruption), a symbol of mainland China, as the troublemaker in a modern, progressive and cultured Hong Kong household. In such narratives, the *biaojie* eventually underwent a transformation and was elevated to the status of actually marrying a Hong Konger demonstrating that "What Hong Kong does to her is to arouse in her the universal longings of a woman and regender her into a feminine role" (ibid., p. 300). The politics of 1997 independence from Britain and unification with the mainland were strong subtexts of these narratives.

An important point that emerges from the above examples is that media texts offer up a variety of ways in which the gendered nation and its female subjects are to be consumed. As state apparatuses of a hegemonic system, the media facilitate parallels between the development of a nation and its women. At the same time, through its images and narratives, it provides the ideological basis for the discipline of this population that can misbehave to the extent of asserting its independence. Curtailment of women's freedoms takes on a new urgency; their reproductive capacity across class and caste lines breeds hegemonic anxiety regarding a loss of control in policing borders.

In a neo-network era then, characterized by decentralization through multi-layered networks of production, consumption, and distribution (Curtin 1999), the representation of diversity becomes a challenge. This is because of the financial risk involved in catering to minority populations. Yet it is this diversity that is a gold mine for private, indigenous, and foreign networks that can cater to audiences hungry for programming in regional languages and regionally specific cultural themes. Women gain a new significance in projects of economic development, as suggested in this section. They acquire new roles as consumers of modernity without giving up their old ones as keepers of tradition, simultaneously opening up new avenues for expression and subjectivity.

Beginning around the 1980s when television received a boost around the world due to various international and national events described in the next chapter, national governments, particularly social democracies, mined television for its commercial potential. The tension between the opening up of new avenues for expression and efforts to contain old ones becomes an intriguing site for analysis in international media studies. As we shall see, this tension often translates into lucrative marketing strategies where state and private goals of economic expansion work hand in hand, reentrenching social hierarchies that have endured through time. Yet, structural edges are giving way to new formations of community and experience.

Chapter Five

Competing Networks, Hybrid Identities

In the mid-1990s and 2000s, market narratives have become co-opted into nationalistic ones, intertwining national and economic growth in a way unprecedented before the advent of satellite television. Cosmopolitanism is now a nationalist project and the cultivation of the consumer becomes as important for the state government as it is for private corporations (Abu-Lughod 2005). This chapter details the political and economic context for media liberalization in tri continent countries and provides extensive examples of the various forms of hybrid television programming that have resulted. Using postcolonial theory, the chapter critiques the myriad positionings of gender and ethnic minorities in such programming. It ends with a discussion of the cultural implications of hybrid programming that characterizes much of the transnational television industry today.

Structural Adjustment Programs in the 1980s mandated by the IMF and the World Bank forced many nations of the Middle East, Africa, and Asia to deregulate state control over industry and privatize certain sectors such as the media and open up indigenous industries for foreign investment. The World Bank repeatedly advocated the partnership of states and markets to effect overall human development. The aggressive deregulation in the United States in the late 1970s, which picked up momentum in the 1980s under President Regan, and the corresponding privatization in Great Britain in the 1980s under Prime Minister Margaret Thatcher created ripple effects across the world. Capitalist economic development received impetus in Japan in the 1950s, Hong Kong in the 1960s, Taiwan, Singapore, and South Korea in the 1970s; and India and China in the 1980s. Newly independent governments inherited the British colonial legacy of state dependency where state-financed organizations dominated economic growth and in keeping with socialist welfare philosophy, ensured equitable economic distribution, at least in theory. The corresponding complex bureaucracy that ensued urged many governments to seek opportunities to privatize and open up markets to remedy the waste that had accumulated during the decades of state intervention (Zaharom 2000).

Nyamnjoh writes in the case of Africa:

> Cultural production in Africa is caught between control by the greedy and aggressive pursuit of profit by the global media on the one hand, and repression at local levels by states marginalized as global players and reduced to flexing their muscles vis-à-vis their own populations...What neoliberalism wants of African governments is national and regional policies in tune with the profitability expectations of global capital, policies that minimize countervailing traditions, customs, world views and expectations of continuity. (2004, pp. 60–1)

The commercial potential of television was recognized by national elites and businessmen, and governments gave way to private investment and broadcasters in postcolonial countries. Those military dictatorships that already had strong connections between government and private media entrepreneurs expanded opportunities for media commercialism. Impetus to television in tri continent countries was propelled by various international events (for example, the 1964 Olympics for Japan, the 1972 Olympics for Senegal, and the 1982 Asiad Games for India) where although still cost-prohibitive, television sales skyrocketed especially with the introduction of color. Other national spectacles that boosted the sales of television sets were political funerals that simultaneously reinforced the idea of a unified hegemonic nation-state. Examples are Indira Gandhi's funeral in India in 1984 where the blazing orange flames of the funeral pyre, the red and saffron *sari*-clad corpse, and the white *kurta-pyjama* clothes of Rajiv Gandhi, Indira's first born, who lit the pyre according to sacred Hindu rituals, made for vivid and dramatic television (McMillin 2001; Mitra 1993). Similarly, the Thai King's mother's funeral in 1996 was a gripping testimony to the power of color television where the teeming crowds of mourners dressed in black were connected through the medium, to the rest of the nation watching at home. The funeral rites were a revival of the royal past; officiants wore costumes from earlier dynasties and some rode elephants that wound through the streets in a stately procession (Hamilton 2002). In such contexts, television established itself as a space for the expression of national mourning and collective identity.

In Europe in the 1990s, Morley and Robins (1995) write that the public service media philosophy shifted to a neoliberal one where individual consumer interests based on ethnic, religious, and linguistic (to name a few) groupings became marketing strategies for aggressively commercially driven enterprises. In fact, the concerns of the public service enterprise such as democracy and national identity are considered, in the new privatized media context, to hinder the development of viewing and consumer communities. This change in philosophies had a tremendous impact on developing countries where privatization was encouraged in the media, to meet the demands of globalization, and the consumer identities of the people were sought after as marketing niches rather than their identities as citizens (see Algan 2003, in the case of Turkey; La Pastina 2003, in the case of Brazil; and Kraidy 2003, in the case of Lebanon, for example). Morley and Robins (1995) argue that the objective of transnational corporations such as Time Warner, Sony, Matsushita, and Rupert Murdoch's News Corporation, is to break down national boundaries in favor of global markets, and thus is antithetical to the objective of national governments which seek to contain the nation through centralized broadcasting services. Price (1995) adds that government control over broadcast media diminishes in the age of globalization. While initially regulated as tools for the propagation of democracy and national identity, media industries are now no longer confined to national or regional boundaries. Direct broadcast satellite transmission allows the flow of messages across national borders, and national governments are fearful of the implications of this flow for national identity and cultural integrity. Loss of control over the definitions and circulation of national culture translates into loss of power and control over national boundaries – a reason for hegemonic anxiety.[1]

Certainly the overriding motive of global channels is not solely profit since tri continent markets are among the poorest in the world. Yet the middle class in these countries is growing and the channels serve to sustain the colonial language as a crucial language of currency and administration. In an attempt to manage increasingly chaotic media environments without curbing their economic potential, national governments established loose broadcasting policies that gave entertainment media a relatively free hand, but curtailed news programming. Specifically, entertainment media in various tri continent countries experimented with format and content, using strategies of hybridization, dubbing, cloning, and collaging (Moran 2004) to achieve and sustain high ratings, while news media became more conservative, reflecting the voice of the government as it did in the early days of broadcasting. The role of television in many postcolonial countries, then, oscillates between national development imperatives imitating the positivist paradigm of development communication, and market imperatives, following the aggressively commercial, private network model of the United States. Subsequent sections in this chapter deal with government and programming strategies to tap the commercial potential of television. An appropriate point of entry to the discussion is the arrival of Star TV in the Asia region.

Star TV and Transnational Media Networks

Any discussion of the liberalized global television environment has to begin with the media significance of the Gulf War in 1990–91. CNN's coverage of air raids against Iraq by American-led allied forces in Kuwait was of tremendous interest for audiences in Middle and Southeast Asia who were limited to poor quality and scanty coverage by their own national networks. In Mumbai, India, high-rise hotels and apartment buildings installed satellite dishes, bypassing draconian telecommunication laws (Mankekar 1999). Similar equipment was used across the Middle East to receive CNN's signals of the war. The establishment of Star TV in 1991 in Hong Kong by Li Ka-Shing of Hutchison Whampoa and his son Richard Li, owner of the Pacific Central Group coincided with liberalization and privatization efforts in various Asian countries. By April 1991, Star TV's footprint covered as many as 38 countries in Asia (K. Kumar 1998). Realizing the potential of the liberalized environment in Asia, Australia-born media baron Rupert Murdoch purchased 64 percent of Star TV, which uplinks to ASIA SAT-1, and bought the remaining 36 percent of Star TV in July 1994 ("Murdoch buys balance," 1994). Despite the fact that many governments were caught unaware with the influx of Star TV programming (their permission was not sought even though required by ITU and World Administrative Radio Conference (WARC) regulations), Star TV, with its "multidomestic" rather than "global" strategy, was able to convince various governments that it would stay respectful of local cultures, engaging in such strategies as dubbing and subtitling to ensure programs resonated with local audiences. Star TV split its beam between Greater China (Hong Kong, Taiwan, and the PRC), and the Indian subcontinent, Southeast Asia, and the Middle East (Sinclair 1998). So powerful is Murdoch's presence on the global media scene that his approach to global entertainment and infotainment has been termed "Murdochization," which can be characterized by global media technological convergence, market-driven journalism, international production and distribution of US-inspired media formats, and a focus on infotainment that places the media as the central venue for public information. It is instrumental in the standardization of global media products that are adaptable for local contexts, leading to hybrid products that contain elements of both global and local (Thussu 1998).

Star TV's use of satellite-to-cable systems and direct-to-home (DTH) broadcasts ensured easy accessibility and good quality reception. With Hong Kong as its headquarters for network production, distributions, marketing and sales, public relations, graphics and creative services, administration and management, engineering and satellite uplink; and with Jakarta as its Southeast Asia headquarters, Star TV was able to extend its platform of Star Movies, Star Phoenix, and Phoenix Chinese Channels (in China), Star Chinese Channel (in Taiwan), Star Plus and Channel [V] (in India), to name a few examples, to Asia, providing a welcome alternative to staid programming from national networks.

Star TV was followed by other foreign channels such as CNN, TNT, and Cartoon Network (owned by Turner Broadcasting Services), ESPN (owned by Disney), HBO Pacific (owned by Time Warner), and MTV and its local clone, Channel [V] (owned by Viacom) (Sinclair 1998). The presence of foreign channels provided a tremendous boost to local economies because the objective, as stated in a Star TV advertisement, was primarily to connect consumers to local businesses. As the following examples illustrate, the advent of satellite television particularly in Asian countries, paralleled government policies to liberalize and privatize their markets.

In India, the establishment of Star TV coincided with the nation's June 1991 economic liberalization policy. In keeping with its objective of encouraging open investment and liberalized trade, the Indian government did not curb the flow of Star TV channels such as MTV (now on the Doordarshan platform), Prime Time Sports, and BBC World Service (Shields and Muppidi 1996). Murdoch acquired 50 percent of Asia Today Limited (ATL) in 1993, which runs Zee TV, and the network provides an exhaustive menu of Hindi films and film songs to Asian audiences (Bhandare 1997; Pathania 1994). Star TV and Zee TV became a source of anxiety for Doordarshan because by 1993, the two satellite channels were estimated to enjoy a combined 20 percent of total television advertising in India.

To counter the competition, Doordarshan and private television networks alike launched genre-specific channels, such as Doordarshan's "Movie Club," Zee TV's "Zee TV Cinema" and Star TV's "Prime Sports." Star TV and Zee TV's success as business networks was recognized by politicians and entrepreneurs in various states in India. Many also recognized the potential of these networks for political propaganda. By 1993, private, regional, vernacular language television production centers had been established in various state capitals:[2] Sun TV in Chennai, Raj TV in Hyderabad, and Asia Network in Trivandrum. Prevented from uplinking to government satellites, these networks uplink to RIMSAT (Doordarshan 1995), and provide a wide variety of programming in regional languages, from Indian films and variety shows for entertainment, to serials and documentaries for education and development (McMillin 2001).

In Malaysia as well, Prime Minister Mahatir Mohammed's Look East Policy and Malaysia Incorporated and Privatization Policies in the 1980s built upon the nation's 1960s New Economic Policy (NEP). They propelled the nation to economic prosperity and did much to alleviate ethnic conflict. Mahatir, while staunchly protectionist and anti-imperialist, was not anti-capitalist, and regarded transnational investment as crucial for the country's economic growth. As with other Asian countries, the mid and late 1990s saw an increase in complexity and diversity of the Malaysian television environment with five television stations, of which three were commercial, five subscription cable channels supplied by the Mega TV cable company, and 15 satellite subscription channels through Astro, a satellite broadcasting company. In 1969, MegaSat-1 (Malaysia East Asia Satellite) was launched from Kourou, French Guyana. Political and media alliances were strong where, for example, the Melewar (media) Corporation is controlled by a Negeri Sembilan royal house member Tunku Abdullah, also a close associate of the Prime Minister (Zaharom 2000).

Hong Kong, under the weak Hong Kong Special Administrative Region (HKSAR) government, is a symbol of China's progressiveness and liberalism. Although very much under the control of the Chinese government, Hong Kong's Western-influenced media serve as a template for China's own goals of liberalization. Even before 1997, Hong Kong's local television productions and US music programs and movies were popular and available in China largely through piracy networks. The launch of Star TV in 1991 in Hong Kong and its take-over by Murdoch led to a collaborative venture between Murdoch and Chinese entrepreneurs in the form of the Phoenix Satellite TV Company facilitating the broadcast of US sports and entertainment and regional programs from Star TV to China. To ensure long-term success locally, co-productions, joint ventures, international forums, and film festivals are routine between transnational conglomerates and local media companies. A consequence of liberalization of the media environment in transnational China (which M. Yang 1999, describes as including Taiwan, mainland China, Hong Kong, and the Chinese diaspora across the world) is that the media have shifted from being the voice of the government to fulfilling a variety of entertainment, education, and information needs of the audience. They provide refreshing alternatives for the public who had been limited to state-mandated media until then.

Yet, Ma (2000) cautions against romanticizing the new character of media in China. It is free to experiment and diversify as long as it is within the norms of political and economic interests, leading to sometimes blatant media promotion of these interests. The relationship among media, government, and market also translates into fewer programming options for those who do not have the purchasing power to consume the products advertised. Rural populations are largely neglected in this context. The free media market is therefore not antithetical to the imperatives of the state, but closely managed by it, for its enormous economic potential. Entertainment media are less susceptible to censorship because they are considered to be frivolous, feminine and primarily a generator of revenue and ratings.

In the 1990s in Latin America, privatization was allowed to a greater extent in the media. Mergers and acquisitions and transnational collaborations allowed those media organizations that enjoyed government support in the authoritative regimes from the 1960s to the 1980s, to become giants in the area. For example, in Argentina, Citi Corp Equity Investments (CEI) owns Canal 9 and Canal 11 (two of the four television channels); Brazil's Globo is a veritable media empire with vertical and horizontal expansion in financing, banking, food, mining, telecommunications, and insurance, to name a few industries; and in Colombia, Arcilla Lulle and Santo Domingo media groups lead the field. In Peru, Panamericana Television stands out in scale (Waisbord 2000). The result is that, as in India, the future for independent and small-scale operations is bleak.

Liberal ideas of the freedom of the press may be said to have been introduced in Latin America by the Miami-based Inter American Press Association (Hallin 2000). As described in Chapter Four, Latin American media's complicity with state policies is because of the strong symbiotic relationship between capitalists and government (Hallin 2000; Sinclair et al. 1996). For example, Televisa's needs drove Mexico's media policy rather than the PRI. Azcárraga's affiliation with the PRI meant the party's needs were often synonymous with that of Televisa. Televisión Azteca in 1972 (formerly the Imevisión government network) became Televisa's competitor. Although both continued as voices of the party and, later, of the three major political parties in the latter 1990s, their competitive status led to more bold, insightful, and investigative political stories (Hallin 2000).

The Middle East also experienced a boom in the development of television with the Gulf War. CNN's 24-hour broadcasts virtually monopolized the news arena in these countries where state-supported news media lacked the resources and coverage to compete. Specifically, the Egyptian Space Channel (Space Net) produced by Egyptian Radio Television Union (ERTU) launched its international television service followed by MEBC in 1991, broadcasting from London and sponsored by Arab investors and Saudi royal family business connections. The Egyptian film industry has been revived through television productions and ERTU has invested in "Hollywood on the Nile" to maintain the nation's presence as a leading film producer in the region. By 1994, there were 20 transregional satellite television channels, most notable of which is Orbit (comprising 16 television channels including CNN, Hollywood Channel, Discovery and Music Channel). The BBC was cancelled as part of this platform due to its controversial human rights documentaries. Besides television channels, Orbit has four radio networks in Arabic and English. Emerging leaders are the Qatari broadcasting system and the Al-Jazeera Satellite Channel, Arab Radio and Television (ART – a 4-channel network broadcasting from Rome), and foreign competitors such as Showtime (sponsored by GULFDTH, a collaboration of Viacom and Kuwaiti Investment Properties Co.). Other examples are Lebanon's satellite channels, LBL and Future, full of game shows and entertainment oriented programs. The governments in countries such as Jordan, Qatar, and Saudi Arabia have established MMDS (multichannel multipoint distribution systems) to censor programming they deem distasteful to the public. For example, in Bahrain, undesirable channels are encrypted and in Qatar, delayed programming allows quick censorship. Also, encouragement is provided for Arab-language programming to establish a pan-regional audience and value system. Local programming for national audiences is increasing as are culturally relevant programs.

In Egypt, the state has maintained control over the ERTU. The arrival of satellite television in the early 1990s, although slow to gather momentum, caused the government to seriously consider ways to counter the competition. As in India, commercialism was the answer and national programs carry a high proportion of advertising. Also, the government invested in the satellite station NILE-SAT and in Egypt's Media Production City, a conglomerate of 29 film studios, editing units, hotels and an amusement park. In 2001, the government established Dream TV, full of music videos and political discussions (Abu-Lughod 2005).

Policing the Skies

Trends of deregulation and privatization of media industries around the world in the 1980s and 1990s were not uniformly accommodated, of course. As mentioned earlier, China's "Six Nos" policy was influential in limiting foreign television programs in the country. Similarly, Indonesia's Broadcasting Bill withdraws licenses from broadcasters who exceed the 30 percent air time limit for imported programming (Staff 1998). Singapore, Malaysia, and Vietnam have banned private ownership of satellite dishes (Chan 1994). In Korea, foreign satellite programming triggered strong protectionist policies with downscaling of media organizations and institutions and subscription fees, leading to mass protests against the Korea Broadcasting System (KBS).

Independent papers in the latter 1980s such as the *Hankyoreb* (started by fired journalists) and *Media Today* and *Labourer's Newspaper* by labor groups have provided an alternate voice in Korea (Park et al. 2000). The country has renewed state power, even withdrawing from the IMF in rejection of its open-door economic mandates. Kim, Park, and Sohn write:

> [I]n the case of Korea, state power is being reinforced. Since there is no alterna-
> tive power to replace the state which will work to cope with the tendency of
> globalization, the government is wielding the strongest hegemony in the process
> of restructuring. (2000, p. 122)

Beginning in the early 1990s, newspaper companies in Korea (such as *Chosun, Joongang,* and *Dong-A*), expanded their services to include new media sections incorporating electronic bulletins and electronic newspapers. Commercial television companies were granted licenses and by 1991, the Seoul-based commercial television channel, SBS, began service. In 1995, cable TV was introduced, with service on 29 channels. Between 1995 and 1997 eight other commercial television companies were established. The rise of the state in an era of globalization is strongly evinced in the case of Japan, Singapore, Korea, and Taiwan. It plays a significant role in facilitating processes of internationalization within these countries (Weiss 1998).

As in Korea, the climate of press liberalization in the 1980s meant further control over broadcasting in Taiwan. By the late 1970s, cable operators offered illegal cable service through VCRs and crude transmission facilities. The first competitor to the KMT stations was the DPP pro-democracy station in 1990. The declining strength of the KMT and the microwave technology of the cable transmitters allowed this station to continue. Overseas satellites such as Japan's BS-3a and BS-3b, and Indonesia's Palapa-B2P allowed the entry of American and Chinese programs into Taiwan. After pressure from the US, Taiwan extended its copyright law to include films, music and computer databases in 1992, and in 1993, ratified the Cable TV Act to avoid US trade sanctions (C-C. Lee 2000). The Government Information Office (GIO) has to clear all imported programming before broadcast and a minimum of 70 percent of programming on terrestrial television stations and 25 percent on cable channels has to be locally produced (Chan 1996). Although the cable market has exploded with small merchants making use of satellite spillovers and pirated videos to cablecast to small communities, the cable audience is still a minority. The state is no doubt weakened in its capacity to maintain its central influence over its people. Yet it is still dominant and negotiates and competes with private networks to develop relationships that are fluid, consonant, and dialectical, altering the terms of internal debates on media ownership and autonomy.

The tightening of media freedoms was experienced in Africa as well. As in much of the tri continent countries, liberalization in the African media industry arrived in the late 1980s and early 1990s. Yet, for the most part, Nyamnjoh (2004) notes, African journalists, academics, artists and writers who question the policies of the state are immediately disciplined. Government declarations of cultural renaissance and freedom of the press belie quick and strict disciplinary actions against individuals, no matter how high in rank or prestige, who may express opposing or controversial views on public matters. Such a structure certainly influences media productions by African journalists and the political reality is that it is easier for a "Western production team" to produce documentaries of African society than it is for a local one with its own interpretations of reality. Critical press is often subdued (Lush 1998) even in Nigeria, a country of a relatively rigorous press (Oloyede 1996).

In South Africa, the end of apartheid has not quite resulted in greater representation of diversity in its newspapers (Pityana 2000). Academics continue the tradition of self-censorship (Nyamnjoh 2004). The media are often manipulated to reflect the voice of the central authority, as in the case of President Omar Bongo of Gabon (Ngolet 2000), and censor creative endeavors by artists and intellectuals (Soyinka 1994). Nyamnjoh (2004) documents political and cultural repression in Cameroon under both Presidents Ahidjo and Biya who took over in 1982, where pro-government academics and intellectuals were elevated to lofty government positions. President Biya chose for his cabinet those who were of the same Beti ethnicity and who supported productions that were sympathetic to this ethnic region. Priority was given to Bkutsi music on both national radio and television over that of music from other ethnic regions. Such rigid control over state media means a hesitance on the part of private investors in wanting a part of Africa's media. Because of the lack of funds and resources, journalists are generalists, unable to specialize in specific areas. Most newspapers have only a single person as staff and many push personal agendas rather than report the events of the day.

Since the 1990s, however, there has been significant private investment in the media with the BBC and RFI broadcasting regularly on FM in prominent urban African centers. Malawi's first TV station opened in January 1999, Botswana's in July 2000, and Lesotho and Swaziland have commissioned M-net, a South African commercial broadcaster to serve as a national system, bringing to its people mostly foreign programs from South Africa and the West. In South Africa, the South African Broadcasting Corporation (SABC) has significantly moved away from its role as the voice of the apartheid and has entered satellite television with its subscription M-net since 1986, owned by a group of South African newspaper publishers. Multi-choice Digital

110

Satellite Television (DSTV) provides around 23 satellite channels and 48 audio channels and Canal Horizon Plus provides predominantly entertainment programs. The elite population is well catered to, with Canal Horizon for Francophone Africa, and DSTV for Anglophone Africa. All satellite channels have a predominance of standardized soaps, talk shows, dramas, music shows, movies, and sitcoms from the west. Local productions get limited sponsorship through the Union of National Radio and Television of Africa (URTNA). Community radio in Africa has received a boost, however, and more than 100 licenses had been granted by 1988. As Fair (2003) writes in the case of Senegal, the expansion of TV5 in the country into a consortium of five member channels: three French (TF1, Antenne 2, FR3), one Belgian (RTBF), and one Swiss (TSR) into TV5 Afrique; and the dubbing of programs in French on Canal Horizons, maintained the goals of francophonie and Senegal's connection with the French-speaking world.

It is obvious from the above examples that privatization in media industries in tri continent countries have been accommodated with varying degrees of political freedom and control. In general, however, commercialization of media has opened up new spaces of expression, diversity of formats, genres, and better-produced programming. Decentralization, specialization, and diversification in processes of production and distribution have allowed media professionals to experiment with content as well, drawing into the media stage a discussion of social, political, economic, and cultural issues never witnessed before under more authoritative or communist political environments. Rather than the core–periphery, one-way flow of media technology and products documented and critiqued in the 1970s, in the 2000s, interconnected and interdependent hybrid networks have emerged, making profits off copying and adapting program formats.

Hybridity and the Globalization of Television Formats

As global media networks such as BBC and CNN circumvent the globe, satellite networks such as Canal Horizons (in Africa), BskyB (in Europe) and Star TV (in Asia) cater to broad geolinguistic and regional audiences, and private vernacular language networks cater to domestic and expatriate populations, national governments struggle to maintain a stronghold over centralized broadcasting networks. Recognizing the enormous potential of privatization, many national governments, as we have seen in the previous section, allow aggressive private investment and relax legal restrictions on mergers and acquisitions. While news media continue with strong, almost propagandic representations of the government as is the case in many countries in Asia and Africa, entertainment media are given a relatively free hand to experiment and innovate.

Hybrid programming becomes a key strategy in the latter domain, to meet the rising demand for programs that contain elements of the global, yet are charged with local relevance in terms of language, themes, actors, and contexts. Hybrid programming allows lighthearted combinations of global and local programming elements. The average consumer is able to appreciate the humor in the caricature of both global and local and recognize her or his membership in a media world that transcends national borders (McMillin 2001). The result is endless entertainment in the form of talk shows, call-in music programs, sitcoms, soaps, variety shows, game shows and the like, with little space and time provided for political news analysis or, much less, debate.

As developed by poststructuralists Bhabha (1994) and Canclini (1995), the concept of hybridity is useful in international media studies because it allows the study of non-linear, disjunctive phenomena such as the flows and appropriations of religion, clothing, music, media, and other cultural commodities and rituals around the world. According to Bhabha, hybridity represents a liminal space between global and local where this "interstitial passage between fixed identifications opens up the possibility of a cultural hybridity that entertains difference without an assumed or imposed hierarchy" (1994, p. 4). Bhabha, in his critique of literature from the margins of colonialism, argues that it is in these liminal spaces that the nation is written. Imperialist temporalities that clock progress through linear, dichotomized phases (for example, pre-colonial vs. post-colonial) fail to account for minority voices that encounter the past even as they accommodate and speak to the present. In the context of television, Roome (1999) observes that through marketing, advertising, and audience research, the commodification of culture becomes a global phenomenon. In the hybrid formats that emerge, the global and the local may be intertwined. However, the local, the authentic, is altered in the dynamic process of the domestification of foreign cultural goods.

Canclini's (1997) notion of the intermingling of global and local influences in urban spaces proved provocative to the study of, for example, food as a site for intercultural flavours (Sokolov 1991), MTV as a venue for "glocalized" programming in the United States and abroad (Brown 1997), and of reggae music as a blend of Caribbean calypso and rumba, European ballroom dance, African drumming, Agro-Protestant revivalist hymns and US rhythm and blues (Manuel 1995). Yet such studies of hybridity do not adequately consider cultural implications, as explained later in this chapter. Although global and

112

local meanings intersect, the local production, interpretation, and consumption are recognised as crucial to the viability of the capitalist framework that provides the economic base for the local community's consumption. Canclini explains the logic of the market:

> "Popular" is what sells massively, what the multitudes like. As a matter of fact, what matters to the market and the media is not the popular but popularity. The media are not concerned with maintaining the popular as culture or tradition; the culture industry is more interested in constructing and renewing the simultaneous contact between broadcasters and receivers than it is in the formation of historical memory. (1995, pp. 187–8)

Canclini writes that the alliance between the hegemonic and the subaltern translates into conflict and what remains to be analyzed are the political consequences of moving from a centralized and dichotomized construction of socio-political relations to a decentralized one that caters to multiple groups. As discussed earlier in this chapter, the late 1980s and early 1990s were a time of significant change in the television environment across the world with many postcolonial countries deregulating, liberalizing, and privatizing their markets. Satellite television in Asia through, most predominantly Murdoch's Star TV, added diversity of programming choices in countries that were already witnessing the multiplication of television channels with the emergence of private regional, vernacular language networks. Initially, reliance on low-cost programming quickly led to a decline in ratings and the demise of foreign channels because of unfamiliarity of language and cultural contexts and themes. The increasing accessibility of television in remote parts of the world, the expansion of the middle classes in countries of the tri continent, and the increasing demand for entertainment programming have led to frantic and large-scale cloning, developing, collaging (D-H. Lee 2004), and illegal copying or pirating of program formats (Moran 2004).

Such format transfer and adaptation between media markets necessarily lead to competing state and market definitions of nation, community, and citizen and consumer identities. *Hybrid programming*, which may be used as a blanket term to include such format manipulations as cloning, collaging, and developing, simply refers to the cooption of a foreign program for a local market, sustaining the format but injecting local actors, sets, and cultural themes. The success of hybrid programming may be attributed to the shift in the locus of power. Specifically, pedagogical programs on state-owned networks projected the nation as still having to catch up, of not quite having made it in a postcolonial, rapidly industrializing world. Power and prestige were the prerogatives of developed countries. The United States as the perceived

113

trendsetter and the Great Britain, as the colonial overlord, were global leaders to be imitated in terms of language, lifestyle, music, fashion, and so on. Hybrid programming, in its cohabitation of global and local, accommodates the tensions among competing spheres and allows viewers to see their own communities represented in tandem, not as lagging behind, those who historically led the field. Yet, the hybrid is also hierarchical and the term should not obfuscate the very real struggles of representation of the local *vis-à-vis* the global (McMillin 2001). Bhabha's notion of hybridity has received criticism from any number of postcolonial scholars who point to the ahistoricity of the "stripped subject" in the hybrid context (see Ahmad 1992). It has been attacked for its abstraction, its vague spatial location, its bland mixing of metaphors, and the instability of the concept itself. Hybridity is problematic because of its ambiguity. It implies that diverse identities exist peacefully side by side, uncontaminated, setting self and Other on equal footing when in actuality, historical processes that involve stark violence, may separate them (Dirlik 2002).

In an era of media globalization, hybrid representations of global and local, and of traditional and modern, have serious implications for ethnic and gender minorities. Harvey (1989) contends that in a context of intermixing of cultures, styles, and behaviors, nationalist imperatives to contain the nation become more urgent and stringent, resulting, in extreme cases, in devastatingly violent wars of ethnic cleansing. Loomba (1994) adds that Bhabha's hybridity thesis does not address the gender, class, caste and other differentiations of the colonial subject. Donadey (2001) points out, however, that Bhabha's thesis is not so much an assertion of happy pluralism over contested dualisms but an urging to displace and unsettle fixed categories that have persisted through time. Ultimately, the value of the notion of hybridity is its disruption of the hegemony of knowledge hierarchies.

Hybrid programming as a lucrative strategy

It is safe to say that in the 2000s, rampant plagiarism and copying of television formats occur in every television industry in the world. Keane (2004b) identifies three ways in which television industries come to copy each other: (1) coercive morphism (when an organization is forced to comply); (2) mimetic morphism (when an organization follows the market leader); and (3) normative morphism (when an organization chooses those norms that have become "best practices"). Formats that have proven lucrative in one market are sometimes used with permission in another market and, more often, without.

Manipulation of formats rather than context seems for the most part, a foolproof method to dodge detection of plagiarism and punishment, particularly in Asian countries. The complexities of manipulation of elements in a program to suit popular tastes may be understood through an explanation of the television format. Moran (2004) defines a television format as a "set of invariable elements in a programme out of which the variable elements of an individual episode are produced" (2004, p. 5). Formats have overlapping but distinct forms: the paper format containing a summary of the key elements in the program; the "bible" which provides extensive detail (including graphics, photographs, and studio plans) of the programs; printed information on scheduling, audience demographics, and target ratings and audience; scripts from previous productions of the program; and finally consultancy services by owners of the format, advising new producers.

Formats could be imported (as in the case of programs from Hong Kong, Japan, the United States, and South Korea in Taiwan), licensed (legally purchased from another company), clones (unlicensed copying where variations in new formats complicate prosecution), adaptations (closed or open), and reproductions (where footage is from the original and only the anchor is swapped for a local one).[3] Format usage could be closed or open adaptations. In closed adaptation, the industry format is followed closely whereas in open adaptation, certain generic elements are used (Liu and Chen 2004).

Despite the 2000 Formats Recognition and Protection Association (FRAPA) which mandates punishment for piracy, rampant plagiarism occurs, particularly in the highly successful television industries of China and India. Under the FRAPA Act, producers have to pay a license fee for complete use of a format and can adapt it according to local tastes and needs. However, variations created by adaptation become a part of the format with ownership still belonging to the original owner. Specific legal protection is awarded formats through copyright, breach of confidence, and passing off. As is indicated in the terms of protection, copyright refers to the elements in the format and their overall combination. The plagiarism and imitation that characterize the Asian television market may stem from a Confucian advocacy of imitation over originality (Keane 2004a). Copyright infringements in China are generally overlooked and foreign companies seeking to do business in China find such an environment a frustrating one to work within. Many opt for program sales and focus on profits from accompanying advertising packages rather than worry about policing domestic plagiarism.

The continuation of copyright infringements and plagiarism in a time of national and transnational copyright laws indicates the highly profitable and capricious nature of the industry. Keane asserts:

[L]icensed formats reward imitation and provide an exchange of economic rents between agents. The format in this sense creates a chain of value that can be modified and extended across national boundaries as well as within national media systems. In this sense we are telling a more multifaceted story: that formats are instrumental in promoting industry development, particularly in marginal systems and that in the process they extend the stock of televisual ideas. (2004a, p. 11)

The existence of legal protection for copyright infringement therefore, does not mean a tightly controlled international television production environment. The format industry is plagued with legal conflict. Although formats are registered for copyright reasons, license fees are paid and format libraries purchased and sold, yet violations are the nature of the game (Moran 1998). The success of formats in one market is obviously more attractive for producers in another, who prefer to adapt it to local needs rather than create new, indigenous programs that may be financial flops. Besides, a great degree of flexibility is available in adapting a format to a local environment. Contrary to other copyright materials where originality is sacred, format adaptation hinges on flexibility and the more economic profit generated from a single format, the better.

Big names in the television format licensing business are the BBC (whose Format Licensing Division was established in 1993), BRITE, a marketing consortium of Granada Television, London, Weekend, and Yorkshire Tyne Tees of the British ITV Network; and Globo TV which began marketing formats in 1993 (most notable is its licensing of *Voce Decide* or *You Decide*) in 12 countries (including the United States and 11 in South America) with 18 productions in Western and Eastern Europe, six in the Middle East, one in China, and one in Angola (Moran 1998). Leaders in the formatting or program production business are All American Freemantle International (AAFI) with production companies in Great Britain, Australia, Germany, Portugal, Greece, Spain, Turkey, and India. Besides productions and adaptations of US game shows, AAFI engages in co-productions especially in smaller markets. Some popular productions are *The Price is Right*, *The Pyramid Game*, and *Family Feud*. Another leader is King Pin (whose primary productions include *Wheel of Fortune, Jeopardy, Inside Edition*, and *American Journal*). The sale of formats deters accusations of cultural imperialism because content can be manipulated to a certain extent – only the structure is borrowed. Yet as is obvious, structure is itself powerful in mandating certain norms – focus on the grand prize, individual vs. collective triumph, and victory at any cost.

Formats that are most translatable across cultures are those that have minimal "cultural discount," which refers to native elements such as accents, language, cultural themes and local settings (Hoskins and Mirus 1988); are "culturally odorless," in that the very local, or the very ethnic, is absent or not obvious (see Iwabuchi 2004, for a case study of Japanese television formats); that have cultural proximity in that they reflect regional cultures (Straubhaar 1991); and that are culturally transparent or translatable across cultural, ethnic, geographic, and linguistic boundaries (Olson 1999). For example, Japanese programs carry a high level of cultural discount; yet Japanese animation is highly popular, because like video games, it is culturally odorless. Animation is primarily intended for export with just 1 percent of animated films in Japanese. *Pokemon* is now produced in ten languages (English, French, German, Spanish, Portuguese, Italian, Mandarin, Cantonese, Korean, and Greek) and in major media markets across the world. *Super Mario Brothers*, although a Japanese production, was created within an Italian context for greater translatability across cultures.

Cultural odorlessness and transnational success

A prominent example of culturally odorless and transparent format is Celador's (UK) production, *Who Wants to Be a Millionaire*. Its format has been purchased by Fuji TV in Japan and broadcast under the same name (Iwabuchi 2004), by MBC in Korea as the *I Love Quiz Show* (D-H. Lee 2004); by TVB and ATV in Hong Kong as *Baiwen Fuweng* and *The Happy Millionaire for Charity* (*Kaixin Baiwan Wei Gongyi*), respectively (Fung 2004); by CCTV Channel 2 in China as *The Dictionary of Happiness* (*Kaixin cidian*); by MediaCorp in Singapore as *Who Wants to Be a Millionaire Singapore* (Lim 2004); by ABS/CBN in the Philippines as *Are You Ready for the Game?*; and by Star Plus in India by ABCL as *Kaun Banega Crorepathi* (an unlicensed version, *Sawal Das Crore Ka* is produced on Zee TV; see Thomas and K. Kumar 2004).

Other popular formats are BBC's *The Weakest Link* (purchased by Fuji TV Japan and produced under the same name, by TVB Hong Kong as *Yibi OUT Xiao*); by Star Taiwan as *Wise Men Survive* (*Zhi Zhe Sheng Cun*); and by Nanjing TV China as *The Wise Rule* (*Zhi Zhe Wei Wang*). CNN's *Larry King Live* (purchased by TVBS Taiwan as *2100 All the People Talk*), CBS's *60 Minutes* (purchased by CTV Taiwan and produced under the same name, and by CTV Hong Kong as *60 Fen Zhong*), and Columbia Tristar's *Russian Roulette* (purchased by TVB Hong Kong and TransTV Indonesia and produced under the same name, respectively), are further examples.

British and American-based production companies are not the only leaders in the format field. Japan poses the second largest television market in the world, exporting as well as importing software and hardware (Iwabuchi 2004).

Ninety-five percent of television programs in the country are produced domestically. After World War II, Japan was at the receiving end of a barrage of American programming and through imitation and appropriation, was able to create localized versions of US programming. Japanese television began in 1953 with a high content of US programming but by the mid-1960s was able to reduce this significantly. By the 1980s, only 5 percent of Japanese programs were imported (Keane 2004a). Japan therefore is an example of a market with strong local content with flagging ratings for such American shows as *Beverly Hills 90210, ER,* and *Ally McBeal*, compared to local television dramas. American influence is pervasive in Japan, yet the latter's appropriation of this influence, giving it what Iwabuchi (2004) calls a "Japanese odor" (p. 23) is evidence of the dynamics of accommodation of transnational media and products across the world. Examples of format sales in Japan are: TBS's *Waku Waku Animal Land* to the Netherlands in 1987; Nippon Television Network's (NTV) quiz shows including *Show-by Show-by* to Spain, Italy, Thailand, and Hong Kong in the mid-1990s; TBS's *Katochan Kenchan Goki Gen Terebi* home video segment to ABC in 1989 which made it into the globally recognized *America's Funniest Home Videos*, and *Takeshi Castle* to Hong Kong, the United States, Germany, and Spain. It must be noted that *Takeshi Castle* in the United States on Viacom's Spike Network is dubbed over by extremely racist and sexist caricatures of the Japanese. The sale of Fuji TV's *Iron Chef* (*Ryouri no Tetsujin*) to America's Paramount network (later cloned as Iron Chef America on E.W. Scripps owned Food Network) and TBS' *Happy Family Plan* to China's Beijing TV (BTV) are other examples of Japanese format transfer.

The stripping of "cultural odor" on television programs is a key state and market strategy in Singapore because of the government's language policy and the nation's multiethnic population. Eighty percent of MediaCorp Singapore's programming is local including drama and current affairs. Numbers of game shows are increasing and the company has bought format licenses for *Who Wants to Be a Millionaire, The Weakest Link,* and *The Wheel of Fortune Singapore*. MediaCorp's competition with its rival, SPH Media Works (Mandarin) Channel [V] (beginning in 2001) has led to an increase in game shows on both channels such as *Youth Quest* and *Exchange Lives* on Channel [V], and *Tic Tac Toe* (the Chinese version of *Celebrity Squares*) on Channel 8 (Lim 2004).

Cloning, developing, and collaging

Unlicensed adaptation of programs may be divided into cloning, developing, and collaging. Cloning refers to those that completely copy the original model (for example, in 1993, Korea's *Challenge, the Mystery Express* on MBC was accused of cloning Japan's NTV program, *Quiz, the Magical Brain Power*; and in 1999, Korea's SBS was accused of copying Japan's TBC's *Tokyo Friend Park 2*). Despite local flavors such as actors, accents, and jokes, format and objective of the show are identical. Most popular formats for cloning are quiz shows and game shows that feature exorbitant prizes, celebrity anchors, and guests.

Developing refers to those programs that extend only part of the original format to create a new format. An example is Korea's (SBS) 1998 *Seo Senon's Making a Good World*, which copied the 3-minute *Silver Quiz* segment on Japan's *Samma Supertrick TV* where members of the rural elderly community were quizzed on various items, mostly their knowledge of English. First denounced by viewers and the Korean Broadcasting Commission for its disparagement of elders, the program rose in popularity as it began depicting this community more realistically and with respect.

Collaging refers to combining features of different shows into a new program. The Korean (SBS) *Paradise for Curiosity* for example, lifted elements from variety Japanese infotainment shows such as *Alarm Clock TV* (Fuji TV), *Experiment and Nod* (NHK), *The Laws of Fear* (ANB), *Discovery*, the *Great Aru Aru Cyclopedia* (Fuji TV), *Dokoro's Megaten* (NTV), *Gonnomisako's Science Hall* (ANB), and *Dakeshi's Book of Genesis* (ANB). To a lesser extent, Korea buys licenses for shows such as MBC's 1999 purchase of *Boys and Girls in Love* from Japan's Fuji TV, for its own *Love Train* segment of *Eve's Castle* where "the participant who confesses his/her love rides a special train whose track can veer in different directions depending on the partner's reply" (D-H. Lee 2004, p. 46). Korea has also copied formats from the United States (for example, MBC's *Three Boys and Three Girls* and *I Love Quiz Show* are based on NBC's *Friends* and ABC's *Who Wants to Be a Millionaire*, respectively).

The Japanese idol-drama is phenomenally successful in Taiwan, adapted from Japanese manga (comic stories). It appeals to younger audiences for its use of young, attractive, often unknown actors, liberal use of traditional and popular Japanese culture, and has led to Taiwanese clones (for example, CTS' *Meteor Garden* and *Poor Aristocrat* were licensed adaptations of Japanese manga; and the cable network SAN-LIH's *Lavender* and *MVP Lover* were local scripts co-produced with the terrestrial TTV and CTV, respectively). The idol drama is extremely profitable because of its expediency (in terms of shooting and scripting), merchandising (product placement), potential for spin-offs, and co-production, which facilitate dual broadcasting on cable and terrestrial stations. Liu and Chen note, "With formats increasingly being incorporated into trans-cultural flows the Taiwanese idol-drama, itself a hybrid cultural form, provides an opportunity for local cultural industries to survive the challenge of trans-national hegemony" (2004, p. 72).

Japanese formats are popular in Chinese, Taiwanese, and Korean markets although in Korea, formats are unofficially "copied" because Japanese media were banned in Korea for 30 years after the latter won independence from the former in 1945. Japan's media influence on Asian countries grew in the 1990s and Korea emerged as a strong contender in the mid-1990s. What results is not just "global localization" that marries the global common element to the local specific context, but "local globalization" (Iwabuchi 2004, p. 34) as well that allows audiences to feel they can participate in a global society through their recognition of local elements in globally circulated formats.

The blatant copying of Japanese programs and the Korean government's 1998 liberal policy and its allowance of Japanese sports programs, documentaries, and news shows in 2000, led to scathing critiques in the Korean press. Questions of the integrity of national and cultural identity were raised and the implications of such large-scale cloning or adaptation on local creativity were vociferously argued. Cultural subordination to Japan was a palpable fear especially in the shadow of Korea's 30-year colonization under Japanese rule. Korean producers claim they are inspired by such formats and have not plagiarized them. Their use of American formats is far less a concern than use of Japanese formats. Informal copying may be attributed to the structural inconsistencies in the Korean television industry. The aggressive battle for ratings in the 1990s and the inadequate production infrastructure led to countless amateurish productions that had little capital investment and poor business plans. Prime time early evening time slots were particularly vulnerable to ratings slides and with meager resources to support the production of solid storylines, producers often resorted to plagiarism to meet the high demand and stay afloat (D-H. Lee 2004).

As in Korea, the Taiwanese television industry struggles with a small market and not enough resources to make indigenous productions profitable (although Taiwan did not import programs from the United States in the 1960s and 1970s when accusations of cultural imperialism were at their peak, in the 1980s, it imported heavily from Hong Kong, and in the 1990s and 2000s, from Japan and South Korea). Taiwan banned Japanese programs until 1992. After the 1993 Cable TV Law, programs, particularly dramas, could be indigenous productions or imported from Hong Kong, Japan, Korea, and Mainland China. Taiwanese networks in general copy each other's programs rather than develop alternate programming, which leads to almost identical news, talk shows, and dramas across channels. For example, the successful *Fair Judge Pao (Bao Qing Tian)* on CTS was highly rated in China, Hong Kong, and other Chinese markets and copied by Taiwan's CTV, only with a female judge (*Female Judge – Nu Xun An*), but the latter flopped. Taiwan's 1976 Broadcasting Radio and

Television Law mandates that total program content should contain less than 50 percent of entertainment to ensure a balance among its news and government, education and culture, public service, and entertainment categories. The highest number of imports in Chinese programming are from mainland China and Hong Kong and non-Chinese programming from the United States, Japan, and Korea. The major source of television programming in Taiwan is domestic productions (Liu and Chen 2004). The law also mandates that local productions be not less than 70 percent on terrestrial channels and not less than 20 percent on cable channels. As in Korea, Taiwan uses Japanese formats for "incidental inspiration" (Liu and Chen 2004, p. 58). Taiwan constitutes an important regional format production center as well. Its *I Love the Matchmaker* (*Wo Ai Hong Niang*) and *Special Man and Woman* (*Fei Chang Nan Nu*) have been successfully exported to mainland China. Co-productions with the mainland (as undertaken most notably by the All-Round Production Company (Quan Neng Zhi Zuo Gong Si) are increasingly common in the face of rising production costs.

The similarity of programming across channels is evident on Chinese television as well. Through mimetic morphism, programming, formats, and set designs are similar if not identical in the smaller Chinese networks despite large vertical mergers such as the China Film, Broadcasting, and Television Group; the Beijing Radio, Film, and Television Group and the Shanghai Media and Entertainment Group. China's blatant plagiarism and copyright infringements are actually difficult to prosecute because of the lack of an efficient international prosecuting body, and the difficulty in arguing exactly what and how much content in a program have been copied. Also such copying or "borrowing" is seen as a positive move, an indication of liberalization against the stark backdrop of the centralist, bureaucratic control of media by the Chinese Communist Party.

Popular shows in China are the *Zhengda Variety Show* (*Zhengda Zongyi*, 1990), a co-production between Zhengda Consortium (a Thai-Chinese company) and CCTV. Including a quiz show format and celebrity guests, the show was soon cloned across Chinese networks by 1997. The show dropped its quiz format and reinvented itself as a clone of the British distributor ECM's *Dog Eat Dog* with the disclaimer that it wasn't plagiarizing the latter, just injecting it with Chinese characteristics. Hunan Satellite Television's *Citadel of Happiness* (*Kuaile da ben ying*) was similarly copied across Chinese channels. CCTV has bought other formats such as TBS's (Japan) *Happy Family Plan* (*Shiawase Kazoku Keikaku*) and transformed it into *Dreams Become Reality* (*Mengxiang Chengzhen*). Phoenix TV (Hong Kong) distributed Taiwan's *Special Man Special Woman* (*Feichang Nannü*) and *I Love the Match Maker* (*Wo Ai Hongniang*) to mainland

China. Programs from Hong Kong and Taiwan are also very popular in China. Shanghai Television licensed the *Sesame Street* format from Children's Television Workshop and has broadcast it as *Zhima Jie* since February 1998, featuring characters Xiao Meizi (Little Berry) and Huhu Zhu (Puff Pig). Examples of co-productions are Granada Media's venture with Hong Kong-based Beijing Yahuan Audio and Video Production to create *Joy Luck Street* (*Xing fu jie*) based on *Coronation Street*. The challenges to convert English working-class plots to Beijing street life, not to mention constant script intervention and supervision by Granada, were considerable, but the show eventually became a success (Liu and Chen 2004).

In India, American formats provided fodder for shows resulting in such programs as *Good Morning India* (from *Good Morning America*) on Doordarshan 1, *Crime Stoppers* on Doordarshan Metro, and *India's Most Wanted* on Zee TV (both based on *Cops*) (Bhandare and Joshi 1997). Star Plus' *Kaun Banega Crorepathi* (the Indian clone of ABC's *Who Wants to Be a Millionaire*) consistently topped the ratings every week of its telecast. The Hindi-language Zee TV also provides a refreshing alternative to pedagogical programming on Doordarshan. Game shows and talk shows are abundant, produced by Zee Telefilms. Star Plus' Hindi-language serials, soaps, and game shows, brings it into direct competition not only with Doordarshan and its affiliate Zee TV, but other commercial, predominantly Hindi language networks such as SonyET (Sony Entertainment Television).

As for private regional networks, Sun TV caters to South Indian Tamil-speaking audiences and diasporic communities in Sri Lanka and Singapore. Asia Net, targeted to the Malayalam-speaking populace in Kerala, attracts expatriates in the Middle East, and Gemini and Eenaadu cater to Telugu-speaking audiences in Andhra Pradesh. By the 2000s, the nation boasted over a 100 channels, reaching primarily urban audiences. With India's rich film history that has always included heavy borrowing of Hollywood plots, and with the industry's common practice of shooting films abroad for audience appeal and producer tax benefits (Thomas and K. Kumar 2004), it is difficult to determine exactly what constitutes a domestic and/or foreign production on television, especially when much of its content is drawn from the film industry. Unlicensed "inspirations" on Indian television include *Movers and Shakers* on SonyET based on NBC's *Jay Leno*; *Hello Friends* on Zee TV based on NBC's *Friends*; *Tanha* on Star Plus based on *The Bold and the Beautiful*; *Sawal Das Crore Ka* on Zee TV based on ABC's *Who Wants to Be a Millionaire*; and the *Amul India Show* on Star Plus, based on *Oprah*. Licensed formats include *Family Fortunes* on Star Plus based on *Family Feud* and *C.A.T.S.* on SonyET based on *Charlie's Angels*, and *Kaun Banega Crorepathi* on Star Plus based on *Who Wants*

122

to Be a Millionaire. In the case of *C.A.T.S.*, a license wasn't necessary because production by UTVI (United Television of India) was commissioned by Sony, which owns Columbia Pictures, owner of the rights of the US television program (Thomas and K. Kumar 2004). Copycats include MTV's *Bakra* similar to *Candid Camera*; *Yehi Hai Right Price*, after *The Price is Right*; and *Bol Baby Bol* after *Kids Say the Darnedest Things*. Also, television networks in India blatantly copy formats from each other. Suroor (1995) comments, "If Zee TV is cloning the Bombay cinema, then Doordarshan is cloning Zee TV, and ATN and Jain TV are cloning both of them. The only difference is who packages it better." He cites Vinod Dua, an independent television producer, who says, "Almost every channel is so similar that if you walk into the middle of a programme, you can't tell which is which" (ibid., p. 7). The lack of variety in programming is due to the fact that only a handful of production companies provide programs to these channels. Whether it is talk shows, music and video countdowns, sitcoms, or dramas, Doordarshan and the cable and satellite channels strive toward a hybrid Indian/western identity. A pan-Asian character is evident with commercials for Taiwanese, Japanese, and Hong Kong-manufactured automobiles, electronics, and domestic appliances. Anchorpersons and actors intersperse comments in the vernacular with those in English.

The imitation of Western formats in India is hardly new. Bollywood, India's film industry, has merited its name for its blatant copying of Hollywood formats and themes. Indianization of Hollywood films becomes a crucial project in Indian cinema. Ganti, in her study of the process of Indianization as a dialogue between filmmakers and producers, suggests that, "Because the practice of adaptation is motivated by a conscious desire to manage risk, Indianization tends to be a conservative process that precludes innovation in narrative and generic practices" (2002, p. 289). If an Indianized film is successful in one language, it is quickly remade in other languages to ensure its profitability in regional markets. It is not uncommon for the multilingual Indian viewer to see all versions of a film and compare quality and acting. To merit imitation, Hollywood films should lend themselves to high emotion and complex narratives, with intricate subplots, parallel tracks, flashbacks that take the viewer across generations and eras, and songs to allow for narrative complexity. In Indian films, songs constitute an intricate system that provides a space for the artistic expression of sexuality without being explicit. In this way, both the conservatism of the audiences and the censorship codes of the state are not threatened (Ganti 2002). Song sequences are completed months in advance of the film and marketed for preview on television. Audio tapes of film songs hit the market long before the film does, setting the stage for its grand entry.

Just as Hollywood films are adapted for an Indian audience, hybrid programs are manipulated to reflect local cultural values for Asian markets. For example, reality shows such as *Survivor* in Hong Kong and Japan focus on collective harmony rather than sexual and economic competition as do its North American and British versions (Fung 2004). As a multicultural, multilingual society, Singaporean programming emphasizes Asian moral values rather than specific ethnic or religious groups. Such values are multiracial harmony, kinship, and multicultural equality (Lim 2004). The host of *The Weakest Link* in China is reticent and cheerful, a contrast to the dour Anne Robinson of its original. Such shows mark a shift from the elite to the popular where the average citizen could be the face of television rather than the usual line-up of politicians, celebrities, and actors (M. Yang 2000). Formats represent a process of structuring difference within repetition (Moran and Keane 2004).

The possibilities of hybrid programming and their relevance for local audiences have resulted in locally produced shows topping popularity lists for television programs in most Asian countries. For example, in China, local Mandarin and Cantonese soap operas and historical dramas receive top ratings (Brent 1998). In India, Hindi films and Hindi-language serials are the most watched (Thussu 1998), in Indonesia, the majority of the top shows are locally produced (Ryanto 1998), in Taiwan, local or Hong-Kong produced dramas are most popular (Chan 1996), and in Singapore, Malaysia, and South Korea, local programs far outrank imported, particularly western ones (Chadha and Kavoori 2000).

Critiquing the hybrid

The discussion on hybrid programming points to the role of local production companies as active players in the media markets of their own countries, not as impotent components of an imperialistic media environment as theorized in the 1970s. The examples of various forms of such programming may lead to a sense of complacency regarding the transnational television market and the choices it provides for consumers. It glides over the real frictions between global and local that exist in format adaptations. An overt focus on deconstructing dichotomies, of looking for interstitial spaces of expression and life, of uncovering ambivalences and hybrid cultures, can also lead to a focus on the "happy medium," away from the real violence that existed and continues to exist between colonizer and (post) colonized (Donadey 2001; Parry 1996). Going back to Bhabha's (1994) notion of hybridity, Donadey writes, "A consequence of this deconstructive move is that the position of the desiring subject endowed with agency becomes unmarked, since part of Bhabha's point is to show that colonial discourse generates its own oppositional space from within" (2001, p. xxiii).

The concept of hybridity has generated much debate and scholarship in international media. The general trend is either to describe the hybrid product in terms of its capitalization on diversity and cultural difference for global economic profitability, or to question whether it embodies resistance, accommodation, or both. Little empirical analysis exists in this area, however (Murphy and Kraidy 2003). Although Bhabha is not denying friction in the interstitial and is attempting to unmoor the fixity of categories such as global and local, what needs to be underscored is the struggle for representation that the local, the subaltern, undergoes.

The hybrid formats of contemporary media texts have to be placed within their historical contexts. The task of creating global–local narratives and translations has its roots in imperialist missions in colonized countries. Sudhir (1993) provides an intricate analysis of hybrid texts in colonial times. The mission of the British imperial government in particular was to create bilingual dictionaries and history texts where British intellectuals, versed in local languages, would create these works for use by both the British and native elite. Although the input of native scholars was crucial for the completion of such projects, the trajectories the texts took were determined by the colonizer. Writing in the context of Indian lexicographies, Sudhir observes that the interaction between the British and Indian scholar was always fraught with tension, with competing frames of reference resulting in a dialectical process where the imbalances in power always played out such that the British interpretation of the text endured over the Indian one. He notes that both colonizer and colonized participated in the production of new vocabularies. Yet such a production was conducted within the social and cultural framework of colonialism. The "complicity" (ibid., p. 343) of the Indian counterpart must be understood as a product of the power relationship between the participants. Bilingual dictionaries, in particular, served as important channels of communication between colonizer and colonized, yet these were not value-free documents. The interpretations of words were heavy with ideological import, providing yet another frame of reference exhibiting the positional superiority of the colonizer. Therefore bilingual dictionaries were very much the output of power differentials created by colonialism. Such dictionaries were manipulated compilations, with the power to shape not just speech and syntax, but consciousness and ways of thinking as well.

The critique of hybridity and the brief account of its colonial roots bring to the fore the importance of assessing the cultural implications of format adaptation – a much-neglected area in international media studies. The trend is to point to global–local combinations in televisual texts and consumer products as examples of a new age of expression and identity that allow even citizens of the global south to partake of narratives of progress and modernization, once the privilege of industrialized Western countries. Yet these combinations, while poking fun at the global, fall back onto time-tested caricatures of local subalterns, be they gender, ethnic, class, or religious minorities. Privileged for the most part, are Western and national elites. The next section illustrates a few examples of the imbalances in hybrid programming and raises salient issues to be considered in the evaluation of the efficacy and utility of such programming.

Cultural implications of hybridity and format adaptation

As highlighted in Chapter One of this book, the availability of multiple program and product choices in the media marketplace leads to liberal pluralist ruminations on the empowerment of the consumer. Globalization does not sit paradoxically to nationalist imperatives, but is undertaken as a state project in itself and is redistributed through nationalist narratives. The urban middle class is invariably the audience for such narratives of globalization, modernization, and progress, and women come to be identified as prime targets to build the national economy, through both their consumerism and economic productivity.

Hybridity has serious implications for the middle-class woman because, as Fernandes (2000) and Sunder Rajan (1993) have theorized, the woman has the dual function of grabbing the modernity project by the horns, exploring the public sphere, and making a lucrative career in it for her family; at the same time, she has to keep the traditions of her home and of her in-laws, ensuring festivals, religious ceremonies, and daily rituals continue uninterrupted.

Hybridity in advertising, products, and television programs becomes a key marketing strategy to grant consumers membership in the intermingling flows of global, national, and local. Specifically, they provide further avenues for women particularly to expand their complex roles in society without interrogating the necessity of this complexity or dual private *and* public burdens. Hybrid programming is considered a symbolic representation of transnationalism, and hybrid television programming is upheld as an indication of the market's attention to local needs and wants. Yet such a focus on micro choices and cultural experiences distracts from its very limited trajectory *vis-à-vis* a capitalist structure which plays a significant role in defining "autonomous" needs and wants. For example, Appadurai (1996) argues that various free-trade zones have emerged particularly for high-tech commodities, fetishizing production and concealing its transnational relations. Local sites of production, be they the sweatshop, factory, or the nation-state itself, are glorified while the dispersed forces that drive production are disguised. At the same time, global advertising spins narratives of consumer agency that are so heady, so fevered, so immediate, and so continuous, that the consumer willingly buys into this distorted world, convinced that she or he is a free agent when in reality, she or he is a mere chooser of products.

The disjunctures of globalization where the potency of national and political borders is diminished, where remote centers mobilize and organize outsourced labor populations, where choices on the market increase yet true freedom is curtailed, also increase the possibilities of violence and oppression, particularly for women. As reflectors of the cultural ethos, television programs in particular play a vital role in ordering place and rank for a nation's citizens, in an environment where these places and ranks are being complicated by competing narratives of identity and citizenship. As described in Chapter Four, women emerge as protectors of an ideological past while men are partakers of a modern present, legitimizing discipline and punishment of women in the private sphere, a theme explored further in Chapter Six. Films and television programs invariably fall back on time-tested tropes that stereotype women and caricature minorities.

For example, Fernandes' (2000) fieldwork in Mumbai among print media professionals and middle-class consumers in 1996 and 1998 showed that print advertisements fetishized the hybrid, deliberately juxtaposing traditional and Orientalist depictions of Indian life with modern technologies or global persona (such as a *sadhu*/priest sitting beside an air conditioner or a *sari*-clad woman with pan-Asian features) to erase national boundedness and replace it with transnational possibilities. Embedded within such advertisements was the assurance that the essence of India (the Indian accent or traditional clothes, for example) was not lost, but perfectly capable of confronting the global and welcoming it. The marketplace and its commodities lent the nationalist project its rhetorical strategies, equating consumerism with nationalism and brand loyalty with patriotism. Fernandes suggests that hybridity is integrated with processes of capital formation and contained within the boundaries of propriety of the modern nation. It is linked to the class identities of the urban middle class. Contemporary globalization facilitates the reconstruction of social inequalities. Disruptions created by competing meanings of womanhood or citizenship are carefully managed through hybrid constructions of global and local, curtailing the freedoms of the latter awarded by the former.

To use another example, F.L.F. Lee's (2004) study of the representation of female Hong Kong officials in the *Ming Pao* and *Apple Daily* newspapers from

1998 till 2001 showed that news coverage was generally positive, emphasizing that these women possessed the rationality and strength of males, and the tenderness of females. Also, female officials were portrayed as very traditional wives and mothers, doing household chores without domestic help, and appreciative of the traditions of their in-laws. Conveniently ignored was the fact that the burden of modernity in the juggling of private and public spheres was squarely faced by women; the focus of the news articles was that the challenges of modernity could easily be handled, it was just a matter of efficient time management. F.L.F. Lee sums up (2004, p. 220): "The perfect woman image would not harm the women politicians, but it may nonetheless fetter other women by its failure to problematize, or even its attempt to trivialize, the work–family tension."

In television formats that pit men against women or that draw women into the center stage of debate, topics discussed may be considered progressive, and may include political, economic, and even marital and relationship issues. Yet, the terms of the debate are carefully controlled so that the norms of propriety are never threatened. A case in point is Zhong's (2002) analysis of China Central Television and Singapore Television Corporation's joint staging of the Biannual International Mandarin Intervarsity Debating Competition (BIMIDC). The study revealed various levels of control in terms of the stage settings, terms of the debate, and interpretations offered by the moderator. Specifically, although the debaters professed they did not indulge in the customary deference to Confucius and Laozi, or cite the poetry of the Tang and Song dynasties (a bold display of youthful rebellion), the chairman or moderator played an important disciplining role:

> He compared the debate (between the teams from the People's Republic of China and the Mandarin debating team from the University of New South Wales) to a family quarrel (*jiating zhengchao*) between naïve little girls (*xiao meimei*) and their mature, rational elder brothers (*da gege*) [and]...asserted that males were inherently rational and logical and females were born emotional. (ibid., p. 44)

Other examples of policing strategies by local conservatives are the Malaysian government's 1989 ruling that television commercials include distinctly ethnic models (Malays, Chinese, and Indian) rather than pan-Asian or Caucasian models as a backlash against its earlier 1980s policy of using pan-Asian faces to propagate a sense of Malaysian identity (Ang, 1996); and the reinterpretations of women's opinions on the Indian hybrid game show, *Adarsha Dampathi-galu* (*The Ideal Couple*) (McMillin 2003b). To explain the latter, the program on the private, regional, Kannada-language Udaya TV, loosely based on Fox's *The*

Newly Wed Game, showed that women's responses on the show were blatantly corrected or edited by the male host to ensure that they conformed to conservative norms of husband and wife behavior. Women who asserted their independence were told that such was possible only because they had noble and progressive husbands; and love marriages were described as threats to masculinity because only aggressive and domineering females would go against the family to enter such alliances. Vernacular language networks, therefore, took on the nationalist project of containing the nation within patriarchal narratives so much so that even shows that thrust women onto center stage did so in a way that established their subservience to men. McMillin (2003b) notes that British colonialism could be, to a certain extent, limited to the external material sphere of public affairs. Private satellite television, however, crossed private–public boundaries and entered the inner spiritual sphere of the Indian household. The narratives that accompanied some shows on these channels such as individualism, freedom, and universalism, became a source of hegemonic anxiety as it presented counter-narratives to national dominant ideology. The policing strategies on hybrid shows served to assure conservative audiences that the boundaries that constrain the childlike subaltern stood firm, and that competing claims to entrenched ideologies of class, caste, and gender, crumbled in the face of patriarchal power. Television game show formats in particular provide powerful spaces for the exercise of consumerism. The focus on winning the grand (usually monetary) prize, on settling for a variety of consolation commodity prizes which could range from detergents and jewelry to foreign trips and automobiles, all set up a narrative of desirable capitalism. Using the example from *Adarsha Dampathigalu*, winners received silk saris (for women) or suit materials (for men) and jewelry – items they would receive at a Hindu wedding. The commodities themselves reiterated the theme of the show, tying in consumption with an essential expression of gendered Hindu identity.

Similarly, the rising volume of B-grade films that are cranked out in major film production centers in the world such as Hollywood and Mumbai, recreate standard sexual and racial stereotypes, further entrenching hegemonic structures of power. In this context, Appadurai observes:

As fantasies of gendered violence dominate the B-grade film industries that blanket the world, they both reflect and refine gendered violence at home and in the streets as young men (in particular) are swayed by the macho politics of self-assertion in contexts where they are denied real agency, and women are forced to enter the labor force in new ways on the one hand, and continue the maintenance of familial heritage on the other . . . Because both work and leisure have lost none of their gendered qualities in this new global order but have acquired ever subtler fetishized representations, the honor of women becomes increasingly a surrogate for the identity of embattled communities of males, while their women in reality have to negotiate increasingly harsh conditions of work at home and in the non domestic workplace. (1996, p. 45)

Stereotypical representations of women extend to that of minorities as demonstrated in Curtin's (2003) analysis of Hong Kong's *The Good, the Bad, and the Ugly* (TVB, 1979). The 80-episode, highly rated serial, juxtaposed Wai, the good, law-abiding son of a modern Hong Kong family, with Ah Chian, his flip-flop-wearing, tobacco-spitting, heavily accented, long-lost brother from mainland China. The dramatic strategy worked well to clearly demarcate the differences in modernity and desirability between the two brothers, serving to create an identity for Hong Kongers that reflected diligence, education, and refinement, a stark contrast to the backwardness, disorder, and cronyism of mainland China (see also Fung 2004; Ma 1999). Similarly, McMillin's (2002a, 2004) analysis of game shows, talk shows, music programs, soaps, and dramas on Indian television in the 1990s demonstrated that people of lower caste and from rural areas were portrayed as servants, as objects of development projects, and as comedic elements.

In Indonesia, MTV Southeast Asia's incorporation of *dangdut*, a derivation of indigenous North Sumatran music blended with flavors of Indian film music, Arabic popular music, and western rock, was a show of attention to the local. However, its positioning of VJ Jamie Aditya who parodied this form popular among lower-class Indonesian youth allowed the hybrid program to maintain its position of global glamour by inviting Indonesian youth to partake in the condescending humor directed at this form of popular culture. Sutton (2003) states that although representations of localness in the insertion of Indonesian, Javanese or Minangkabau elements are widely available, they stand as marginal representations. They are exploited for their fringe positions to the larger cultural core of society.

Another striking example of local caricature is Channel [V] in India, which describes itself as a "sort of lunatic asylum run by the inmates. And loony tunes are really their signature . . . End result: a reasonable part of the nation is on its knees laughing – at themselves" (*Star TV Annual Report*, 1996). Through liberal use of such phrases such as "Music is public garden and I am its humble fertilizer," or "Mind it" (meaning, "watch out," or "beware"), by its educated, stylish, urban, usually foreign-born Indian anchors, Channel [V] pokes fun of locals and by inviting them to laugh at themselves, allows them privileged membership with the in-group of those in the know. Such programs caricaturing the local work well because they appease national government's anxieties of cultural imperialism. Chow (2002) contends that:

> There is a way in which...the current euphoria about hybridity must be recognized as part of a politically progressivist climate that celebrates diversity in the name of multiculturalism...In this context, the criticism voiced is often not so much an objection directed at multicultural hybridity itself as an attempt to call attention to what is effaced by its ostensible celebration.

The provision of new spaces of identity and expression through hybrid television programming is not under attack here; what is, however, is the easy use of historically oppressed minorities, be it the colonial, gender, or ethnic subject, for huge economic profit, further exacerbating their real exploitation in private and public spheres.

Hybrid programming and subjectivity

It is well worth pondering the lessons on subjectivity and personhood conveyed through the narratives of hybrid programming. Frantz Fanon's treatment of the psychological effects of colonialism and systematic subordination are relevant here. Fanon's *Black Skin, White Masks* (1952) and *The Wretched of the Earth* (1961) have been critiqued for their reduction of colonialism to white oppressor and black oppressed and for their equation of all colonial experiences to each other, respectively. Yet Fanon, a psychiatrist, is much respected for his advocacy of political activism and for his study of how subjectivity and the systematic internalization of colonialism could be transformed into self-empowerment, specifically, through anti-colonial violence. Fanon's work at the Blida-Joinville Clinic in Algeria brought to life for him the double decimation of violence – that of the oppressor and the retaliating subject. Fanon, of course, was writing and acting in a time of devastating violence in the context of the Algerian war of liberation from the French (Algeria gained independence in 1962, a year after Fanon's death). His writings on subjectivity have tremendous relevance for the seemingly innocuous hybrid programming around the world.

Specifically, Fanon addressed the internalization of the colonizer's construction of the backward, depraved, colonized subject, within the latter himself or herself. As the numerous examples in this chapter have demonstrated, racist and sexist frames in imperialist cinema caricaturing ethnic and gender minorities are now unquestioningly co-opted by ex-colonized populations. In an attempt to gain power, to slide into the director's seat, and retain a lucrative partnership with ex-colonizers, local media producers transform caricatures of the local into a profitable marketing strategy. Urban idioms, "quaint" native accents, native (mis)use of English phrases and their intermixing of vernacular and English phrases are all mined for their humor potential.

The ability to laugh at oneself may be romantically interpreted to mean the emergence of a certain postcolonial confidence and maturity. The painful awareness of local inadequacies in terms of etiquette, vocabulary, and accent compared to Western counterparts is particularly acute in societies that have been colonized and that have been subjected to reminders of their backwardness through centuries of media and cultural propaganda. Such an awareness may be compared to the embarrassment nationalist leaders in pre-independence, 1940s India felt with the loin-cloth-clad Gandhi as their leader, speaking for them at various international summits and meetings with British royalty. While Gandhi used his "always out of place" (Young 2001, p. 328) image as a semiotic device to demonstrate the defiance and disobedience of the Indian peasant to British colonialism, this "out-of-place" Indianness is now a marketing strategy, an object of humor, allowing spectators to breathe a sigh of relief and make fun of this raw display of backwardness. Laughing at oneself, then, is an extension of the subjective positioning of the colonized that Fanon theorized. The acceptance of self-caricature as a legitimate space for ridicule is an internalization of the positional inferiority of the postcolonial.

No doubt these expressions of hybridity serve to contest the flux in society and the newer forms of structural pressure. Again the power of the hybrid can be overestimated. In fact the hybrid itself may provide a safety valve for popular resistance – a space where difference, rebellion, and individuality may be articulated, yet in a format and venue (commercial television) that uses this very expression for its profit, safely insulated from the real spaces of power where resistance could take a nasty turn and face drastic consequences. Young addresses this pressure-venting strategy in his example of the funding of the 1999 WTO dissenters in Seattle by the very corporations they were demonstrating against such as Unilever through Ben and Jerry's Ice Cream and the British National Lottery. He poignantly states:

> The danger comes from the way in which there seems to be a new kind of self-deconstructive politics at work, designed to sustain the new world order by *staging its own forms of dissent*. Capitalism has apparently even managed to commodify resistance to itself to the extent that it also organizes and increases production of that resistance. (2003, p. 137; emphasis added)

Despite the skepticism we may award to hybrid programming, we have to also acknowledge the structural changes they *do* effect. For example, Algerian *rai* music has provided a significant venue for Algerian youth to rebel against conservative Islamism in the country. Also, the very presence of women on the public screen on particularly hybrid game shows, gives them a voice not available before such formats made their appearance, and over time, could lead to possibilities of activist agency. We should continue to be cautious about these possibilities because all too often, those voices of "freedom" are co-opted into the dominant structure that defines the parameters of that freedom.

Important questions to be addressed in analyses of hybrid programming are: what are the historical structures that make possible the caricaturing of the local, particularly at a time when it is gaining currency? How may we theorize the complicity of local media producers, living off pay checks from transnational media conglomerates, in constructing such spaces of humor? How do indigenous, private, television networks continue the task of policing borders and disciplining citizens in an environment of cut-throat competition from other indigenous and foreign television networks? And, finally, what cultural transactions take place, what is gained and what is lost, in hybrid programming as a lucrative strategy for both indigenous and foreign networks?

A radical politicization of textual analyses of contemporary media is crucial if we are to adequately address its cultural implications. Obviously, such analyses lead to questions of reception, a complex issue dealt with in the next chapter.

Chapter Six
Grounding Theory
Audiences and Subjective Agency

The preceding chapters have laid out several important arguments: First, master narratives of modernity born in the context of European Enlightenment do not account for how "pre-modern" processes such as traditionalism, religious practices, and caste systems, for example, can be co-opted into modernizing, nation-building strategies of postcolonial countries. Second, a cultural continuity exists in mechanisms of hegemonic control among pre colonial, colonial, and postcolonial eras – ruptures in draconian rule and true emancipation of oppressed subalterns rarely occurs with a change in guard. Culture and identity have to be thought of in terms of flows, transgressions, complexities, and transboundary dynamics that overlap and influence each other intimately. Third, the symbiotic relationship between state governments and private corporations has led to a major shift in goals for tri continent countries – from social development to capitalist expansion – significantly altering the construction of people from citizens to consumers. With this shift comes greater viewing and product choices in the marketplace, providing people with a sense of individual empowerment and freedom just by virtue of the presence of alternatives to government-mandated programs, goods, and services. It also means a continuation of dominant structures of patriarchy and the curtailment of subaltern freedoms. Innovations in media products through hybridization and cloning, collaging, copying, and developing of formats are symbolic of the market's recognition of the vital and dynamic agency of audiences and their power to nurture or stifle a program or television network.

Finally, which brings us to the premise of this chapter, the level of audience consumption opens up a wide array of theoretical and empirical questions such as: what is the nature of audience agency? How do we study and theorize audiences' choices without romanticizing their autonomy, yet giving voice to their positions as negotiators of meaning and agents of change? How do we identify variations in class, caste, gender, religion, and language (to name but a few) that texture subjectivity?

Perhaps nowhere else is the theoretical gap in international media studies as glaring as it is in audience research in non-western countries. As will be detailed in Chapter Eight, the expense of funding, logistics of fieldwork and infrastructure, academic time constraints, and a privileging of Western audience experiences, limit audience studies to primarily viewers located in North America or Great Britain, or if "international," to students or diasporic communities from foreign countries studying or living in British or American environments. An extensive exploration of international audience studies yielded, literally, a handful of studies that critically and empirically addressed issues of media consumption and the implications of globalization in tri continent countries. Some of these will be cited as examples in this chapter, to draw out the need for further audience studies and suggest directions such analyses should take.

As explained in Chapter Three, the postcolonial approach to media studies is charged with a politicization that continually interrogates configurations of power in mediated experiences. When it comes to the study of audiences, such an approach is quite distinct from that of North American reception studies, which are largely descriptive (if from the social science perspective) or that focus on cultural meanings audiences make from media texts (if from the cultural studies approach). Critical studies and its attention to power differentials in society did much to texture the cultural studies approach to audiences, yet most studies incorporating such an approach limit observations to gender differences without adequately addressing class, ethnicity, nationality, or religion, for example. The following section provides a summary of British and North American traditions of audience research and the contributions of anthropology to media reception methodology. It is followed by a detailing of the postcolonial approach to audience studies, highlighting the attention to issues of subaltern agency and subjectivity. The need for this approach to media reception is argued for, particularly in an age of globalization where subaltern politics continues to be marginalized in the overall capitalist complacency that views opportunities for advancement as abundant to those who just make use of them. Also, the postcolonial approach is appropriate given the differences between Western and non-Western viewing contexts as addressed at the beginning of the last section of this chapter.

International Audience Studies

Chapter Two suggested that the ruptures in dominant theory in international media studies around the 1960s and 1970s also led to new ways to study media audiences. This critical turn has been labeled the "interpretive paradigm" (Drotner 2000a), "new audience research" (Ang 1991), "reception theory" (Jensen 1991), and "new revisionism" (Curran 1990). Contributions of literary studies, cultural studies, and anthropology most significantly altered the way in which media audiences were conceptualized and studied.

The positivist approach to audience studies

Early mass communication research could be considered a branch of American functionalist sociology. Such research in the 1940s and 1950s drew from social psychology and sociology (Livingstone 1997). North American audience research was significantly influenced by the experimental method of the Yale School (Hovland et al. 1953) and the positivist social psychology approach (see Ball-Rokeach and DeFleur 1976; Katz and Lazarsfeld 1955) of the Columbia Bureau of Applied Social Research. The latter led to the persuasion model encapsulating two theories of audience behavior, namely, diffusion and selectivity. Katz developed the latter as the Uses and Gratifications model. Essentially, this model argued against monolithic constructions of viewing contexts and audiences, a reaction against the magic bullet, direct, and powerful effects communication model of the time, which was integrated in the critical European social psychology approach that informed the (Frankfurt) Institute of Social Research (see Adorno 1969; Horkheimer and Adorno 1972). Katz and Lazarsfeld's *Personal Influence* (1955) was concerned with the institutional context, democratic processes, and interpersonal networks that mass communication encompassed. Katz, with Lazarsfeld, has been criticized for examining only those effects that could be measured quantitatively (Gitlin 1978). Their work derived from the normative tradition and examined media effects and public opinion to demonstrate the individual agency of the consumer against the power of the mass media (Livingstone 1997).

Much of the conventional audience research that followed in North American communication departments drew heavily from the tradition of social science effects research of Blumler and Katz (1974) and McLeod et al. (1991), and from positivist scholars influenced by sociology and social psychology (Gerbner and Gross 1976). Social science methods typically include experiments, longitudinal field studies, and surveys, following Bandura's (1977) social learning model to study, primarily, the effects of television on children (see Liebert and Sprafkin 1988; Paik and Comstock 1994) and on international audiences (Cohen 1998; Melkote et al. 1998). These studies are useful in the scope of their research questions and broad-based audience surveys. Yet critical commentaries on how gender, class, and ethnicity differentiate viewing experiences and how programs reconfigure interpersonal relationships still comprise the minority of such audience research. Liebes and Katz's (1990) *Export of Meaning* and Dayan and Katz's (1992) *Media Events* have sometimes been touted as evidence of the convergence between mainstream mass communication research and the more critical audience studies approach of the British cultural studies scholars in that both highlight diverse viewing contexts and show how disempowered groups resist media dominance through individual interpretations.

However, Ang (1996) differentiates between the sociological (including the political economy and uses and gratifications approaches) and semiological approaches (that examine television as a system of representation, not as a mere technological transmitter of messages). Early functionalist mass communication research situated audiences within the ideology of a conservative modernist framework where viewers were either watching too much television, or the wrong type of television, most undiscerning (particularly children, women, the elderly, and ethnic minorities) in their tastes. Television audiences have been projected as a passive, invisible mass inhabiting a suburban wasteland, malleable as subjects of objective social science and marketing research alike who could define and shape their standards of taste, morality, and social order. The dominant, positivist, functionalist view of audiences constructed them as a coherent monolith, a view that was ironically reiterated in neo-Marxist critical theory, which posited that audiences were, as a whole, subjected to a dominant ideology that was hegemonically imposed on them. Both opposing paradigms did not entertain the possibility of individual agency and, in their research questions and empirical explorations, took the passive audience as a given. Ang (1991) charges that academic mass communication researchers rely on an institutional point of view to know their audience in an epistemological sense. They too, like market researchers, draw on ratings and broad audience data to substantiate their conclusions about the ideological power of institutions or media texts. Such studies further entrench an institutional perspective because of their organization of individuals and social phenomena into measurable variables such as demographics, personality types, uses and gratification variables, and so on. What results is not knowledge of the viewing experience or of relationships surrounding it, but of the isolation of viewer types and viewing contexts. Ang calls for a grounded audience study where the absence of response, even silence, provides rich data when taken in context (see also Bausinger 1984).

Contributions of literary and cultural studies

The postmodern turn in audience studies signifies its attention to the local. The traditional, Marxist, or structuralist view to the study of audiences regards them as socio-economic constructs. The Foucauldian or New Historical Approach follows the deconstructionist tradition of dismissing grand narratives of linear progress, yet in its construction of "historical knowledge as anonymous, dispersed discourses organizing society as well as the body" (Machor and Goldstein 2001, p. xiii), retains the complexity of the text and the autonomy of the critic. Postmodern reception studies pay attention to multicultural literatures, pop culture, and their reception by particularly ethnic and gender minorities. They draw on the classic cultural studies mission to examine low culture as well as high culture and the ideological environment that demarcates the two. Increasing attention is also given to middle brow culture where scholars urging this level of scrutiny argue that attention to the socially constructed extremes of media artifacts may in themselves reify the artificial divide between high and low cultures.

Reception theory in literary studies informed critical conceptualizations of audiences. Jauss (2001) introduced the idea of dialogue between a text's author and its reader, the former situated in a historical time and place, and the latter, in the contemporary present. Through a circular hermeneutic experience, the reader's expectations do not distort the author's intent, but allow a range of subjective interpretations by the reader resulting in a certain transformative power of the text. Fish (2001) takes this further to establish that the *reader's* interpretive position defines the meaning more forcefully than the author's ideological intent. Lest we are too dejected with this delineation where the onus of interpretation is on the reader and the text has limited transformative value, Mailloux (2001) notes that change does happen – only, it is evolutionary, not revolutionary. Essentially, these literary theorists sought to answer the classic realist/idealist question: where is meaning located – in the text or reader, or both? Marxist structuralists, mostly political economy scholars, locate it in the author and text. Quite simply, this means an anchoring of meaning production to media organizations and producers who spend exorbitant amounts of time and money to meticulously research and construct messages that are packed with ideologies of race, gender, class, citizenship and so on, to induce people to consume products that will lend them membership in privileged urban communities.

British cultural studies contributed much to a contextually rich understanding of domestic and international audiences. The surge in ethnographic studies in the 1980s was a response to overtly structuralist approaches that placed the audience as passive recipients of media messages. British cultural studies recognized the active audience and sought the study of it in such micro spaces as the family and such unconventional spaces as the street, and urged international reception studies toward a more critical and cultural direction. This turn was also propelled by an introspection in other fields such as literary criticism and its interrogation of "text" as a site of ideology, and anthropology, where the encounter between researcher and field was heavily critiqued for its perpetuation of social and cultural hierarchies (Morley 1996). Cultural studies scholars embraced the idea of interpretive communities theorized by Jauss, Fish and Mailloux. Bennett's (2001) nuanced poststructuralist Marxism (which he describes as "a Marxism that comes after structuralism, that is responsive to its criticisms") privileges the interpretive audience yet concedes that a certain dominant or preferred meaning is foregrounded by the institution, relegating others to the background.

Hall's (1980) premise of the polysemic nature of televisual texts whereby viewers could derive the *dominant* or *preferred* meaning embedded in the text, develop an *oppositional* reading to the text, or *negotiate* between preferred and oppositional meanings, positioned them as active partakers of the televisual context, not passive recipients of ideological messages. Hall's further writings on the relationship between text and context paved the way for a variety of empirical analyses that sought to understand how audiences responded to media and popular culture texts based on their social and gender differentiations. British cultural studies, in its focus on ideology and cultural hegemony, drew in scrutiny of the role of the mass media in facilitating and sustaining structures of power (Hall 1980, 1997), and how these structures were appropriated and resisted (Fiske 1989).

Ironically, the polysemic nature of media texts as proposed by literary and cultural studies scholars also signaled the study of the *text* as a point of entry to audience analysis, reinstating the text over audience hierarchy. Sadly, then, the bulk of audience research theorizes ground rather than grounds the theory (Morley 2003). Theoretical ruminations regarding the pros and cons of doing fieldwork, of the imbalance in power structure between researcher and researched, and about the politics of writing up and representing respondent voices are plentiful. Empirical analyses of audiences are relatively few, particularly for non-Western viewing communities. Those that do exist are, for the most part, reception analyses that use qualitative methods of inquiry deriving most significantly from the fields of sociology and anthropology. While the ethnographic method of anthropology seems the most logical and rigorous to address issues of culture and micro experiences, much of the research on audiences that emerges from cultural studies scholars is considered reception analysis, not ethnography.

To explain, reception studies use qualitative and quantitative methods and some elements of ethnography such as case analysis, participant observation, and immersion in the field. Ethnography, on the other hand, includes intensive participant observation (Clifford 1992), physical presence in the field (Hastrup and Hervik 1994), and long-term immersion in the social and cultural life of the researched. Many reception analyses are passed off as straight ethnography, leaving some audience researchers to despair at the diminishing integrity of methodology (Drotner 2000a; Nightingale 1993). The studies that do endure in their relevance for scholarly conversations on the social role of media technologies, that provide a commentary on television's ideological and cultural influence in an era of globalization, are those that are most meticulous and rigorous in their methodology where site, respondent base, and respondent and media contexts are clearly delineated. Reception analysts concern themselves with immediate decoding contexts; media ethnographers address the larger context of the viewer's daily lives. Drotner states that media researchers reach out for alternative methods like "analytical octopuses" (2000a, p. 174), and, in general, those from the Anglo-American tradition engage in relatively short observation periods, and mine data through in-depth interviews and informant diaries.

The cultural studies framework led to various reception analyses of communities and practices hitherto ignored in media studies. Significant in this tradition are Hebdige (1979), Jameson (1991) and Hall and Jefferson (1976) who studied youth subcultures in Britain for patterns of counter-hegemony in terms of youth fashion and music. The notion of the active audience was compelling, and scholars such as Radway (1984) and Grossberg (1984) examined audience engagement in and contestation of preferred meanings in romance novels and rock music, respectively. Others such as Bobo (1995) and Modleski (1986) established that audiences brought different subjective positions to media texts and took from it, meanings influenced by these positions. In the area of international audiences, scholars studied diverse audience engagement with exported US shows (Ang 1985) and gendered responses to television as a central and nation-building commodity in everyday life (Morley 1992), showing that different social groups may view the same text differently. Methods involved analyses of viewer mail (Ang 1985; Bird 2003), and participant observation and interviews (Gillespie 1995; Jhally and Lewis 1992; Morley 1980) to address the use of communication technologies within the household and interrogate the construction of national identity in transnational media.

A significant body of work in this framework is Morley's ethnography of BBC's current affairs *Nationwide* (1980) program audiences, where the viewer–text interface was considered a site of struggle and negotiation over meanings, resulting in the same text being interpreted differently by different people based on their subject positions. As part of a larger reception study sponsored by the center for Contemporary Cultural Studies at the University of Birmingham, Morley studied *Nationwide* audiences within their domestic arenas and found that women preferred fictional programs, romances, and local news, while men preferred factual programs, sports, and realistic fiction. He argued that the men and women in his study could be articulating their gendered roles because they were living up to social expectations, an artifact of their being interviewed in the presence of their families. While men devoted almost all their attention to television viewing, women did a host of other activities with it. Social status was also a factor in how men and women watched television where women who were dominant in the household, or who were breadwinners, did not follow the usual gendered pattern. In this analysis, Morley underlines the link between the macro and the micro, the private and the public, the real and the trivial, and so on, and argues that macro-structures are reproduced in micro-processes.

Radway's (1984) *Reading the Romance* is another much-referenced study for its analysis of how 40 romance novels readers in a mid-western community in Smithton could escape a routine-filled environment for a fantasy world where they could feel romanced and loved. Radway's work is well known for her connections between text and subject, neither sealed off from the other. Evidence of the active audience was provocative for other audience analysts who examined fan culture and individual appropriations of pop culture. Fiske is a prominent name in the analysis of the popular and, in his analysis of Madonna fans, writes:

> [I]f her fans are not "cultural dopes," but actively choose to watch, listen to, and imitate her rather than anyone else, there must be some gaps or spaces in her image that escape ideological control and allow her audiences to make meanings that connect with *their* social experience. (2001, p. 247)

The romanticization of audience agency has its roots in the eighteenth-century Romantic philosophies where individual freedom was considered an important component and prerequisite of social order. Objective knowledge was considered to be contingent upon subjective human understanding and on the organic unity of society (Shalin 1986).[1] The Romanticists in essence, invented a past into which they injected their modern values of human dignity, autonomy, and freedom in order to construct a utopian future and thus subvert the adverse effects of industrialization and capitalism.[2] They perceived society as progressing as an organic whole. In an organic society the individual was not just an actor but a self-conscious and critical author. This view is circular because the whole is explained through its parts and each part is explained through the whole and is called the "hermeneutical circle." Shalin asserts,

"The language of Romanticism confers on the individual a crushing responsibility for the well-being of the whole society. At the same time, it stipulates that man's liberty is contingent on his ability to embrace the whole, to incorporate its ways into his self" (ibid., p. 106). Philosophers such as Kant, Goethe, Hegel and Emerson rejected rational thinking as divorced from judgment and prior beliefs and values. Specifically, Kant acknowledged that value is important in understanding and that biases should be made into premises. Kant's *Critique of Pure Reason* influenced sociological hermeneutics, which focused on uncovering authorship and untying the bonds of the institution.

The principles of Romantic hermeneutics were extended to the social sciences in the early twentieth century. While this could lead to microscopic analyses of society, Shalin (1986) observes that it also provided a framework for the analysis of class, inequality, and exploitation. The ideas of the Romanticists reappear in the rhetoric of the "active audience" theorists. Specifically, the movement from the magic bullet theory of audience reception of media messages to the critical reception of media messages derives from the Romanticists' view that individuals are not just actors, but critical and self-conscious authors of ideas. Such a notion drives studies of media consumption in particular and consumerism in general.

Criticisms of reception analysis

Murdock (1997) dismisses the tendency among media scholars to pass off interviews, focus groups, and other qualitative data as ethnographic material, as poor attempts at thick description. The result is a superficial inquiry into complex and changing phenomena. The tendency in cultural studies to focus on textual analysis of television programs the researcher is a fan of, and to examine successful shows as true representations of reality, following, ironically, a social science tradition where the media are taken to be a commentary on contemporary society, have also been critiqued (Nightingale 1996).

The fan status many researchers award themselves (Acosta-Alzuru 2005; Ang 1985) has been lauded for the insider perspective it provided *and* criticized for its "tainting" of research observations. As Bird (2003) notes, no doubt the researcher needs some cultural competency in the texts audiences are engaged in, yet the equation of researcher with respondent as if both are part of the same viewing community is obviously problematic, leading to "the now large body of literature about certain genres of rock music, written by a couple of generations of academics who grew up on it, and who accept its value" (ibid., p. 121). In their attention to viewing pleasure and fandom, reception analyses have been critiqued for their tangential treatment of structural issues and for their limited scope. Such analyses have conventionally focused on the popularity of the text, on explaining the applications of British cultural studies, or on demonstrating audience pleasures with the text. Rarely were the social and political contexts of audiences and texts interrogated (Nightingale 1996).

A few notable studies that connect reception to social context are Press' (1991) *Women Watching Television* and Press and Cole's (1999) *Speaking of Abortion: Television and Authority in the Lives of Women*, which looked at the way women's class identities informed how they responded to television's portrayal of social issues. Much of cultural studies theory on television watching that followed continued to place the medium in the domestic space, at home where viewing is an isolated or familial activity, usually conducted alongside other activities such as eating, talking, and conducting daily chores (Dahlgren 1988; Ellis 1982).

The attention in cultural studies to varied subject positions resonated with mainstream mass communication researchers who touted the uses and gratifications approach as offering similar contextual openings, allowing the researcher to understand the various uses audiences made of media and the gratifications they derived from this usage (Blumler et al. 1985). Despite Clark's (2005) assertion that the roots of social science and the humanities could be drawn together in a context of globalization to study audiences, we would do well to remember Ang's (1996) reminder of the stark differences in the two approaches. While the uses and gratifications approach derives from a liberal pluralist construction of society comprising of autonomous and free individuals, the critical cultural studies perspective is always mindful of context and power differentials. The attention to limited agency is a relatively recent academic development. As a shift from extensive use of qualitative methods and components of ethnographic fieldwork, critical media reception scholars are now calling for greater rigor in method and a return to some of the traditions of anthropology.

Contributions of Anthropology to International Media Studies

The examination of media as part of everyday ritual in anthropology began, most significantly, in the 1980s (Ginsburg et al. 2002). Most studies on reception focus on responses to specific media texts as in Abu-Lughod's analyses of cinema audiences in Egypt (1997); Dickey's (1993) analysis of Tamil cinema and audiences in South India, and Mankekar's (1993) analysis of the epic

Hindu serials *Ramayana* and *Mahabharatha* and their reception by viewers in North India.

The contributions of anthropology to audience studies in communication are its multi-sited approach and its recognition of postcolonial, minority, and diasporic communities as integral constituents in the study of the historicity and diversity of media audiences (see Cunningham and Sinclair 2000; Gillespie 1995; Marks 2000; McLagan 1996; Mohammadi 1994, Shohat and Stam 1994; and Sreberny-Mohammadi for studies in these communities). The opening up of epistemological boundaries in the study of audiences positioned them as embedded with a cultural context that also included forces of production and distribution. Audiences no longer constituted a community of objective study, "out there" and distanced from the researcher.

Anthropologists engaging in international media studies draw from, most significantly, Benedict Anderson's (1991) notion of the "imagined community" and Jürgen Habermas's "public sphere" (1989) because both conceptualizations allow for the study of communities that come together across boundaries to partake in a collective identity (Ginsburg et al, 2002). It must be noted here that feminist critiques of the public sphere[3] injected a pause in how reception theorists accommodate Habermas's theory.

For example, Fraser (1995) and M. Yang (1999) have both noted that Habermas's public sphere assumed equal and democratic participation without critiquing the stark reality of the time, and that persists in most societies today, where men and their issues dominate the public sphere while women and subalterns are confined to the private sphere. Appadurai (1990) urges attention to the vital role of the media as a collaborator in national and transnational processes, producing notions of culture and identity in contemporary society.

Media ethnography may be described as the empirical analysis of cultures based on intensive and exhaustive prolonged fieldwork in specific contexts. Attention is paid to micro processes rather than macro structures and products. Through scrutiny of the local, of people's thoughts, perceptions, and behaviors, the ethnographer is able to read the world through the eyes of her or his respondents (Gillespie 1995). Such a method allows the researcher to make connections between the private and the public, the domestic, local, national and global, and finally, between micro issues of power and macro structures of power in society. In media studies, the term "ethnography" represents an expansion of reception studies along empirical and methodological trajectories. Empirically, the environment under study is extended to include areas beyond the immediate viewing context. Methodologically, the in-depth interviews that characterize reception studies are supplemented by participant observation, informal conversation (Drotner 1993), archival research, and textual and policy analyses. Methods cannot be rigid and orthodox, but are adapted to the context and community under study (Mankekar 1999). Nightingale (1993) and Schrøder (1994) seek a return to rigorous field-based ethnography, not quasi audience research loosely based on the methods of ethnography.

The rigors of the ethnographic method are more obvious or strictly adhered to in Latin American and Nordic audience studies (see Buarque de Almeida 2003; Drotner 2000b). Contrary to the trend among some communication scholars to develop audience analyses from letters and fan mail, Murphy (2003) and Abu-Lughod (1997) assert that being *in the field* is crucial. The site of research should be approached with the understanding that it is always, already hybrid (Kraidy 2003). Buarque de Almeida (2003) argues for long-term immersion in the field and contends that the ethnographer is in an intersubjective liminal space, crossing gender, class, and ethnic boundaries to get to the data and at the same time, is subjected to it by the respondent community.

Two primary concerns define ethnographic studies. The first is how the plurality of ethnographic voices is represented (Clifford 1988), and the second is how to ground ethnographies such that they truly show the correspondence between power and culture in the world system (Marcus 1992). Power discrepancies become more acute when it is the Western, Caucasian researcher who studies the non-Western respondent. Feminist ethnographers have produced extensive literature on the power differentials in the field that confound their interactions and observations. White researchers are accused of essentializing the respondent of color, while white feminists are criticized for equating their experiences with those of the non-white women they study (see Ong 1987).

Media ethnographers may find themselves co-opted into a system of representation where, unwittingly, they may work in tandem with media producers in representing and thereby objectifying the very audience subject-positions they hoped to give voice to (Dornfeld 199; T. Turner 2002). An inversion of the ethnographic subject may also occur where the community under study frames the ethnographer as an object for its consumption (see Himpele 2002). Zavella (1996) writes that the insider ethnographer, the returning native (see also Acosta-Alzuru 2005), is constantly negotiating her status since the members of the community being studied often make assumptions of the researchers' intents, skills, and personal characteristics. Some ethnographers have even resorted to deception to gain access to their communities[4] (C. Katz 1996). The native researcher has the unique limitation of always having to be accountable to the community studied. Zavella (1996) notes that the researcher has to decenter her or his own narrative to avoid investing herself or himself with too much power over the subject. Finally, important to note here is that ethnography can, by its very methodological attention to local practices, privilege the cultural rather than realistically situating the cultural within the larger political and economic structure.

Besides representing the plurality of voices and connecting figure to ground, media ethnographers are concerned with how locality of the study is selected and theorized. The site of the study provides rich data on social structure and lived experience (Gupta and Ferguson 1997) where the "production of locality" (Appadurai 1996, p. 181) becomes an important endeavor of ethnographers, themselves embedded in this localism.

Himpele writes:

> there is no neat separation between media and producers and the terrain of cultural representation...The ethnographic self-awareness that emerges from being compounded into the multiple layers of representation, being co-opted into the political projects, and articulating unspoken cultural strategies of such public spaces may be an aspect of modernity itself...it is available as an analytic and vertical angle, blurred as it is from a parallax position, from which to grasp the competing and convergent configurations of power and authority with which we and others produce and represent culture in public. (2002, p. 314)

Conventional anthropological ethnography has itself been criticized for its unrealistic expectations. Such a method is also encased in an assumption of researcher objectivity where, miraculously, the researcher, immersed in a culture for long periods of time, can emerge and document, with clinical detachment, the interactions and social relationships of the research subjects (Amit 2000). Okely (1992) identifies the effort of anthropologists to unhinge personal experience from academic report in the pursuit of scientific objectivity as a symptom of larger structural demarcations of personal and private in industrialized capitalistic societies. Callaway (1992) points to the contradiction in the notion that only prolonged immersion in the field can produce authentic results when, simultaneously, distance between researcher and researched is also considered crucial for the reporting of scientifically detached results. Although the ethnographic site that is away from the home of the researcher is considered more valid (Gupta and Ferguson 1997), Malkki (1997) writes that fieldwork turns to the study of the banal and the mundane to draw connections between the exotic and the familiar. According to Caputo (2000, p. 19), such boundaries contribute to an "evaluative hierarchy" that reproduces a colonizing study of the world.

Anthropology's attention to the ethnography of media production and consumption (see Guerevitch et al. 1982) spawned a new, critical, and in-depth analytical framework for the study of television reception. Yet, despite its significant theoretical contributions, anthropology's approach to media studies, as does dominant theory in communication, assumes the centrality of the media in everyday life as it is in Western societies, without adequately acknowledging that for most of the populations in tri continent countries, the media, particularly television, constitute a small, albeit important, part of their daily existence. As stated in the introduction to this chapter, reception analyses in non-Western countries are scarce and further declining in favor of analyses of media texts and institutions. For the postcolonial scholar, such a retreat is bewildering, especially when structures of power are all the more manifest in tandem with strident local voices embracing, resisting, and appropriating the same.

Postcolonial Interventions in Audience Research

For critical scholars who continuously interrogate boundaries of positivism, for feminists whose lived experience translates into an activist methodology, and for postcolonialists who claim critical and feminist standpoints to draw connections between macro institutions of power in public spheres to their micro manifestations in the private spheres (Hegde and Shome 2002), ethnographic fieldwork offered by British culturalists is not enough. More efficient is a structuralist framework as developed by Althusser and Gramsci which postulates that ideologies are conceptualized and perpetuated through unconscious lived conditions and experiences, not as surface forms and contents of ideas (Hall 1980). Postcolonial scholars engaging in international media studies advocate a deconstruction of gender, ethnic, and class hierarchies, to name a few, to contest notions of a monolithic women's consciousness or a unitary mediated experience, for example (Mohanty 1987; Minh-ha 1987, 1989; Visweswaran 1996). These scholars draw from British cultural studies and European structuralism to contest positivist reception studies as limiting to the understanding of women and subalterns. For such researchers who undertake reception analysis, who are interested in uncovering power differentials in the field, a singular, unified method is elusive and even suspect. Postcolonial scholarship, in particular, is not anchored to a specific method. Its methods of inquiry are driven by the larger social contexts it interrogates. Interdisciplinarity characterizes the methods of such scholarship and could include anything from textual analysis to ethnography (Shome and Hegde 2002).

Critical postcolonial scholars use ethnographic fieldwork to interrogate structures of power and to negotiate politics of access in the field and of representation in academia. Postcolonial feminists "encourage a conceptualization of feminist epistemology as a heterogenous enterprise with multiple strands" (Wolf 1996, p. 5). Reception analyses by scholars using a postcolonial approach (Mankekar 1999; Rajagopal 1996) show that the researcher and the researched are complex individuals with multi-layered identities. These scholars note that neither the researcher nor the researched should be essentialized, but should be regarded through interdisciplinary perspectives as divided and dynamic beings (Lal 1996; Wolf 1996; Zavella 1996).

Such critical perspectives are indeed liberating to the postcolonial, feminist scholar who desires an integrated theoretical and methodological framework to point to the continuity of historical structures of colonialism in the contemporary environment of globalization. Although the validity of Marxist, feminist, deconstructionist, and psychoanalytical perspectives in informing postcolonial scholarship has been described extensively and considered empowering to the subaltern scholar (Shome and Hegde 2002), much of the research in this area remains in the realm of theorization and not empirical study.

In integrating such interdisciplinary audience research theory into empirical design to address the interdependency and interconnectivity of media globalization, certain hitherto fixed entities such as place and people become problematized. These need to be reconceptualized in terms of flow and dynamic process. A cautionary critique of flows and fluidity with respect to tri continent fieldwork is provided later in the chapter.

Unmooring place, de-anchoring subjects

Ethnographic fieldwork can no longer privilege the rootedness of place as the defining context of study. Couldry (2003) proposes a liberation from place itself so that the media ethnographer conducts research not at specific points of production and consumption, but follows patterns of power and their manifestations at various locales.[5] No doubt the shifting and transient nature of the site means that prolonged observation or immersion of the researcher in the true sense is not possible, but the purpose of the research is to observe sites where significant practices occur. Therefore, the emphasis should be on the action itself, not so much the place. Such a conceptualization derives from earlier theory where Massey (1997), for example, suggested that a place should not be considered as *being*, but *becoming*; it is transformative and changes with the conditions of the research, the participants, the researcher herself or himself, not to mention the social, cultural, and economic environment of the time. Further, Clua (2003) differentiates between "space" and "place": "For 'space' was an abstract concept that became concrete when turned into 'place.' 'Place,' thus, was the lived, perceived, experienced space invested with human values" (ibid., p. 58). She attempts to de-anchor spaces from processes where spaces of media activity, whether the sitting room (Morley and Silverstone 1990) or elsewhere, take precedence over the activity itself. Similar to Couldry (2003), she seeks a broader understanding of spaces as places that are continuously being reproduced through forces of capitalism and other social structures. Morley's (1996) attempt to detour fieldwork from the open spaces of the city to the intimate space of the living room should further be critiqued for its privileging of one space over another, asserts Clua (2003).

Applying a critical geography (see Hay 1996; Massey 1997) to the study of media audiences requires awareness not just of changing landscapes but also of the mobility of subjects (Grossberg 1988). Murphy (2005) shifts conceptualization of audience from fandom to "community" and examines its connections to extended family, neighborhood, work, school, and other such local contexts. Lest we feel lost in this unmooring of space, people, researchers and structures (Ang 1996) cautions us that we need to start from "somewhere"; we need to avoid generalizations and highlight contextualized particularities.

More importantly, for all the dismantling of the fixities of the research field, the postcolonial scholar has to keep in mind that viewing communities are very much bound to structure. The freedom of nomadism (Fiske 1989) is a privilege of those with the cultural, economic, and social capital to "flow." The following sections address the fluidity of people, spaces, and culture, yet underscores that fluidity does not necessarily mean autonomy, agency, or freedom. Structures of power are very much in control of such flow. At the same time, the limited agency of audiences *does* alter structure cumulatively, over time (see Mailloux 2001), resulting in new interpretive media communities and rituals. Minority discourse (see JanMohamed and Lloyd 1990) allows us a way to address this agency against the overwhelming pessimism of some postcolonial scholars who believe the subaltern cannot speak (Spivak 1988a). Chow addresses just this point:

> Unlike the absolute certainty of a negative conclusion such as "the subaltern cannot speak," minority discourse analysis offers hope: their recognition of subordination (as evidenced in the word "minority" as opposed to "majority" or "mainstream") is accompanied by a persistent belief in the possibilities of expression, articulation, and agency (as evidenced in the word "discourse").
> (1998, p. 3)

Before entering a discussion of agency and subjectivity, however, it is useful to outline a few differences between Western and non-Western viewing experiences as identified by media ethnographers.

Differences between Western and Non-Western Viewing Experiences

Viewing contexts

Much of early audience research methodology derived from the case study method (Morley and Silverstone 1990) and indicated that television and media technology consumption takes place in the private, domestic sphere, bracketing the living room as the site for participant observation. In many non-Western countries, however, television viewing is, to a large extent, a collective viewing activity in low income, urban, and semi-urban homes. This considerably limits our understanding of media as public commodities, a status common in non-Western countries. Internet cafés, roadside television, video parlors, and marketplace radio are some of the sites where interactions with media may be observed (Algan 2003).

For example, a study of domestic laborers in Bangalore, India, showed that open doors in a television household in the evenings were a sign of hospitality and community friendship where neighbors would trickle in over the course of the entire evening to watch the game shows and dramas that occupied prime time (McMillin 2002b). Discussing cinema audiences in India, Srinivas (2002) adds that audience behavior is remarkably different from the silent filmgoer in Western cinema theaters. The Indian cinema experience is characterized by boisterous audiences who whistle, cheer, and berate the stars on the screen, a far cry from the silent, orderly movie environment of Western countries.

In the case of Latin American countries, although urban television watching may be a central feature of nuclear family units (Murphy 1999), Tufte (2000) notes that semi-urban or even rural television viewing very often takes place even *in front of* the front door, because most homes in this strata do not make clear distinctions between the living room and the street space in front of it. Doors and windows are open throughout the day with only the inner chambers such as the bedroom or kitchen screened off from the very public areas of the rest of the house. Such an environment complicates distinctions of private and public so carefully theorized in Western media theory (Meyrowitz 1985; Thompson 1990).

Likewise, Spitulnik (2002) reports from her fieldwork among radio listeners in Zambia that in very poor communities, it is even considered antisocial to stay inside during the day. Most activities, especially radio listening, are conducted outside among neighbors. The radio shifts from outside to the living room in the evenings (if the home has one) and then is secured in the bedroom with other household valuables at night. The radio travels with its owner – to work and family functions, for example – and thus is a highly mobile and visible symbol of its owner's prosperity. The differences between Zambian and Western, particularly US, media use outweigh the similarities, and a different sensibility is required for Zambian media ethnography. The romanticized image of a single viewer or the nuclear family huddled around the radio or television set may exist only in the imaginations of media producers and policy-makers. In Zambia, the viewing context is the site for the dynamic interplay of a variety of activities: children playing, visitors arriving and departing, women baking buns or pounding maize, and so on. Ethnographers attempting to describe media cultures and viewing behaviors should "wander in this field – beyond the living room – and welcome the unboundedness of its subject" (ibid., p. 351). No doubt ideological demarcations between the public material and domestic spiritual persist (Chatterjee, 1993), yet in terms of the geography of viewing space, the ritualization of community viewing (where these could also become social events for the exchange of gossip, political views and most often, refreshments), translates into a very different viewing experience from that of Western audiences.

Religious and emotive content

The emotive quality of indigenously produced programs is quite different in particularly Asian and Latin American countries as compared to the soaps and dramas of the United States, Great Britain, Australia, New Zealand, and countries of Europe. This quality cannot be underestimated especially in the case of Latin American *telenovelas*, which carry a high pedagogical content resulting in actual changes in viewing behavior. Fuenzalida (1992, cited in Tufte 2000) underscores the importance of treating *telenovela* emotion as a pedagogical element with effects more far-reaching than straightforward education or news programs.

The intimate relationship among religion, politics, and media is another feature that distinguishes non-Western from Western televisual content. Religious programming on television in particular, has proven to be a powerful vehicle to foster citizen and national identity, most notably in the case of Egypt (Abu-Lughod 2002), Iran (Abrahamian 1999), Lebanon (Kraidy 2003), Southern

Chile (Rodriguez 2003), South Africa (Tomaselli and Teer-Tomaselli 2003), and India (Mankekar 1993; McMillin 2002a, 2002b; Mitra 1993; Rajagopal 1996). The embeddedness of religious tropes within such societies makes it possible to use highly stylized techniques that may be understood only by the informed viewer. For example, television in Iran, far from touted as an external "bad" influence on local cultures and traditions, was coopted by Khomeini under the Islamic Republic to propagate his philosophies. Television brought home to the people not just the faces and voices of religious conservatives and monarchists, but also the trials of left-wing activists (Abrahamian 1999).

Burch's (2002) analysis of the popularity of the Hindu epic, the *Ramayan* in Nepal, offers an explanation of the phenomenal success of this religious narrative even in a non-Indian context, and the cultural literacy that was required to ensure its resonance among its viewers. For example, the use of blue color for the skin of the Lord Vishnu, white clothes to depict death and mourning, and generally bright hues to convey divine grandeur, would not be aesthetically pleasing to the Western eye, yet provided important symbolic shortcuts to the Indian and diasporic Hindu viewer. The use of music to relay dramatic tension, and the frequent songs and dances to connote emotion and devotion resonate with India's strong film tradition and oral culture.

Liberation theology, according to Rodriguez, which "assumes that the mission of all Catholics is to make the world a better place by repudiating poverty, which implies struggling against the evils of external domination and internal colonialism" (2003, p. 178), found its way to the masses of Southern Chile through community media and alternative media projects. Religion and media are intimately intertwined and correspond with the culture of the faith-based community. The interweaving of liberation theology and the media was a source of grave concern for the apartheid government in South Africa, particularly in the 1970s and 1980s. The Steyn Commission of Enquiry into the Mass Media was charged with exploring the politicized theology in the alternate press. Tomaselli and Teer-Tomaselli explain:

> In the legitimating doctrine of apartheid – Christian nationalism – the Calvinist original doctrine of Salvation by Election had been reconstituted into a theology of white supremacy. Followers of this predestinarian faith saw Catholicism as a threat, because the latter, like many other religions, makes provision for a *will* to salvation. Thus, Afrikaaner nationalist ideology had for many years demonized the Roman Catholic faith as the *Roomse gevaar* ("Roman threat"), on a par with blackness and communism. The matter was not helped by the Catholic Church's prosocial stance, which provided solidarity and income to the burgeoning black opposition to apartheid. (2003, p. 197)

Although the Catholic Church has historically been opposed to popular media which it considered as catering to low tastes, in the context of anti-apartheid struggles, the South African Catholic Bishop's Conference actively used the press to fight against apartheid and for social justice. Notable papers in this regard are the *Southern Cross* (established in 1920) and the *New Nation* (that ran from January 1986 to May 1997). The latter reported the activities of the Congress of South African Trade Unions, United Democratic Front, and various anti-racist church organizations. The Church's role in the fight against apartheid cannot be underestimated in South Africa and delivered a momentous blow that exceeded the force of either the labor movement or the press in general (Tomaselli and Teer-Tomaselli 2003).

If religion can be used to forge a national consciousness (or in the case of South Africa, an anti-nationalist consciousness where nationalist here refers to the apartheid state) through the media, we also have to examine how the media are used to mobilize resistance against religious consciousness in nation-states that abhor such leanings. The Chinese Communist Party's extreme measures against Falun Gong practitioners in the 1990s, is a case in point. Falun Gong, it should be noted, is not a religion, but draws upon the "Dharma Wheel Practice" (its literal meaning) to channel *qi* or vital energy throughout the body through various meditative and physical exercises. Zhao observes that Falun Gong "is a multifaceted and totalizing movement that means different things to different people, ranging from a set of physical exercises and a praxis of transformation to a moral philosophy and a new knowledge system" (2003, p. 211), that was contradictory to the Chinese state's technocratic policies of modernization. Falun Gong's surge in popularity in the mid-1990s coincided with the commercialization of the media, facilitating its spread to millions of Chinese and foreigners across the world. Mainstream and underground book publishing houses and audio and video companies took on the highly lucrative project of reproducing Falun Gong lectures and principles leading to increasing alarm in the Chinese state. Although the latter initially supported Falun Gong and some of its members were also members of the group, its media activism and its international support resulted in the Chinese state using a variety of strategies – from counter-press to highly publicized executions, to quell the movement. The role of the media is significant in this context – websites, videos, books, alternate journals – to name a few, provided a sympathetic space for the Falun Gong and anti-Jiang Zemin diatribes. The emancipatory struggles of the Falun Gong may be critiqued for its use of authoritarian propaganda, yet it is an example of a resistance movement, a fight against modernity as defined by the bureaucratic Chinese state. It is also another example of the powerful use of the media by what started as a marginal group, to promote

153

its philosophy much like the examples of states using religion disseminated through the media, to garner public support.

The rigidity of television itself as a two-dimensional medium constricted by short programming time frames, formulaic formats and interruptions by advertisements has been a bane in countries that have thrived on live theater, lengthy music and dance performances and interactive melodrama (for example, see Hobart 2002, in the case of Bali; Rajagopal 2001, in the case of India; Abu-Lughod 2002, in the case of Egypt; and Mandel 2002, in the case of Kazakhstan). Strategies of live theater or melodramatic cinema are coopted into television formats, most often failing miserably in the beginning, then gaining momentum as they graft in the immediacy and structural efficiency of global formats. Papa et al.'s (2000) extensive analyses of the entertainment-education format in Latin American, Asian, and African countries, demonstrate the parasocial interactions generated between viewers and program protagonists to effect changes (albeit limited) in behavior and social structure.

Political content in programs for entertainment

The political edge in many melodramas from particularly Asia and Latin America are absent in their Western counterparts. In fact, in Brazil, attempts to inject overtly political themes in Brazilian *telenovelas* were met with protest from female viewers who wanted them to retain their melodramatic, romantic roots (La Pastina 2003). In contrast to American soaps, Egyptian melodramas depicted characters who personified the Arab socialist and national development objectives of the state government (Abu-Lughod 2002). Egyptian melodramas, then, develop protagonists to communicate lessons of desired citizenship and morality.

In the case of India, Rajagopal (2001) provides an intricate analysis of the 1980s Bharatiya Janata Party (BJP) government's use of national television to politicize and propagate Hindu cultural values. Through the airing of the Hindu epics, *Ramayan* and *Mahabharat*, on the state-sponsored Doordarshan national network, it elevated Hinduism as *the* code of conduct for all citizens committed to a prosperous, progressive, and uniquely Indian state. The unfolding of particularly the *Ramayan* epic, which told the story of the Hindu God Ram, and the simultaneous unraveling of the violent Ram Janmbhoomi-Babri Masjid battle in Ayodhya, North India, between Hindus and Muslims who respectively believed the site was the birthplace of Ram and a sacred place of worship, powerfully upheld Hindus as the righteous claimants of Indian land and culture. The ancient epic was tailored to meet the needs of the ideological mission of fundamentalist Hindu politicians of the BJP. In tandem with politicizing the epics, the BJP government engaged in a "retail Hindutva" or Hinduness (Rajagopal 2001, p. 64), providing a range of consumer products such as buttons, posters, shawls and stickers, through which consumers could express their Hindu identities. The destruction of the Babri Masjid mosque on December 6, 1992, and the death of thousands of Hindus and Muslims led to the fall of the BJP in key states of the country such as Madhya Pradesh and Himachal Pradesh. Nevertheless, the BJP effectively wove economic liberalization within its own Hindutva policies and the progress of an economically prosperous Hindu state became its crucial political strategy. Rajagopal writes:

> Commodity images of Hindutva, however, became absorbed as part of the symbolic apparatus of liberalization, providing the semblance of a self-sufficient indigenous modernity unruffled by the developmentalist state's retreat, and coming into its own, paradoxically, amidst globalization. (2001, p. 26)

Chatterjee (1993) comments that the conflation of Indian nationalism with Hindu nationalism is by no means a retreat of the modern state to pre-modern religious conceptions. It is a very modern and rational framework that legitimizes a central role of the state as a unified and sovereign entity. The premise of this framework is not religious but secular. Politics of inclusion and exclusion are pinned to the nation's history, not just to ideologies of Hindu supremacy. The study of television in such a charged environment, then, has to take into account the intimate influence of political and religious structures and cannot rest with a mere description of micro viewing pleasures and experiences.

Social differentiations among audiences

The social differentiations among media audiences have to be theorized differently in non-Western countries than they are in Western countries. The classic definitions of class – as referring to those who own land, means that although women are implicated by this definition, they are classless because in reality in most tri continent countries, women are denied land ownership. A common frame of reference for class analyses of Western viewing communities is the socio-economic index, which provides clear demarcations of income brackets. In non-Western societies, semi-urban and rural populations may not think of class solely in terms of income, but in terms of caste, sect, and religion as well. The caste system and concepts of being untouchable common in societies in India and Japan are interlocked with class and need to be addressed as much as socio-economic differentiations. In addition, people's communal affiliations (in shared faith, ethnic, and language experiences, for example) and their perceptions of personal status have to be considered when drawing interpretations of their social standing (Vickers and Dhruvarajan 2002). For example, class distinctions in India are complex, where the urban poor see themselves as laborers, people who suffer, or people who have nothing, and regard the upper class as "big people" or "rich people." No single hegemonic class can be identified in India, capable of imposing a hegemonic rule in the Gramscian sense (Kohli, 1987, cited in Dickey, 1993). Dickey suggests that, "[O]pposition between classes has equally to do with values and aesthetics as with economic inequalities and relationships" (ibid., p. 11). The cultural definitions of class, she asserts, have to be taken into consideration as well as the economic.

Social positioning of media

Perhaps most important, media in general and television in particular, are not as central an influence in non-Western societies as they are theorized to be in Western ones (Harindranath 2003). For most tri continent populations, television is still a luxury, and, if accessible, is a minor component of daily rituals. Television viewing is limited to 2–3 hours a day, and is often dictated by whoever has the most control over leisure activity in the household. The presence of invariably one television set per household does not mean that micro viewing communities within each family do not exist, it just means that the development of fandom or articulation of responses to television is quite different from such processes in the United States or Great Britain. The study of media representations in tri continent countries such as billboards, posters and popular tent cinema (Dickey 1993) or epic serials (Rajagopal 2001; Mankekar 1999) certainly provide strong evidence of the "mass" character of media viewing. Yet these analyses could distract the reader from the reality of most citizens in the country where the relatively inexpensive cinema, let alone television, may well be beyond their reach. Such a reality reminds us that the ground is where audience research should begin, not from the text or theory as has been the convention.

Algan (2003) identifies the dilemma in international media research, where the audience is discussed *after* a thorough treatment of the ideological content of the text it is watching and the political economy within which the text and audience are embedded. Such a conceptualization quite literally, turns audience studies into a commentary of text and its interpretation rather than that of audience and the place and function of the text in their lives. This is a crucial point because a focus first on text and ideological context may easily lead to a skewed assumption of the pervasive power of media in the audience's lives when such media actually constitute part of a complex matrix of other social structures that define and texture audience's lived experiences.

For all its unmoorings of epistemological fixities of place, people, and research design, media ethnography still carries with it a naturalized "Westphalian ideological discourse in that it has taken for granted the nature of civil society and the history of governance in relation to consumer democracy" (Murphy 2005, p. 174). Further, in the 2000s, globalization and its shifting places and subjects have led scholars away from audience studies in general: the messiness is overwhelming, even paralyzing. Renewed scrutiny of the ground is essential if we are to make any substantive progress in our understanding of how global and local media are really accommodated, and what symbolic meanings media flows take on as they course through viewing communities across the world. In addressing the dynamics of media reception, audience agency and audience subjectivity are important points to be addressed and critiqued in international media studies.

As described earlier, North American reception analyses that explored meanings consumers made from popular media were criticized for their romanticization of the active audience, as if individual choices automatically translated into autonomous freedom and social power. These studies were significant in their revelation of audiences' multiple reading positions, yet to a large extent privileged their pleasure over the social and capitalist structure they were ensconced in, only thinly drawing comparisons between subject location and subjectivity. The partiality toward conclusions of agency is strongly evident in international audience studies as well. Much of this tendency may be attributed to the reaction against bland claims of cultural imperialism that also assumed the passivity of non-Western media audiences (see Strelitz 2003). Besides, the postcolonial framework that focuses on the subaltern, and the ethnographic method that scrutinizes culture and micro experiences on the ground, exacerbate the trend toward highlighting resistance (Corner 1998).

Agency, Subjectivity, and Subjective Agency

From an extensive survey of international audience studies, two dominant themes emerge. First is the broad trend of highlighting *audience agency* and *resistance*. The sites of examination of such resistance include mediated political protests and demonstrations, the internet, *telenovelas* and development soaps, grassroots communication, hybrid programming, and local-global cultural appropriations. Second is a surge of recent studies that squarely address the issue of *limited agency* and *subjectivity*. These studies either place the *media as central to social life* or, more realistically, as part of a larger *matrix of mediations* that inform consumers' perceptions of self. The following sections provide brief examples of each to address the diversity of such research.

Audience Agency and Resistance

Activism in protests and demonstrations

It is true that where there is domination, there is also resistance. The character and trajectory of this resistance make for fascinating analyses of audience reception. Many accounts of popular and press activism are embedded within larger analyses of media coverage of political upheavals, particularly in the case East Asian countries. For example, Ma (2000) describes such resistance in the case of China during the June 5, 1989 Tiananmen Square incident. Despite the government's attempts to frame the tragedy as a consequence of youthful fanaticism, journalists and students subverted this dominant coding by planting their own anti-government messages in newspapers. Such subversion had to be conducted within relatively safe parameters, however. He writes:

> In the 1990s the Chinese mediascape was characterized by conspicuous discrepancies in different "reading zones"...Although it is an open secret that many party members and officials are engaged in widespread corruptions, the media are very timid and only cover cases officially condemned by the party. But in everyday discourses, there are all sorts of jingles, rhymes, and poems which criticize the government and corrupt officials with biting sarcasm. (ibid., p. 30)

In the same vein, the active audience in Korea is located within a context of political response. An example is the support from college students, professors, and journalists for the 1974 *Dong-A Ilbo* newspaper's "Declaration on Practicing Freedom of the Press" that demanded non-interference from government and other institutions on press freedom as well as illegal arrests of journalists (Park et al. 2000).

The internet as a democratic space for participation

Besides public protests and demonstrations, international media scholars examine the internet as a space for democratic expression and activism.

Drawing from Habermas's conceptualization of the public sphere, these scholars regard the internet as a participatory space, facilitating free and oftentimes anonymous participation and therefore fostering equality. Recent studies on internet chat rooms highlight the notion of agency and identify this medium as a site for transnational connections and the development of an idealized public sphere. For example, Tanner (2001) describes an internet discussion forum on the October 1998 arrest of Augusto Pinochet in London, which resulted in 1,670 letters facilitating membership of its authors into a larger process of Chilean reconciliation. Other examples of online campaigns are the protest of NBC's coverage of Chinese athletes in the 1996 Olympic Games, the 1996 campaign against the construction of a lighthouse on the Diaoyutai (Senkaku) Islands by Japanese ultra-nationalists, and the 1998 online protest against ethnic violence in Indonesia that accompanied actual demonstrations in the country and led to the resignation of Indonesian President Suharto the same year (Marcus 1999). The Net movement of the Zapatistas in Chiapas, Mexico, and the *Free Anwar Campaign* and *Justice for Anwar* websites in Malaysia that cropped up right after Malaysian Deputy Prime Minister Anwar Ibrahim was fired leading to widespread anti-Prime Minister Mahatir Mohammed sentiment in 1998 (Ling 2003), are other cases of political activism mobilized through the internet.

Mitra's (2004) study of the discursive strategies used by the web portal SAWNET (South Asian Women's Network) for South Asian women is an account of women's agency in cyberspace. He documents South Asian women's activism in pre-independence protests, in guerilla warfare to protest domestic abuse, and in the mass media where he cautions that the danger of the latter is that minority voices can be co-opted into the hegemonic system and retransmitted within its own ideological constraints. SAWNET's lack of an institutional voice, editorialization, or audience information indicated that agency was deferred. The very fact that women had a voice on this website at all was liberating, and could ultimately contribute to a collective "hypervoice" of South Asian women. Although the conclusions of the author could be critiqued for their glamorization of the democracy and equality awarded SAWNET participants of the power of their hypervoice that "could transcend the power of unions, protests and the surrogate voice on institutional media" (p. 506), the study does provide some direction for the analysis of popular agency.

Similarly, G. Yang (2003) conducted a "guerilla ethnography" (p. 471) of portal sites (containing website directories, news and weather information, and stock quotes, for example), newsgroups (such as popular.alt.Chinese. text and ChinaSite.com) and online magazines (such as *China News Digest* and *China's Scholars Abroad*), and bulletin boards (such as Chinese language university and media websites). The author's long-term immersion in these venues showed that although some restrictions to democratic participation existed, the high volume of posts per day (as low as 50 and as high as 3,000 for some bulletin boards) and the content which indicated strong resistance to censorship and enforced decorum, indicated active participation on such issues as democracy, economic development, morality, and religion. The conclusion of this study is that the internet provides for Chinese both within and outside the country, cultural spaces that are linked to global networks to facilitate worldwide protests. They perform an important political function both at national and international levels and may be regarded as a transnational cultural sphere. Further, the internet forum connects intellectuals in mainland China, Hong Kong, Taiwan, Indonesia, and Singapore in struggles that are common to all.

To cite another example, Nyamnjoh (2004) observes that African activists have used new Information and Communication Technologies (ICTs) to argue against giant pharmaceutical companies in South Africa and to fight against aggressive globalization at the WTO and G8 summits. Websites represent the interests of indigenous minorities by the Baha Pygmies of the rainforest and the Bushmen of the Kalahari and the large community of the Yoruba of Nigeria and Zulu of South Africa. No doubt these concerns are articulated by elite intellectuals, NGOs, and activists on the behalf of minority groups, but at least they are represented in good faith. Although telephone and internet lines are scarce in villages and even in cities such as Bamenda in Cameroon, people often write messages to be transmitted by internet business staff who wait for replies and print them out for their customers. Cell phones have also proven to be an empowering technology. In 1998, the Cameroon Telecommunication Company (Camtel) was formed through the merger of Intercam and the Department of Telecommunication at the Ministry of Post and Telecommunications. Camtel Mobiule (Cameroon Telecommunication Mobile Company) was given the task of installing mobile phones in the country. Cameroon now has over 200,000 cell phone subscribers. Cell phones have allowed local resistance groups to mobilize without fear of being monitored as could be the case if they were using land lines. Diasporic Grassfielders and migrants supply relatives with cell phones and stay abreast of marriages, feasts, funerals, and other village activities.

While it is true that the internet allows anonymity and freedom to express a wide range of views, research on the democratic function of this medium is complicated by the difficulty in discerning exactly who the participants are. Several feminist studies of internet chat rooms and listservs have demonstrated that these spaces are perceived as hostile arenas for female participants. Accessibility to computers is limited in most countries of the tri continent and a study of the use of the internet by teen girls in India showed that cybercafés were male-dominated spaces and those girls who did venture online, did so primarily to email friends and family. They considered chat rooms just as restrictive as the public spaces of their neighborhoods where they were likely to be harassed (McMillin 2005). Besides, as Castells (2001) reports, 66 percent of internet users in the world are from North America and Western Europe. Only 5 percent are from Africa and Latin America. Curran (2003) adds that so-called "global" magazines supported by related websites, such as OpenDemocracy, for example, are overrepresented by participants from America and northern Europe while Africa and Latin America and even Japan are grossly underrepresented. The nature of the discourse in these venues itself is skewed toward exchanges between like-minded liberals in the United States and Europe. Curran rightly points to the impotence of the "public sphere" created by magazines and web forums where participants other than public officials can safely and anonymously remain in their own enclaves, acting as mere viewers but not active members of such forums.

Further, Lim (2004) suggests that the emancipatory and participatory power of the internet may be inflated. For example, the argument that the defeat of President Suharto in Indonesia was net driven is far-fetched since at the time the proportion of Internet users in Indonesia was less than 1 percent of the population. However, newer technologies thrive when they slide into structures of the old. The internet café in Indonesia, or *warnet*, once located only on university campuses accessible to these privileged populations, now imitates the space of the *warung*, a small coffee and snack house typical in middle-class and lower middle-class neighborhoods, where family and friends congregate. While allowing increased access to the internet, the *warnet*, by duplicating the *warung*, can, as suggested by Curran (2003) also send small groups back into their private, comfortable spaces, while large private companies invade this sphere, making it more cosy for its users, and distracting them from larger social concerns. The global corporate institution exercises social hegemony as did Suharto's development state in its construction of state–corporate relations that thwarted the emergence of a politically active society.

Despite cautionary tales of the internet, M. Yang (1999) reiterates that this medium should persist as a site for scrutiny particularly in its potential for a transnational public sphere for Chinese women. Its state monitoring and commercialization notwithstanding, the internet provides the most effective and efficient way for transnational Chinese to build solidarity. The video compact disc (VCD) is also a commodity to examine for its capability of storing films from the 1920s and 1930s and the Maoist Era, and more recent ones from industries in Hong Kong and Taiwan. Films could be used to stimulate debate and discussion among Chinese students and others, on the changing representation of the mainland Chinese woman over time.

Telenovelas *and social change*

The transformative function of Latin American *telenovelas* has been upheld as an example of audience agency (Kottak 1990). For example, Tufte's (2000) analysis of the reception of the mini-series, quasi-documentary, *Rebellious Years* (*Años Rebeldes*) aired on Rede Globo in 1992, showed how the program spurred people to demonstrate against and ultimately cause the defeat of President Collor in 1992. Also, the strong fan following of the *telenovela From Body and Soul* or *De Corpo e Alma* resulted in a demand for a revision of the Brazilian penal code (supported by 1.3 million signatures) after the untimely death of its star, Daniela Perez.

In a similar vein, Mandel (2002) conducted participant observation in Almaty, Kazakhstan, between 1995 and 1998, among 100 viewers of the British government-produced *Crossroads*, based on the US soap and Latin American *telenovela* format, to facilitate the transition of Kazakhstani society from communism and authoritarianism to capitalism. Sponsored by the British Know How Fund, the show used ample product placement (most notably British American Tobacco products such as Wrigley's gum and Smirnoff vodka) and depicted a marriage alliance between Kazakh and Russian families. Kazakh actors and viewers were disgruntled at the higher status awarded the intellectual Russian family and the lower blue-collar service class status of the Kazakh family. After the departure of the British advisers, Kazakh writers scripted in the divorce of all intermarriages and introduced a detective in the soap since all other self-respecting US soaps had one. The conflict between Kazakh and British realism in the production of the soap is a good example of local appropriations of foreign format and aesthetics. Viewers gradually took pride in *Crossroads* and saw in its protagonists depictions of modernity modeled after US soaps such as *Santa Barbara*. Mandel (2002) observes that *Crossroads* provides an example of the amalgamation of the foreign and global with local Kazakhsthani culture. It catered to the taste of Kazakhsthani students who craved foreign and global styles, but was suitably indigenized to suit local tastes.

In the subfield of development communication, numerous studies from both the positivist, social psychology approach and the critical feminist approach, address the effects of educational media. Using the former approach, Papa et al. (2000) document the pro-social value of entertainment-education formats such as soaps, dramas, popular music and even comic books in developing countries of Africa, Asia, and Latin America, dealing specifically with spreading awareness of such issues as gender equality, HIV/AIDS prevention, drug abuse, and adult literacy. Their reception analysis of the radio soap, *Tinka Tinka Sukh* (Happiness Lies in Small Pleasures) through surveys, in-depth interviews, and focus groups of listeners in the village of Lustaan, India, showed that several processes textured how audiences accommodated the educational themes of the soap. The soap centered on four family units: (1) an ideally constructed family who promoted women's welfare and harmony in the village; (2) a depraved family with a domineering father and a mother who overindulged her son and neglected her daughters; (3) a widow with three daughters who met varying fates based on their independence; and (4) a tragic bride who committed suicide after being persecuted by her husband and his family for bringing in a meager dowry. The authors' conversations with viewers revealed that through parasocial interaction (identification with the soap's characters), interactions with peers, and collective action, listeners were able to relate the lessons of the soap to their own lives. Effects were limited, however, and strong patriarchal conservatism ensured that women and minorities could articulate their freedoms only inasmuch as they did not threaten the structure they were bound to.

Grassroots communication and activism

Feminist scholars of development communication question how differences in gender, ethnicity, and class, to name a few social differentiations, inform access to media technologies. The work of these scholars provides another window to media reception and audience agency in non-Western countries. Based on the premise that women are active producers of meaning, and using models of participatory communication and process video (Riaño 1994), various researchers of development communication have documented how basic media technologies can facilitate activism at the grassroots level. For example, Kawaja (1994) describes three community-based collaborative projects: *Beneath the Mosaic* (about immigrant women), *Video Stores* (about immigrant and refugee teenagers), and *Through Our Eyes* (about teenage girls' stories of alcoholism in the family) where script development, production, and distribution of films all served to bring about awareness of the problems faced by women and teenagers. Similarly, Rodriguez documents participatory video production by women in Colombia. She writes, "the shift from being a televisual consumer to being a producer serves as a catalyst for multidimensional processes that range from the psychological to the political to the existential" (1994,

163

p. 153). Participatory video allowed the coverage of a wide variety of experiences and acknowledged the complex realities that comprised the experiences of these women. Ruiz (1994) discusses a 1984 project called *A Thousand and One Voices: Communication with Urban Aymara Women* conducted by the Gregoria Apaza Center for the Advancement of Women. The film itself provided a documentary frame through which women's experiences could be represented as stark social facts rather than anecdotal situations.

Further, critical development scholars focus on indigenous media forms to convey issues on women's health and progress. For example, Mlama (1994) identifies dance and drama in Tanzania where the artists resided with the community and identified major problems that could be addressed through an art form (dance, drama, storytelling, recitation, etc.). The community as a whole watched the show created by the artists, and participated by discussing the problems identified and solutions suggested. The author reports that women participated as well as men, and the project demonstrated that the concerns of the former (such as schoolgirl pregnancy, failing marriages, unfair division of labor, and so on) were vastly different than those of the latter. Dyer-Bennem (1994) describes a similar participatory ritual, quilt making by African-American women, as a space for political and personal representation. Muñoz (1994) demonstrates from her ethnography of women in Colombian *barrios* that they were avid consumers of *telenovelas* and adapted social messages in their daily lives. Likewise, Protz (1994) examined women's experiences in producing and manipulating media in the Caribbean, Latin America, and Asia. The author notes that the women, by viewing photographs that depicted experiences similar to those they were facing in their own lives, were able to articulate their own frustrations and express sorrow for their hardships. Mensah-Kutin (1994) describes the WEDNET initiative in Ghana to show that traditional interpersonal communication through dance, indigenous drama, songs, storytelling, and discussion were crucial for horizontal emphatic communication with women at the grassroots level because it acknowledged the reality of rural communities and allowed for the discussion of important issues such as women's socio-economic conditions. As these researchers have pointed out, such participatory projects are invariably marked by friction particularly in their early stages because in addition to the challenge to the women's self-identities, family members questioned women's new empowerment facilitated by the projects.

The examples from development communication indicate that change is possible, however limited, at the grassroots level. Mobilization to action facilitated by community leaders and supported by social workers, non-government organizations, and local governments themselves, has resulted in societal changes. Local women's banking schemes and cottage industries have been initiated through grassroots activism, and the media in its rudimentary forms such as puppetry, folk theatre, posters, and street plays, have played a significant role in creating awareness of the potential of such initiatives and sustaining membership and support for them (McMillin 2002a).

Hybrid programs and the texturing of audience choices

Various analyses of the immense popularity of hybrid programming point to the emergence of a strong audience voice as perhaps no other format has. Hybrid programming, as detailed in Chapter Five, allows great flexibility of formats, many of which are interactive and demand audience participation through call-in game and music shows, internet surveys, and online voting opportunities. Game shows and talk shows in particular receive high ratings. Viewer responses to a large extent, fashion the trajectory these shows take. For example, fieldwork at the studios of Udaya TV in Bangalore, India, that produced the hit show, *Adarsha Dampathigalu* (The Ideal Couple) revealed the complex correspondence between the producers of the show and their viewers, where the approximately 2,000 letters from viewers every week played a crucial role in the questions and issues that were addressed on the show. Although the producers ultimately decided the propriety of themes and even curtailed the freedom of their (particularly) female guests, viewers' opinions were carefully discussed each week to ensure that the show met the latter's needs and cemented their loyalty to the network (McMillin 2003b).

Capino's (2003) discussion of the Philippine movie talk show genre is a fascinating account of how a popular form of communication – gossip – spawned the political-showbiz talk show genre that featured typical non-elite, outcast guests such as soothsayers, transvestites, porn actors, and teen mothers. Incorporating women's talk, gay slang, and effeminate discourses, such talk shows as *See True, Scoop* and *Rumors, Facts and Humor,* represented the power of the popular, so much so that a porn star was eventually elected to a political position.

With media globalization, the greater variety of programming in many tri continent countries has also provided greater freedom in viewer choices. The availability of foreign and indigenous programming has allowed audiences to be more discerning in their tastes, selecting programs that resonate more closely with their own needs. In South Africa, Strelitz (2003) writes that radio stations are quite distinct in their music menus and clientele where urban English language stations such as 5 FM play a high percentage of English music while indigenous rural stations such as Ukhozi FM play local music for its listeners who are 99 percent black. How global music and programming are accommodated is significantly structured by class where "for rural black, relatively poor and ill-educated South Africans, local music has a strong resonance, while for white, urban, well educated and relatively affluent South Africans, the opposite is true" (p. 239). Strelitz's audience analysis on the Rhodes University Grahamstown campus, showed that lower-class black students, who felt quite isolated from their black and white middle-class peers, watched indigenous dramas such as *Isidingo* and *Generations* in the "Homeland," their university residence, where they could also freely speak Xhosa. They watched these programs to the exclusion of foreign programs because these dramas resonated with the tribal conflicts and faction fights they experienced in their neighborhoods. Although many of the students watched foreign programming at home and in their neighborhoods, they actively sought local dramas on the Rhodes campus, where they were confronted daily by flows of modernity in their English-speaking peers and Eurocentric curriculum. Therefore, the question of "foreign to whom?" (Morley 1994, p. 145) is an important one to interrogate since as Strelitz (2003) demonstrates, *Dallas* provided a more familiar context for an African rural East Cape student rather than local Xhosa language dramas because it was aligned more closely with his social context growing up on a white-owned South African farm.

In the same vein, Kraidy's 1992–2001 ethnographies in Lebanon, particularly in the Maronite community in the mountains, demonstrated how people shifted among Western, Arab, and Lebanese identities. In particular, Kraidy focused on responses to the locally Télé-Liban produced drama, *The Storm Blows Twice*. The drama, with its representation of social and cultural transitions, struck a chord with its viewers who were grappling with similar tensions between traditionalism and modernity. Incorporating music by a premier music family, the Rahbanis, the show used blended music (European classical, Arab classical, and Lebanese folk music) to symbolize its hybrid themes. Overall, Lebanese youth showed a marked preference for locally produced shows (Kraidy 2003). Similarly, Algan's (2003) ethnography of radio audiences in Sanliurfan in Turkey along the Syrian border revealed that Sanliurfans most enjoyed arabesque and political pop music; in particular, youth identified with love songs that depicted personal and economic turmoil and the problems of being a marginalized population. Herrera's (2001) study of teenagers in Iran showed that the lessons learned in the mosque resonated with popular and club music, revealing the state religion as a central manager of even spaces of youth expression and identity.

Multiethnic communities display a variety of responses to global and local television, and studies documenting such responses demonstrate the dynamics of reception. For example, Wilson's (2001) observations in 1996 of Chinese,

Malay, and Indian students watching the *Oprah* show in Penang, Malaysia, were that some viewers identified easily with the decidedly American context and themes while others distanced themselves from it. Differences were exacerbated along ethnic lines where Chinese and Indian groups more readily identified with overseas, diasporic communities. Viewers developed storied selves, adapting to or resisting characters on the screen. Overall, viewers could agree with general themes of sexism and adolescent growing pains, yet were critical of the public embarrassment of airing personal issues on national television. They simultaneously appreciated the struggles of stereotyped women and upheld local conventions of gender prescribed roles. They enjoyed the show for the spectacle of "Americans making fools of themselves every Sunday" (p. 95).

Analyses of multilingual audiences in India have shown the complex interplay among class, caste, religious, and gender identities and television viewing. An analysis of cable and television audiences from varying socio-economic and religious backgrounds in India revealed that conservative, middle-income, Hindu and Muslim viewers watched a high degree of religious programming. Muslim viewers preferred programs from the Middle East and welcomed this alternative to the Hindu-centric serials on the national network, Doordarshan. Lower-income Hindus, Muslims, and Christians enjoyed the hefty menu of films and film-based, call-in music programs and most reported that they had not been to the cinema ever since they had access to a television set. Upper-income viewers of all religions positioned themselves as global citizens, relating to American sitcoms, dramas, and game shows far better than the vernacular language programming on national and private networks (McMillin 2002b). To cite another example, a Muslim family in Monteiro and Jayasankar's (2004) study would not watch television during Ramadan, but watched news on the national network Doordarshan, presumably because this was educational and informative, not catering to prurient interests as perceived to be the case by entertainment television.

Ethnographies on youth and television reveal multiple subject positions among these young viewers. For example, Grahamstown youth in South Africa believed the immorality and disrespect to elders in such serials as *Sex and the City* and *Ally McBeal* were undesirable social values (Strelitz 2003); Brazilian youth seemed more conservative than their parents; *telenovela* audiences, particularly female viewers, although envious of the rich lifestyles of the characters, also idealized their own contexts stating that the rich were plagued by unhappiness and an insatiable quest for power and money (Tufte 2000); and youth in India situated MTV and Channel [V] styles as something they might try but that wouldn't change their core Indianness and family values (Monteiro and Jayasankar 2000).

Clearly, the wider variety of program choices and media products in the urban marketplace leads to a certain sense of empowerment in the viewer. She or he is in a position to flit among networks, programs, languages, formats, and genres, based on the need of the moment. Here as well, we need to be reminded that variety comes with a price, and many urban and rural homes in tri continent countries cannot afford cable connections, let alone a television set. Collective viewing practices no doubt encourage wider participation in the medium, yet, in particularly rural environments, familial chores for even young children such as harvesting fields and milking cows after the end of a full day of work, school, or domestic labor, leave very little time for television watching (McMillin, forthcoming). Participation and agency, then, are a privilege of urban and some semi-urban populations.

Local appropriations of the global

Local appropriations of the global provide another avenue for the study of consumer agency. Murphy (2003) discusses the consumption of Coca-Cola in San Miguel Canoa, Mexico, as an example of cultural appropriation. While the chilled and fizzy soft drink is represented on television and billboard advertising as a glamorous, sexy, global product, it is consumed at room temperature, warm, often poured into a plastic bag "to go," representing more the local connotation with warmth and life rather than cold death and sickness. Murphy's (1999) ethnography in Querétaro, Mexico, makes a strong case for the non-reception contexts that reveal mediated experiences. His discussions with the leader of a *conchero* dance group revealed how intricately Mexican television influenced the traditional dance in that costumes now reflected the skimpy sequin and feather attire of *telenovela* star Thalia depicted in music videos and advertisements.

Similarly, Hobart's (2002) report of his ethnographic observances of the Balinese play, *Gusti Syu Ratih* set up in Tengahpadang (a pseudonym) village by the famous Bhara Budaya troupe and serialized on Balinese television between March and April 1991, is a fascinating account of the dynamic relationships among producers, actors, and audiences, and the prevailing popularity of indigenous performance art. The televised version incorporated jokes about Javanese culture which, Hobart speculates, possibly resonated with Balinese audiences who knew they occupied peripheral status in Javanese-dominated Indonesia. The jokes and insertion of pop music were enjoyed by audiences, but their reception was starkly different from the live theater version that played to sold-out audiences, juxtaposed between temple ceremonies and gambling and food stalls. The antics of the actors were larger than life, ebbing and flowing based on audience response. For such actors, television was dead and Hobart states, "The dialogic world of Balinese theater enables us to see better how Europeans and Americans tend to fetishize texts and presume the naturalness of producer-centered models" (2002, p. 377).

The examples highlighting the democratic function of the internet, *telenovelas*, grassroots media projects, hybrid programming, and variety of media choices, give us an idea of the dynamics of local media production and reception. Truly, diversity of media products and economic opportunities in liberalized or quasi-liberalized countries opens up a wide array of alternatives to state-sponsored goods and services. The increased presence of women on the public television screen, as game, talk, and music show hosts and participants; as news anchors, and protagonists in dramas and sitcoms reconfigures, however slowly, the dynamics of gender relations, resulting in greater female assertiveness in private and public spheres.

We need to be cautioned here by two primary criticisms of audience research, however: romanticization of the audience, ignoring the ideological power of the media, and the lack of a political and critical edge. No doubt there is evidence of audiences truly changing the course of events as seen in shows that have been revamped, extended, or cancelled based on fan mail (most prominently in the case of soap operas), yet as Bird states, "this kind of transformation from consumer to citizen seems rare...Resistance means fighting for the right to have fun" (2003, p. 174). To restore resistance to its structural import, we are brought back to the question of agency.

Limited Agency and Subjectivity

The issue of subjectivation and limited agency is a topic of central concern for many critical, postcolonial scholars. As explained in Chapter Three, Latin American media studies and South Asian postcolonial studies carry the critical and political edge that characterized early British cultural studies. Ethnographies of media audiences are keenly attentive to how social and political structures influence media content and reception. Scholars from this critical tradition argue for a broader analysis of cultural practices and daily rituals rather than a myopic focus on audience and text (Tufte 2000). Recent Latin American and South Asian media ethnographers in particular, have injected a critical political dimension into audience studies to shift it to an exploration of *mediations* rather than text-context or active-passive audience studies. Although these scholars critique the Marxist structuralism of world systems theory scholars for its extremely depressing view of the possibilities of agency, Wallerstein's (1986) view of this concept is relevant here. He addresses the complexities of conceptualizing agency faced by any student of society and culture:

> The issue of agency is not a simple one. It plagues the social sciences. As those who denigrate generalizations in the name of ideographic uniqueness never tire of saying, any structural analysis implies that an individual, a group is caught in some web not of their making and out of their control... If one adds to this conundrum the fact that in virtually any social situation, the actors may be ranked in a hierarchy of power – some stronger, some weaker – it follows logically that the stronger "get their way" more frequently than the weaker... This social reality is transformed into a problem of the analyst when we discuss agency. Should the analyst describe history from the top down or the bottom up? The obvious answer is the analyst should do neither, since the two are inextricably linked. (ibid., p. 65)

The inextricable linkage of structure and culture is what Wallerstein is referring to, giving us some direction in how to pursue international audience studies. Rather than identify a space or medium around which to study mediated behaviors, the focus should be on the dialectical processes of negotiation that audiences and consumers undergo in making meanings from media, intimately informed by their structural and ideological positions in a society. Butler (1997) contends that it is possible to understand the dynamic between subject and agency by regarding the subject as constituted within structure, not as an autonomous, free individual. Resistance by such individuals then is part of the act of subjection, a reaffirmation of it. That is, "A power *exerted on* a subject, subjection is nevertheless a power *assumed by* the subject, an assumption that constitutes the instrument of that subject's becoming" (ibid., p. 11). As Ang (1996) pointedly remarks, romanticization of the consumer or audience revives the linear transmission model of communication, as if audiences' passivity or activity occurs in a vacuum. Connections to their social and historical contexts show easily how limited this agency really is, and how short-lived. In her conclusions regarding the representation of "woman as victim" in the Indian press (specifically relating to accounts of contemporary incidents of widow immolation), Sunder Rajan (1993) argues that these women cannot be considered either as mere pawns in power struggles or as individualistic heroic icons of historical tragedy. Female subjectivity should also be seen as female agency and this is where the analysis receives its political edge. The subject-status of the woman should be reconsidered so that there is a shift from concerns about the subject to concerns about how the subject is personified.

Several recent examples of audience reception anchored within structural contexts are available to illustrate these points. As stated earlier, two themes emerge in analyses that weave the interconnections between structure and culture. The first regards *media as central* to the activities of the viewing community. The role of the media is examined as they influence the viewer's various identity positions and daily rituals. Such an approach is most evident in the work of anthropologists examining, most significantly, the role of television in the construction of religious, gender, class, and caste identities (Abu-Lughod 2002, 2005; Mankekar 1999). The second focuses on a matrix *of mediations*, of which television may constitute a component, through which people make sense of their social realities. Such an approach recognizes that television in particular, may constitute a part of the daily activities of the individual and that its content is a constituent of a larger mix of cultural and social factors that provide interpretive tropes for its consumers. The following sections provide a few examples to illustrate these themes.

Centrality of media in anchoring consumers to structure

In addressing the socializing role of television, ethnographers from anthropology situate viewers as both pedagogical objects of state directives and as performative subjects in their own expressions of identity. The use of the ethnographic method, itself from a field that focuses on the cultural, that is, anthropology, may lead researchers to unduly privilege the centrality of media and the agency of its consumers.

A significant body of work is Mankekar's (2002) fieldwork among middle-class and lower-class audiences in New Delhi, India, which showed that the narratives of the Hindu religious epics, the *Ramayan* and *Mahabharat*, provided crucial lessons on desirable citizenship for its viewers. Incorporating traditions of folk dance and music and employing unsophisticated computer graphics, the televised epics were able to construct hierarchies of religion where non-Hindus were outside the narrative of nation, causing Hindu viewers to believe they were watching an unfolding affirmation of the sanctity of the Hindu state and its goodness for all people. Mankekar (2002) summarizes that Hindu nationalists since the early 1990s have used the *Ramayan's* description of Ram Rajya (or the kingdom of Lord Ram) as an ancient Hindu past that had to be revived from its submergence in Islamic invasions and British colonization to be reinstated as an essentially Indian past. By conflating sacred Hindu nation with the Indian nation, the supremacy of the Hindus and the priestly and royal classes was not questioned, but assumed. Apart from Hindu viewers, Sikh viewers also accepted the divine roles of the mythological gods and found divine philosophies relevant in their daily lives. Muslim viewers, on the other hand, were far more skeptical of some of the adages spouted on the epics and critiqued the immense suffering female counterparts to the male gods went through.

Another much-cited study is Abu-Lughod's (2002) fieldwork on television reception with domestic workers in Cairo and village women in Upper Egypt. It demonstrated the high degree of resonance between the television soap opera and the emotional response of its most ardent fans. Their lives of oppression, domestic abuse, and exploitation were represented in the dramas they watched, each flowing into the other to construct overall lived and mediated universes. An earlier study showed that Middle Eastern women's experiences were being expanded by new and alternative televisual discourses to the highly conservative social ones they were used to (see Abu-Lughod 1997). Despite the various problems of poverty, children's illnesses, household chores, and high cost of food staples, rural Egyptian women enjoyed television dramas that did not even remotely address their economic realities. Soaps and dramas centering on affluent families were watched avidly and the twists and turns of the plots were followed carefully. The vast disparity between lived and televised contexts did not preclude the women from drawing connections to their own lives (Abu-Lughod 2005). As shown in Mankekar's (1999) study of middle-class and lower middle-class female television viewers in Delhi, Egyptian audiences were able to select certain messages to appropriate for their own contexts.

The selection of messages to suit one's reality was observed in M. Yang's (2002) fieldwork in Shanghai (1991–93) among "informal discussion groups as well. Called 'film criticism among the masses' (*qunzhong yinping*)" (ibid., p. 201), the groups were created in state venues of employment such as factories and schools in the 1950s, to facilitate public participation. With her respondents, M. Yang discussed the transnationalizing role of the television drama series, *A Beijing Native in New York*. The series revolved around a Chinese couple in New York who ended up divorcing, the wife marrying the sweatshop owner she worked for, and the musician husband teaming up with a Taiwanese businesswoman to build his own sweatshop. Viewers' discussions of the show clustered around five themes: international exchange, loss of personal status and familial networks, the all-powerful pull of capitalism, the dichotomous roles of the demure, traditional Chinese wife and the hard-edged Taiwanese career woman (whom female viewers appreciated), and the declining power of the Chinese state to contain its citizens. Television then, provided a "third space" of expression (ibid., p. 204) for Chinese residents who could imagine transnational ventures, but could not act them out in real life. Through transnational media, Chinese subjectivity was severed from the state, leaving it free to connect with remote Chinese subjectivities. Transnational Chinese, while displacing state subjects, also became entangled in new configurations of power. Freedom from state subjectivity only meant that the subject entered other mechanisms of power.

M. Yang's attention to nuances of "liberation" is evident in the work of Mankekar and Abu-Lughod as well. All these studies highlight the resonance between lived and represented structures within which audiences are embedded and contribute significantly to our understanding of non-Western media audiences. Arguably, their use of the media text as the point of entry to analysis may give the reader the view that the media play a central role in the lives of the viewing community, a theoretical assumption of a majority of Western media studies. The examples highlighted in the next section draw out other mediating influences more directly.

Television as part of a matrix of mediations

The conservative patriarchal structures that envelope most societies of tri continent countries deploy various micro and macro strategies to ensure the limited freedoms of gender, religious, and ethnic minorities. The few examples that follow describe how, even in the context of fairly progressive televisual narratives, the inhabitants of these structures ensure its enduring strength and viability. Increasing economic opportunities for women in the public sphere are accompanied by melancholic reminders of the limits of their subjectivation. Butler describes specific ways through which to address subjectivity, where the analyst provides:

> (1) an account of the way regulatory power maintains subjects in subordination by producing and exploiting demand for continuity, visibility and place; (2) a recognition that the subject produced as continuous, visible, and located is nevertheless haunted by an inassimilable remainder, a melancholia that marks the limits of subjectivation; [and] (3) an account of the iterability of the subject that shows how agency may well consist in opposing and transforming the social terms by which it is spawned. (1997, p. 29)

What this means is that the analyst should recognize that subjects maintain their disempowered positions because the system that rewards them demands their continuity in those positions. The subject may exercise agency to subvert the constraining structure yet it is at the risk of jeopardizing the identity that is drawn from the position itself. An analysis of audiences' viewing pleasures should therefore be situated within its structural context. Recent media ethnographies take on this task in their identification of audiences not just as media consumers, but as laborers and subjects of interlocking familial and social communities.

The denigration of women's labor and the role of television in limiting their freedoms despite their economic productivity for the whole community, is demonstrated in La Pastina's (2003) ethnography among 30 viewers of *The Cattle King* (*O Rei do Gado*), a Brazilian *telenovela* that was broadcast from June 1996 to February 1997 in Macambria, rural Brazil. The *telenovela* addressed the theme of adultery. La Pastina comments that embroidery was the primary occupation of the viewing community, providing the main source of income. Men and women trivialized the activity, however, denouncing it as the only thing to do in the absence of other economic alternatives. The disparagement of women's labor and social value by the community was reflected in the response of teenagers to *The Cattle King*. Teens argued, based on their viewing of the *telenovela*, that violence against women was justified when women disrespected their male partners (Miranda-Ribiero 1997, cited in La Pastina 2003). Among adults, male viewers declared they would not reunite with their adulterous wives as did the protagonist on *The Cattle King*. Women and men were far more lenient about male than female adultery. Despite both husbands and wives holding full-time jobs, the husbands' work around the house was considered "help" while the women's was unquestioned and demanded. The significant income generated through embroidery had led to men being more open about their expanding domestic duties, but it was obvious this was not considered a generally desirable role. Overall, television watching itself was a relatively small part of leisure activities: it was listed as a primary leisure choice by only a quarter of the respondents and shared relatively equal status with chatting and strolling.

Similarly, the efficacy of local structures of patriarchy was all too obvious in Buarque de Almeida's (2003) ethnography among middle-class and working-class viewers of *The Cattle King* in Montes Claros, a small Brazilian city. Fieldwork showed that viewers perceived the theme of adultery to be experienced more pervasively in São Paolo or other big cities, not in "traditional" Montes Claros. While most women respondents had jobs and were not typical "submissive" females, they explained that they were most curtailed in terms of their sexuality. Female characters on the *telenovelas* enjoyed a certain degree of sexual freedom; in reality, however, sexual activity for women was tightly controlled within a marriage, and severe punishment followed those who indulged in extramarital affairs. Women occupied central positions in Montes Carlos society. Yet this strength was emotional, not physical or material. Women carried the double burden of having to be responsible for both economic and domestic productivity. As observed by La Pastina (2003), even though more men were participating in the care of the home, women were still expected to be primary care givers, with their external economic labor taken for granted.

These findings are reminiscent of Berik's (1996) documentation of the stark realities of women carpet weavers in Turkey, most employed by illegal workshops that had not registered with the Social Insurance Institute. Girls were labeled "factories" by men as soon as they were born, to signify their future economic productivity. Women labored in the workshops while the Koran was read to them by elderly women contracted by the owners so as to conflate religion with work and alleviate the tension among parents who did not want their daughters to work outside the home.

The issue of limited subjectivity is taken up in an analysis of the role of television advertisements among 57 female sweatshop workers in three ancillary assembly factories in Bangalore, India (McMillin 2003a). The women's positions as wives, mothers, and most predominantly, sisters and daughters (a majority were unmarried) made them particularly useful as laborers who worked long hours, had limited coffee and lunch breaks, and who worked under precarious conditions with little to no safety regulations. As stated by supervisors, these social positions had already primed the women to take orders and perform monotonous and complex labor with minimal complaint. Television watching was a small part of daily activities; television advertisements provided a venue for the semi-urban and rural immigrant workers to learn about the modern styles of the city, and gave them tips on what to wear and how to look. The women's income allowed them to indulge themselves to a certain extent, a novelty in the context of extremely constricted roles within their homes and congested neighborhoods. The women who were marginal members of an urban space, were hard working, yet were underpaid and socially devalued. Television advertisements and programs provided them lessons on how to behave and how to dress, as urban residents. Although subject to serious health risks and long work hours, they were also avid consumers of the foods, soaps, and shampoos advertised on television. They set aside a small portion of their income for such items rather than long-term savings schemes, opting for immediate gratification over long-term benefit. The exploitative structure was maintained through the sustenance of the impoverished positions of the workers in the system.

Likewise, in studies of media and modernity in Hong Kong and Taiwan, modernity for women meant greater appliances in the household, aiding in their role as nurturing caregivers (see Ng 1995, cited in M. Yang 1999). In all three Chinese contexts, television simultaneously strengthened and weakened the domestic sphere. It strengthened it by drawing the family together as the target audience for its advertisements for consumer goods and its family-centered program narratives. At the same time, it weakened the domestic sphere in the endless displays of conflicted family life in its soap operas, talk shows, and news segments. Consumer agency therefore, has to be situated within its larger structure for us to be able to realistically evaluate its enduring power, as explained in the next section.

Theorizing Audience Agency and Limited Subjectivity

The intriguing subject of limited agency is taken up by various scholars of psychoanalysis, most notably postcolonialists such as Fanon ([1961] 1965), deconstructionists such as Foucault (1977), and feminists such as Judith Butler (1997). Butler remarks that:

> Power has to be understood as *"forming"* the subject as well, providing the very condition of its existence and the trajectory of its desire, then power is not simply what we oppose but also, in a strong sense, what we depend on for our existence and what we harbor and preserve in the beings that we are. (ibid., p. 2)

The psychoanalysis of the subordination of the subject places this process as an integral part of his or her identity, as meticulously theorized by Fanon (1961). Althusser affirms that rites of interpellation reinforce the awareness of the social subject of her or his subject position. Specifically, how a person is addressed, with respect or with derision, for example, over time, becomes the very criterion through which the subject sees herself or himself. The subject therefore responds in concordance with the unequal power structure where she or he occupies a subordinate position with respect to the interpellator, without dissent. State apparatuses such as the media, particularly television, circulate ideologies and sustain them so that the myriad subjects within that ideology understand and act in accordance to the subordinate positions awarded to them. Everyday discourse, as much as centralized state apparatuses, becomes the terrain where power relations unravel or play out and crucially, where the subject becomes attached to such configurations for his or her existence (Foucault 1975). As Foucault famously writes:

> Power must be understood in the first instance as the multiplicity of force relations immanent in the sphere in which they operate and which constitute their own organization; as the process which, through ceaseless struggles and confrontations, transforms, strengthens, or reverses them; as the support which these force relations find in one another, thus forming a chain or system, or on

the contrary, the disjunctions and contradictions which isolate them from one another; and lastly, as the strategies in which they take effect, whose general design or institutional crystallization is embodied in the state apparatus, in the formulations of the law, in the various social hegemonies...Power is everywhere; not because it embraces everything, but because it comes from everywhere. (ibid., p. 92)

Television, as part of this everyday discourse, with other social structures, plays a vital role in the circulation and maintenance of power hierarchies, through the complicity of its subject-consumers (Thompson 1990). Butler (1997) brings us then to the paradox of subjectivation where the individual, to sustain her or his identity, comes to desire the terms of her or his own subordination. Paradoxically, even though the individual may recognize her or his own oppression, she or he may at the same time support the same system of power and subjugation. Therefore the individual depends on an exploitative structure for her or his existence and identity and in the course of her or his life, simultaneously denies and nurtures this dependency. Important questions that arise here are: is agency always inscribed within domination? How can the instrument of agency simultaneously be the effect of subordination? Are agency and subordination always in opposition to one another?

Ambivalence is an important concept in psychoanalysis to explain how agency is possible in subjection. Agency does not constitute a break in position or identity where it runs in opposition to the earlier subject position, but is constituted in the subject's ambivalent assumption of power where this power simultaneously retains and resists subordination. It would be naïve, therefore, to assume that agency is always in opposition to power. It is also naïve to think of agency as indicative of immediate revolutionary change. Media ethnography, in a context of globalization and privatized local environments, has to examine agency with a constant awareness and interrogation of how exactly it is constituted, what its parameters are, what changes it effects in the long term, and what implications it has for the long term.

The "active" audience therefore should not be considered another hermetically sealed category for analysis as the "passive" one was, but considered a part of a postmodern, globalizing environment where people consume television in unpredictable, contradictory, and dynamic ways. Besides, agency cannot be equated with freedom and has to be viewed as part of the process of capitalist progress (Appadurai, 1996). Tufte writes that two elements should be recognized in a *critical ethnography of mediations* (2000, p. 297). The first is a symbolic resistance that can lead to further struggle for social change. The second is the ability to resist, an ability which explains how oppressed people all over the world can survive the harsh socio-cultural, economic, and political realities they live in.

The strategies of accommodation and adaptation by the subject then become ground for rich empirical study. Ang (1996) recognizes the paralysis that may afflict researchers who want to conduct audience ethnography but do not want to be criticized for their failure to adequately situate the audience within its context and theoretically connect the micro to the macro. One way to circumvent this or work through it is a radical conceptualization of media as a whole, not in terms of their components (that is, radio, television, VCR, and so on). Drotner (2000a) suggests a focus on audience rather than medium. Ultimately, despite Drotner's criticism of Ang's approach to audience studies as an "ethnographic fundamentalism" (2000a, p. 170), ethnography allows the researcher to pay attention to protean micro phenomena as they unravel in rituals of media consumption. Such a scrutiny involves a "methodological situationalism" (Ang 1996, p. 70), which results in concrete, thick, descriptive, and historical narratives rather than nebulous, thin, prescriptive, and ahistorical ones.

Ultimately, the challenge of media ethnography as a pivotal method of international media research is to stay faithful to context, yet connect local contexts to global processes. The privileging of the ethnographic method is not to blandly elevate the micro against the macro. It is to draw attention to the specificities of difference and read such difference against a larger social, political, and economic machinery that seeks consensus.

With the frame of media globalization, Vickers suggests that diversity and difference should be understood in a "one world" context (2002, p. 74), not in the sense that all subaltern experiences can be somehow connected and conflated, but in the sense that they can be described in terms of their relational positioning in a world taken as a whole. The challenge of international media studies is the crisis of representation in ethnographic inquiry, the locational complexity of social and cultural phenomena, and the post-cultural imperialism theoretical malaise. Interdisciplinarity and multimethod analyses seem the best way to approach international media studies, more relevant when accomplished by a mission to uncover where power is located – in the community under study, the researcher, in the writing up of results, in the rewards of the academia, and so on. These challenges are addressed in the next two chapters.

Chapter Seven

Reconfiguring the Global in International Media Studies

To borrow from Tharu and Niranjana (1996), suddenly, the subaltern is everywhere. The hurricanes Katrina and Rita that ravaged the US Gulf Coast in September 2005 swept away surface representations of the happy, blues-singing, beignet-quaffing, New Orleans population and revealed the thick sewage of poverty, racism, and structural abandonment. Volumes of commentary followed in newspapers, talk radio, and news television, blasting President George W. Bush's cronyism in the utter paralysis of action that followed in the weeks after Hurricane Katrina hit. The waves of criticism and accusations of racism in the federal treatment of poor and predominantly black states are an example of the opening up of avenues of discourse about unequal relations in American society. While it is not within the scope of this book to address the various political and cultural reasons for the slow federal response, what is important to recognize is the abject poverty of populations within one of the richest nations in the world. So shocking was the exposure of poverty and its relationship with race that the topic of the "Invisible Poor" occupied popular news and entertainment programs such as CNN's *Anderson Cooper 360* and the *Oprah Winfrey Show*, respectively, in early October 2005. Surprise about the stark realities of the poor whether located in rich or poor countries may be attributed to their marginal treatment in just about every realm – media, politics, and academia, to name a few. It is true that crises prompt public outcry and critical exposure to deep, entrenched structural inequities. Yet, as Tharu and Niranjana caution, we have to be careful how we read these moments of rupture and awareness.

The international media scholar may study these moments as evidence of change, of emergent new voices and images on mainstream media that are counter-hegemonic and that question dominant culture. These voices are often co-opted into dominant discourse itself and marketed on its own terms so that often researchers and activists find themselves part of the mainstream they were reacting against. Too often we see in international media studies, as described in the case studies of agency in Chapter Six, an equation of momentary resistance and media critique of dominant systems, to true revolution and social change. The cumulative effects of such movements must be valued, no doubt; revolution is often slow moving but real. However, limiting analyses to just movements of resistance also inflates the effects of that resistance; we might just mirror in research, the trend in mainstream media to spotlight sensational events without situating them in their historical contexts. What is required is a radicalization of modern concepts of democracy and inclusion to address the stark inequalities that exist in contemporary societies across the globe.

Examining globalization processes from the ground, from the level of lived experiences, is a very different endeavor from examining it from the perspective of institutional power. More immediate and real are the cultural and social implications of global market strategies. As the numerous case studies in this book show, globalization does not simply mean the correspondence between transnational media giants and local consumers. The state, local structures of patriarchy, and grounded traditions and daily practices, all texture how the transnational is accommodated. Regional media giants confound the power and influence of global corporations and the impact of both compete with the impact of other localized institutions of labor and capital. Complex, then, is the environment of media globalization, and complex and intricate should be research designs that address the political, cultural, and social issues that emerge from this environment. While the challenges of conducting international media research is taken up in the next chapter, this chapter draws from the preceding chapters in its assessment of how attention to the local transforms the way we understand and study international media networks and their reception.

The postcolonial framework has allowed several levels of analysis in this book. First, we have examined the Eurocentric construction of the modern nation and have tracked its inadequacy in understanding developing nations of much of the tri continent that have not witnessed large-scale industrial revolution. The unquestioned assumptions of coherence, rationality, and linear progress of the modern nation-state have driven colonial expansion, legitimized postcolonial conflict, provided the ideological basis for the construction of newly independent nations, and set the framework for early research in international communication. The durability of modernity's premises can be attributed to the immense rewards it provides its keepers and protectors. The focus on consensus, not critical struggle, is a far more manageable state project. Mass media, particularly television, play into the safe hands of consensus, reflecting dominant hegemonic interests. Chapter Two has detailed how the attention to hegemonic and dominant interests creeps into international media studies as well. Research designs, particularly those of early development communication, identified, over and over, male respondents as key informants, regardless of the fact that women were primary contributors to households dependent on agrarian economies. No doubt some studies cited the cultural barriers that prevented generally white, male interviewers from speaking to non-white womenfolk in the household. However, no significant efforts were made to remedy this glaring gap in data and male responses were generalized to the whole community. Such a framework resonated with state and academic patriarchal ideologies, deeming it cumbersome, time-consuming, and expensive to addresses "statistically insignificant" populations.

Second, we have addressed the fact that in the formation of a political state, nationalism and patriotism are not the only key processes involved; anti-colonial nationalism and resistance that characterized the independence struggle of colonized countries are key in the birth of the political nation-state. Chapter Three, in detailing the central features of the postcolonial framework, clearly asserts that without drawing those who labor at the margins of a community – be it the global, national, or local sphere, we do nothing but advance the gross imbalance in representation in media studies. The first step is to recognize the diversity of audiences and communities, and then identify subaltern populations and their social, political, and cultural contexts. By working from the ground up, we can make realistic interpretations of the role of the media in creating change, perpetuating hierarchies, or effecting limited transformations – whatever the case may be – within the community under study. Important is the awareness to flows and interconnections, and to shifting identities, so as not to essentialize media behavior to a specific identity position such as gender, class, caste, ethnicity, religion, and so on. Also crucial in this approach is an evaluation of the consequences and implications of subaltern positions and interactions with media. The activist component of postcolonial theory continually seeks avenues for change and intervention, and the scrutiny of the subaltern consumer in relation to her or his social structure provides clues for how change may or may not be effected through the media.

Third, we have learned that the media, particularly centralized television systems, have played a crucial ideological role in sustaining the continuity among hegemonic systems – be they colonial or postcolonial. Chapter Four demonstrated the continuity of centrist constructions of nation and national citizenry. Television and radio played important roles in representing unification strategies of newly independent governments. The structures of political, legislative, and industry control of colonial administrations were very much in place for postcolonial governments to continue their ruling from the center, effecting technological progress and national development along linear, modernist trajectories. Within such trajectories, again, gender, ethnic, class, and religious minorities, to name a few populations, were special projects, budgeted for separately and treated with conservative condescension, not as integral parts of the nation building process. Protests and resistances from these sectors were treated in national policy and television representations as irrational eruptions, hindering the otherwise "logical" progress of the nationstate. International media research has continued to follow this trajectory in the postcolonial era, basing analyses of media representations, for the most part, within unique national contexts, and identifying anomalies to conventional viewing patterns as established by Western theorists, as moments of resistance and audience agency.

Fourth, the ideological role of the media plays a significant part in mapping out the developed and underdeveloped within each country and exacerbates gender, ethnic, religious, class, and caste hierarchies. In the context of transnational media flows, the format industry thrives on strategies of cloning, copying, and imitating, falling back on time-tested hierarchies listed above, to ensure maximum profitability. As explained in Chapter Five, the critical struggles and the incredible diversity of audiences seems finally to be recognized by privatized media networks. Various subaltern communities sidelined by centralized broadcasting systems now find programming in their own languages catering to their local contexts. Hybrid programming injects strong doses of the local, and, encasing this in global formats such as talk shows, game shows, call-in music programs and variety shows, caters to an audience hungry for entertainment that does not treat them as special wards of a socialist state. The postcolonial scholar may relax at this point, with the ample evidence of diverse programming catering to a wide variety of vernacular, religious, and cultural tastes. Yet there is much to be done here as well. As Chapter Five critically evaluates, hybrid programming is certainly an elitist machine, far from the apolitical fluff that some postmodernist media scholars would like to believe. Hierarchies are very much in construction, the local is caricatured, sexist representations of women continue, and local anchors and VJs tread carefully in their onstage personas – be it through their comments or wardrobe – so as not to transgress patriarchal norms of propriety. Do we then despair that the media in subsequent cycles of rule – be it colonialism or postcolonialism – do not do much more than reflect ideologies of power? Do we shut off all possibilities of change? This brings us to the crucial area of audience and researcher agency.

The fifth assertion made in this book is that geolinguistic and domestic media industries undercut the so-called imperialism of global media networks and programming specifically, but nevertheless support a hegemonic social and media hierarchy in their privileging of capitalism at the expense of minority populations. As described in Chapter Six, international audience research has uncovered various degrees of agency and subjectivity. Some authors, particularly those of North American cultural studies, have been quick to privilege differentiated viewing responses, particularly among women, as evidence of resistance against patriarchal norms. Gender-based audience analyses abound in this tradition with fewer that scrutinize the structural implications of viewers' class positions. Postcolonial scholars and media ethnographers also tend somewhat to a romanticizing of the cultural in part because their theoretical frameworks demand scrutiny of the micro, the ground. The postcolonial approach again reminds the international media scholar to situate audience agency within its larger structural context so that what we are analyzing and interpreting are negotiations with that structure, a subjective agency that provides for a sense of freedom, autonomy, and empowerment *even within* institutionalized limitations to such freedom, autonomy, and empowerment. Hybrid and vernacular programming can then be studied as part of this complex environment, providing myriad pressure valves where audiences can safely vent frustrations, vicariously enjoy new economic and social possibilities, and, to a certain extent, imitate such possibilities in their daily lives. The case studies in this chapter revealed that rich and fulfilled lives were led not through a blind inducing of consent but within an awareness of limited possibilities. For particularly societies in the tri continent that have formulated identities precisely within caste, class, gender, and religious hierarchies, such subject positionings are secure, change is disastrous, creating painful ruptures that take a long time to heal and that may result in devastating consequences and further sanctions on subaltern freedoms.

The focus on countries of Asia, Africa, and Latin America has kept with the goal of the postcolonial framework which is quite simply, to turn "the world upside down" (Young, 2003, p. 2). It has shifted the epistemological standpoint to that of the tri continent, taking care to point out differences in colonial and imperial experiences. In doing so, it has also revealed that while we may witness strong influences from formerly colonized countries in terms of media content and formats in Western contexts, overarching structures of capitalism still dominate the world. The postcolonial framework reminds us that a rigorous approach to international media studies demands attention to the complexities of nationalism, identity, and consumerism. Research methods have to address the fluidity of viewing contexts, respondent identities, overlapping structures of media and local traditions, and the variety of media accessed by the individual. The role of the media has to be discussed in relation to other structures such as family, religion, caste, class, gender, and so on, that influence how the individual responds to and is influenced by the media. Most importantly, such a framework continually urges us to question where power is located; that is, to question the notion of agency and place the respondent within his or her larger social context to evaluate, with integrity, the degree of this agency.

At the heart of the debate of the "right way to do research" in international media studies is the split between positivist mainstream social science approach and the critical cultural studies approach. Although the so-called convergence in audience research between the uses and gratifications theory of the former and the ethnographic approach of the latter has been heralded by some as the symbolic burying of the methodology hatchet (see Rosengren 1983, cited in Ang 1996), stark differences exist in their very different constructions of audience agency and the larger structural context. The "decades-long hegemony of positivism and the quantifying attitude in audience research," as Ang (1996, p. 44) puts it, has led to the need for justification of alternative qualitative, ethnomethodological, and symbolic interactionist methods, to name a few. The objectives of critical audience research echo that of anthropology in that they are concerned with accurate representation of the researched without objectifying them, with the understanding that any interpretation is necessarily partial, never complete, an artifact of the current historical, political, social, and cultural environments. The focus therefore, is not in uncovering the "truth," but in providing interpretations of a certain reality. Such an interpretive stance implicates the researcher as well as her or his political and moral subject position. Rather than obsessing over whether social science or humanities driven approaches can converge, research energy may be more efficiently directed to addressing comparative and global questions of media practices. As Boyd-Barrett (1997) notes, although the tension among the positivist, political economy, and cultural studies traditions of international communication endure, all are needed to continue the important conversation on the structure and effects of international media.

We now move on to identify areas in international media studies that need further research. Certainly the objective of the following section is not to push place-based or area-specific studies. As Chow advises:

> Instead of the traditional Euro-centric frameworks of the nation-state, national language, and geographical area that constitute area studies, cultural studies

offers modes of inquiry that require students to pay attention to the cultural politics of knowledge production. (1998, p. 8)

The aim therefore is to address ways in which research can be undertaken to draw out comparative studies on production and consumption in areas that have been sidelined.

The next section urges an expansion to geographical areas neglected in international research, to address the dimensions of globalization from these points of reference.

Expanding International Media Studies to Non-"Hot Spots"

The strong critical tradition of Latin American and South Asian media scholars has resulted in a fairly good representation of media studies from these areas. As indicated in the case studies described in earlier chapters, political economy and textual analyses in such countries as Mexico and Brazil in Latin America; Japan, Korea, China, Taiwan, Hong Kong, Singapore, Malaysia, and Indonesia, in East Asia; and India in South Asia, are quite substantial. These countries are also birthplaces of regional film and television giants, causing media scholars to gravitate towards them as sites of study. Obviously this leaves out a variety of countries particularly other South Asian countries such as Bangladesh, Sri Lanka, Burma, Nepal, and Pakistan, that share some of India's colonial experience and are implicated by the reach and presence of media industries in Hong Kong, Taiwan, Japan, and India. Similarly, apart from a few audience studies in Turkey, Lebanon, and Egypt, media analyses of other countries of the Middle East move little beyond broad accounts of their television and political environments.

Writing about dominant media theory in the Middle East, Khiabany (2003) provides a strong critique of particularly Hamid Mowlana's (1996) work which led the field, stating that the pitting of what the latter calls the Western "Information Society Paradigm" (identified by its focus on capitalism and modernity) and the "Islamic Community Paradigm" (identified by its attention to culture, ethics, and the Tablig principles of monotheism, responsibility, Islamic community, and piety) reiterates the Orientalist divide between modern and traditional. The movement for democratization in Iran struggles against a monolithic construction of culture and society and argues for an engagement with society as opposed to a consideration of just the state. Essentializing Muslim society to a homogenous unit does not account for the complexities

185

and realities of Iran, or any other "Islamic" country. The importance of under-standing a community in varied ways and of being aware of the diversity of experiences based on political, social, and cultural histories, Khiabany notes, cannot be overstated.

Although a wealth of development communication research exists from countries in Africa, critical political economy, textual, or audience analyses that address issues of media globalization are scarce. Media studies on Thailand cluster around issues of representation and production, with theoretical speculations on reception (Hamilton 2002; Berry et al. 1994; Jackson 1999). Similarly, most significant studies on Chinese media discuss the role of state feminism in facilitating a public sphere for women (M. Yang 1999); and how women from mainland China in films[1] (Lin Ho 1999) and on television (Erwin 1999) represent backwardness and traditionalism in narratives that place characters from Taiwan and Hong Kong as progressive, modern, and transnational (Shih 1999). Zaharom (2000) reports that most reception studies in Malaysia follow quantitative media effects methods of enquiry without a holistic under-standing or delineation of context. Ideological, textual analyses that address the cultural continuity of media representations (particularly in Middle Eastern and African countries) would go a long way toward filling some of the geo-graphical gaps of international media research.

Such studies should be undertaken using broad questions of media global-ization as their starting point, not just the locality of the research site. Pertinent research questions that could drive comparative analyses are: what are the cultural processes in the media that demand a consumer rather than informed citizen response? How do social differentiations play into the construction of the consuming persona? How does media globalization with its hybrid pro-gramming and ever increasing spaces for advertising, transform ideologies of gender, race, class, etc. into images of the good and obedient citizen? And, what avenues for solidarity and resistance exist among viewers and consumers across the world? These questions could provide a point of entry into an intri-cate research design that draws in specificity of cultural and geographic con-texts and at the same time speaks to broader comparative concerns of how globalization is accommodated at the local level.

Interrogating Notions of Fluidity of Audiences and Media

The trend toward hitting the "hot spots" in international media studies is a logical output of the structural support awarded in academia. And within these hot spots, certain types of populations are further privileged as objects of study. Dahlgren writes that the "market strategy" (1997, p. 59) of cultural studies equates the popular with youth culture, limiting the scope of empirical analysis and of political perspectives. Rather than engage in critiques of the social order, the trend is to celebrate the popular.

This bias is extended into international contexts where popular culture as it is accommodated in urban contexts is scrutinized resulting in more theory on global–local interconnections. The similarities between tri continent and Western urban contexts are highlighted as evidence of the pervasiveness of media globalization. Appadurai (1996) specifically calls for a connection between local imaginations and social realities. That is, he argues, people's imaginations have expanded to include all sorts of global possibilities by the sheer volume and diversity of media available to them in contemporary urban globalizing cosmopolitan contexts. Other than in areas sealed off from such imaginations such as Albania, North Korea, and Burma, where "state-sponsored realism" (ibid., p. 55) takes center stage, ordinary citizens across the world have access to a repertoire of images and products like never before. The ethnographer examining media effects needs to understand not just what this means to local consumers and their sense of identity – be it global or local, but how it relates to their social realities and how the latter in turn, curbs or fosters their imaginings.

Obviously rural and semi-urban populations in most parts of the world are not the ordinary citizens Appadurai has in mind because they, for the most part, reside outside of this discourse and global imaginings, and constitute a majority of tri continent populations. The material conditions that define the realities of, for example, a slum dweller in a tri continent city who, by occupation, may be a street sweeper, a vegetable vendor, or sweatshop laborer, are obviously very different from that of an urban resident of the same city, who may live in a high rise apartment and work as a teacher, doctor, or lawyer. The role of television in the lives of individuals in these disparate contexts will be very different, yet the bulk of international audience research privileges the experience of the latter simply because fieldwork is easier to conduct in such environments.

Also, several ethnographers have called for a reconceptualization of viewing communities and sites of study as fluid, open, and protean, rather than rooted in space and time (Couldry 2003; Murphy 2003). Marcus (1998) argues for an ethnography that "moves out from the single sites and local situations of conventional research designs to examine the circulation of cultural meanings, objects, and identities in diffuse time-space" (p. 79). This is a marked difference from the call for rootedness by such ethnographers as Morley and Silverstone (1990), who regard the local viewing context as crucial to get a sense of place and immersion in the immediate. This is no doubt an invaluable insight and useful for analyses of media flows such as the transnationalization of masculinity and the localization of effects of this masculinization and its friction or accommodation by local patriarchal structures (Rofel 1999). It facilitates theorization of the urban viewer, for whom media usage could be an important part of daily life. The privilege of fluidity becomes all the more difficult to assess when the community under study is a subaltern one, where the viewer's material conditions, that is, her or his economic base, and caste, class, gender, and religious identities, to name a few, specifically curtail fluidity and, instead, ensure fixity to those conditions. Viewer nomadism (see Fiske 1989) may not be an option.

Shifting the focus to the margins of a community also means engaging in difficult and inconvenient fieldwork; however, it results in the useful exercise of problematizing such notions of fluidity, flow, and flexibility of people and spaces that are heralded by some media ethnographers as characteristic of postmodern urban environments. Notions of fluidity and hybridity in the study of media and society in the context of transnationalism propel the researcher to think in terms of "freedom from the given" (Chow 2002, p. 131), so as to move away from the fixities of paradigms and places. Cheah (cited in Chow 2002, p. 131) calls this a "closet idealism" where for a majority of postcolonials, mobility signifying postnationalism is just not feasible.

For women in particular, childbearing responsibilities may keep them anchored to the home or places close to home while men may transit from rural to urban locales, from national to international spaces. Such realities are important to consider especially in globalization where local infrastructures crucial for women's sustenance may be subject to reconfigurations (Vickers and Dhruvarajan 2002). Research frameworks that address marginal populations, then, have to more urgently draw in the socio-economic conditions of the viewer, identify the role media play in such lives, and honestly portray the extent of fluidity and shifting identities enjoyed by the viewer, and the consequences, if any, of such fluidity.

To cite just one example, postcolonial feminist Suleri's (1996) account of the Pakistani Hadood Ordinances or criminal laws, particularly against *Zina* (adultery and fornication) is a stark example of the tragic rootedness of those at the lowest rung of the social ladder in a society. Under the Muslim *Hadd* (a legal interpretation that runs counter to the Anglo-Saxon legal system created by the British in pre-independent Pakistan), an adult male Muslim could have his hand amputated for stealing if witnessed by two adult males. If witnessed even by several women, he could be tried under the more lenient *Tazir* because women's testimony is not considered credible. In instances of *Zina*, women and children could be accused of fornication when in reality they were raped, as several cases have revealed. The US support of Zia-ul-Haq's military dictatorship in the 1980s and subsequent dictatorships further ensure that these drastic structures stay in place, subjugating the weakest of the weak (Suleri 1996). All the more apparent, then, is the fact that fluidity, hybridity, and nomadism are prerogatives of an elite few "comprador intelligentsia" (Appiah 1996, p. 62) or the "intelligentsia of global capitalism" (Dirlik 1996, p. 315).

As critical scholars, we must continually be rooted in the real and in the lived experiences of our respondents because,

> If we allow the identity formation of postcolonial discourse to construe itself only in terms of nationalism and parochialism, or of gender politics at its most narcissistically ahistorical, then let us assume that the media has won its battle, and the law of limit is upon us. (Suleri 1996, p. 346)

The role of the media in opening up some avenues of discourse in such restrictive societies becomes an important project in international media studies. It is true that the liberation of women in patriarchal societies often runs in opposition to the liberalization and democratization of the nation. Citizenship is generally a male privilege with various avenues for participation available (textured by class, caste, religious, and language differences, of course) in public life whereas women remain largely symbols of purity, honor, and domesticity (Kandiyoti 1994). Measures to contain their freedom, to limit their voices and participation increase with the expansion of opportunities available for them. The project of disciplining women, of giving them well-defined and limited modes of economic and social productivity continues and becomes more urgent as a national one.

The recommendation in extending international audience research to semi-urban and rural populations is a call for attention to structure not so much to anchor analyses to a specific, essentialized community, but to address such questions as: what role does media consumption play in the articulation of the viewer's subjective identity? How do media "work" with other social and cultural factors that inform the viewer's sense of self, place, and reality? What transformative possibilities emerge in the individual's relationship with the media? What narratives on local, national, and global television (depending on the preference of the viewer) lead to the individual's sense of agency, autonomy, and empowerment? How can this be critiqued within the economic, social, and cultural contexts where the viewer is situated? Such questions will necessarily draw in an examination of the community and place, define the media as part of a larger matrix of activities, and address the larger dynamics and flow among these components.

Moving Away from the Nation as a Unit of Analysis

As explained in earlier chapters, globalization theory hinges on the presumption that the nation-state as a central governing agency is on its way out. Boyd-Barrett (1997) argues that the nation-state as a unit of analysis must persist because technological innovations and global distribution networks cannot obliterate its importance and presence. Indeed, we need to keep in mind that for subaltern populations, the nation-state is a crucial entity to ensure basic human rights, when it works as it is supposed to. However, instead of rooting analyses in the macro, in the state, and running the risk of recreating the modernist biases of state-based analysis, what the scholar of international media needs to focus on is how the humanist subject is predicated upon by structures of citizenship, nationhood, consumerism, and other social differentiations such as gender, ethnicity, class, caste, religion, and so on (see Tharu and Niranjana 1996), and the role the media play in legitimizing these structures. Even postcolonial and feminist research that addresses the dynamics of media, globalization, and women, reflects the Eurocentric nation-state bias where experiences of women in a community within the nation are addressed and then generalized as dominant issues of women across the nation (Nelson and Chowdhury 1994).

Particularly in an age of transnational media flows, Bhabha (1994) contends that the unifying discourses of nation, people, and tradition, must be rejected by the postcolonial perspective. Such a perspective should force an engagement with complex political and cultural boundaries that straddle opposed political spheres. The opposed political spheres in the case of media globalization refer to the conflict between the unified, utopian, pristine, traditional past and the complex, technology and speed-defined modern present. A critical postcolonial eye scrutinizes the value and purpose of both spheres as ideological constructions and the strategies of recruitment each awards the consuming subject to transform her or him into a loyal and abiding member. Such a view requires a reading of viewer and consumer choices against the grain of both traditionalism and modernity so that the rights and status awarded to the consumer citizen as subjects constituted within a national frame or transnational one, are continually interrogated for the agency they truly allow.

Moving Away from the Centrality of Media within Society

Theorization of the centrality of media in contemporary society (Thompson 1990) is a distinct product of North American and British mass communication theory that draws from Habermas's public sphere to posit that the mass media, particularly television, provide a pervasive space for popular and democratic expression. In an era of media globalization, Wilkin (2001) postulates that the world order may be divided into four distinct levels: local, national, regional, and global. Communication technology in a modern world facilitates public spheres at all levels where the public is made aware of the important issues of the day through the media, and can discuss them. No doubt the injection of the concept of ideology from cultural studies scholars and the critical Marxist view of feminist and postcolonial scholars complicates this democratizing conceptualization. Yet the bias in international media research continues where television is seen as a medium around which discourse is produced and organized. The internet is considered a generally equalizing playing field for participants of various social, economic, ethnic, gender, and religious backgrounds. The situatedness of the scholar in the field of international communication translates into the need to focus on the media and makes the latter *hypervisible*. It gives them a hyperfunction, even in communities where they are luxuries or where they are consumed for only a small portion of a day that has already been pawned to other immediate struggles in the work and home.

Dahlgren (1997) insightfully comments that the political leanings of Left academics, who do not want to be accused of elitism because of the stark social differences between their own lived realities and that of the subaltern populations they are interested in, cause many to slip into the study of popular culture, a base they can readily share with fellow fans. This leads to a narrowing of the field to numerous analyses of fandom as identified by Bird (2003), and more problematically, a conflation of researcher with respondent, as if both occupy socially and politically equal seats as fans of the same media text. Also, the conveniences of textual analysis lead to a disproportionately large number of such studies.

As described in Chapter Six, for example, Hobart's (2002) report of his ethnographic observances of the Balinese play, *Gusti Syu Ratih* set up in Tengahpadang by the Bhara Budaya troupe and serialized on Balinese television indicated that live theatre was a far more emotive experience for the people than was its televised version. Fieldwork in India among various age, socio-economic, caste, religious, and gender populations has shown that media usage constitutes a generally minor role in the complex lives of individuals grappling with basic logistics of finding transport to school or work, meeting the demands of exams, work deadlines, home chores, and making time for family and friends (McMillin 2002b, 2003a, 2005, 2006). A collaborative project revolving around teens and television in Germany, the United States, India, and South Africa showed clearly that for busy teens even in urban, industrialized global cities such as Munich, New York, Bangalore, and Johannesburg, television watching was a part of a highly complex system of social activities. Teens were absorbed in a variety of spheres such as school, family, peers, church, and so on, and television watching and other media usage were activities they enjoyed at the end of a full and tiring day. No doubt what they did watch played a role in how they perceived themselves and the opportunities available to them, yet such perceptions were also influenced by the other social interventions in their lives (McMillin forthcoming).

These brief notes from the field are not provided to override all the quantitative and qualitative studies that have addressed how a particular show or medium provided a space for identity and vicarious pleasure in its user. However, they underscore the importance of *putting the media in their place* in the social lives of their consumers. Crucial factors such as religion, family traditions, and rituals informed by ethnic roots and class and caste identities texture how the media are accommodated (see Dilley 2004, and Van Dijk 2004, for a treatment of the internationalization of religions).

Another drawback in media studies is that they zero in on the role of television, as is the case in this book. Yet television is still beyond the reach of much of the tri continent population. International media studies must be expanded to include popular culture such as street theatre, puppetry, local rallies, shadow plays, even karaoke bars, video parlors, and cassette tapes (M. Yang 1999), which are, no doubt, cumbersome fields of ethnographic exploration. The intersection of popular culture with mass media in the daily lives of audiences, and ethnographies of how this intersection informs their sense of self and culture will provide a rich understanding of how global interacts with local.

What is required then are studies that are more contextually rich and that do not hesitate to acknowledge that media use is embedded within highly varied and interrelated rituals. This could induce horror and dismay in some media scholars, but the truth is that by seeking those international communities that watch a high degree of television even when they constitute very small minorities of larger populations, we provide a skewed picture of the role and function of media in society, a role that is invariably inflated, reflecting the bias of the researcher and academic field rather than the reality of the ground.

Extending Analyses beyond a Critique of Cultural Imperialism

Much of the theory and empirical research in international media studies discusses issues of difference and cultural identity. Within the broad framework of cultural imperialism, substantial time and energy are poured into assessing the durability of this theory. No doubt, as explained in Chapters Two and Three, the legacy of world systems theory and the modernist paradigm of development communication has led to simplistic assumptions of the coherence of nations and the vulnerability of developing states to Western media and cultural imperialism. The continued focus on proving or disproving that cultural imperialism exists detracts attention and energy from careful structural analyses that address the implications of media representations and consumption rituals. What is missing is a close reading of what this cultural difference actually signifies. Because dominant cultural imperialism theory has labeled tri continent audiences as generally passive, the trend now is to prove they are active. Both are labels that limit our understanding of exactly how this "against the grain reading of active audiences" is produced, and what this agency really means in the long term.

Postcolonial theory is useful here in taking us deeper into an analysis of the cultural difference that is at the heart of contrary viewer response. Bhabha (1994) seeks a shift in the analysis of culture as an epistemological object (where we may superficially essentialize audience response to a particular nationality, ethnicity, or religion, for example) to an enunciatory site (where the audience response is taken as an active articulation of her or his location in a contemporary, complex present and simultaneously in a historical past). Bhabha states that the theoretical focus on the present assumes that cultural identity is articulated in liminal spaces. The contingent and liminal then, "become the times and the spaces for the historical representation of the subjects of cultural difference in a postcolonial criticism" (ibid., p. 179).

What this means is that we should lay open the enunciations of the viewer or the subject and allow her or his interpretations to stand as the truth of the moment, not interpellate them according to academic traditions in our overriding need for theoretical and empirical closure. Such interpellation only exacerbates power differentials between researcher and researched in the field, a topic taken up in the next chapter. However, Lal (1996) cautions that simply laying bare respondents' voices can also recreate the hierarchy of researcher over researched where the former stands disengaged from the latter. The specific positioning of the researcher in terms of her or his ethnicity, class, and gender status within the community under study has to be explained, to demonstrate that both researcher and researched are implicated in the fieldwork experience. Ultimately, the researcher must do her or his homework in understanding the power relations of the community under study and then place herself or himself within those relations as well. Differentiations of class, race, gender, and geography will always mark the fieldwork experience and the objective is not necessarily to overcome these, but to situate and explain them (B. F. Williams 1996).

Historicizing International Media Studies

Another aspect in which international media studies falls short is its historicizing of contemporary phenomena. As Downing observes, certain concepts have enjoyed the privilege of academic scrutiny over the decades: "[I]deology and the state were big in the 1970s, hegemony and discourse in the 1980s, the information society and public sphere in the 1990s, identity and globalization and civil society in the 2000s" (2003, p. 496). The "concept fetishism," as Downing calls it, has led to endless theorizing of their various uses and misuses. Empirical research examining how these concepts have played out address specific moments in time in which media rituals are based. Few studies actually delve beyond the present, to draw in the residual function of colonial pasts or of religious and traditional structures, in informing how viewers interpret and make use of media technologies and texts. Effects of the media, particularly in international contexts, are studied for how they either further entrench local hierarchies or cause consumers to emulate the West. Short shrift is given to the capitalistic gentrifying function of the media, again, primarily television, in preparing and sustaining an urban and semi-urban workforce for an urban marketplace.

Interconnections between states and markets and interdependence among these across the world, be they from so-called core, semi-peripheral or peripheral areas, demand larger and larger numbers of English-speaking skilled and semi-skilled workers. Basic competencies are required to understand the work environment in terms of employee–worker interactions, appropriate modes of dress, cultural and social expectations in terms of interactions with colleagues, and understanding and acceptance of the workload. Soaps and dramas provide story lines that address these cultural competencies. Game shows, reality shows, and talk shows glorify competition and individual success. Consumption of such programming cannot then be merely assessed in terms of it effecting more consumerism, but has to evaluated in the larger trajectory it urges

194

the viewer along so that the latter is understood as part of a neocolonial capitalist machinery, making meaning of her or his existence within a delegated position that awards a limited degree of freedom and pleasure. As Aidoo (1991, p. 152) suggests, we must recognize the contemporaneousness of colonialism.

Engaging in Comparative Research

The whole premise of this book has been to move away from the Anglo American domination of research in international communication and turn the spotlight on tri continent countries. A second important mission has been to address comparative issues and draw in examples from these geographical areas to identify interconnected phenomenon that advance our understanding of the dynamics of interplay among transnational media and how they are accommodated by a variety of populations. Further research is sorely needed that addresses comparative issues of media globalization. Despite the "international" nomenclature of the field, most studies are very clearly national. As stated in the Introduction to this book, even anthologies consist of nation-based chapters with an essay on their interconnections by the editors at the beginning of the book. A way to tear down chapter and nation insulation is to approach edited books differently: to radically change from a mere solicitation of chapters from authors and a collation, commentary, and summarizing by editors to a *collaborative enterprise* where chapter authors read, critique and comment on each other's work. Each chapter can and should address how it relates to, differs from, or flows into the others. The student of international communication will then be able to understand the interdependencies of media phenomena and national systems. Class assignments can be designed to address just this comparative need instead of the conventional nation-based analyses students are encouraged to undertake, time after time.

Relating Research to Activism

Besides focusing on tri continent countries and comparative research, a goal of this book as stated in the Preface and Introduction is, using the postcolonial framework, to seek avenues for activism. The large gap between academic media research and industry market based research is huge. Media effects are the topic of a variety of television news and talk shows, yet rarely are academic researchers called in to be part of the discourse. The industry finds its own experts, usually authors of best-selling books and other media watchers paid by the industry itself. The reason is obvious: academics rarely engage in the realm of social change and for the most part, write and research in isolation from the policy-making world.

The call to link research to activism is far from innovative. Feminist ethnographers, most notably Mies (1983), urged action research, that is, an engagement with the struggles of the community under study, rather than adopt the objective distancing from data and community that has characterized traditional, mainstream research. Globalization makes it all the more pressing for the international media scholar to address social and economic inequity rather than just audience viewing pleasure. The hectic pace of urbanization, increasing demand for a subservient and non-resistant labor force brings to the fore issues of human rights. Downing (2003) points to the need to address this dimension of international media research and expose violations where they need to be exposed. What is required is a radical politicization of the media viewing environment so that empirical explorations are accompanied by a critique of the structural inequities that undergird the viewing experience under study. Scholars themselves should actively seek venues for engagement – perhaps participate or lead media literacy workshops, and work with non-governmental, social, or media activist organizations – to effect change.

The dominant paradigm that regards the nation as a coherent, fixed entity also seals off possibilities of communication for change. To explain, Wilkin (2001) notes that "the dominant model of world order in international relations often follows a Hobbesian account of state–society relations in which the very possibility of society rests upon the necessity of establishing the overriding power of state institutions" (ibid., p. 1). In his study of how human security is conceptualized and prioritized in international relations, Wilkin addresses the limitations of a social scientific understanding of "nation" where such an entity is regarded as a simple, ahistoric and deterministic closed system, reducible to its political definition. Such a view allows social scientists to predict the direction a nation will go in its international relations but does not adequately explain or evaluate why. Through its political, economic, military, and ideological powers, nations are considered to have the ability to discipline and punish its citizens – yet this view does not allow for an explanation of other uses of power – to build community or to foster culture and learning, primarily because it is based on a Hobbesian premise that humans' egoism which is rational and self-interested, is primarily engaged in the pursuit of power for self-preservation. For example, if we were to continue to use the dominant model of communication that focuses on the fixity of nation, we might miss the potential of transnational media connections that facilitate allegiances of empowerment such as the Women's Awakening Foundation in Taiwan and its alliance with women activists in Hong Kong, mainland China, and the United States. We might neglect to examine the possibilities of the emergence of a transnational Chinese women's public sphere in the flows of Chinese Fifth Generation films, Hong Kong New Wave, and popular action films to the United States (M. Yang 1999).

In attempting to uncover ways in which power may be used to build community and create spaces for subaltern empowerment, the postcolonial media scholar may face tremendous challenges. Trained perhaps in broadcast production, or at the very least, in constructing written messages, the media activist may be confronted in the field by vast illiterate populations with deeply entrenched local structures of power that may be supported, even partially, by the oppressed themselves. Spivak (1987) addresses this very dilemma where the researcher stands at a great distance in terms of privilege, from the communities she or he is trying to "help." The first step, she cautions, is to learn to stop *feeling* privileged. The sensitivity to consequences and change should be accompanied by a tremendous humility on the part of the postcolonial researcher where audiences' agency should be recognized and valued as real, not just as products of false consciousness. As M. Wolf (1996, p. 219) remarks, the respondents in such fieldwork may not regard their oppressors as components of a patriarchal society or global economy, but they are not helpless victims either. They have developed ingenious functional strategies to cope with the sexism in their societies and such strategies have to be recognized by the outsider. Quick conclusions of passivity of women will lead to a reification of this population as mere pawns in a misogynist structure that manipulates them. The postcolonial researcher may also be overzealous in her or his mission for activism and may inadvertently imitate the very elitist determination for change and development defined on the researchers' terms, of the power structure she or he is trying to subvert.

Several areas of activist research have been suggested by postcolonial scholars. For example, female sweatshop workers in what Mohanty calls the "electronics global assembly line" (2003, p. 152) including South Korea, Hong Kong, China, Taiwan, Thailand, Malaysia, Japan, India, Pakistan, the Philippines, the United States, Scotland, and Italy, are prime targets within a patriarchal system whose efficiency thrives on unquestioned assumptions of femininity and sexual identity. The satellite or ancillary factory is a crucial source of income for semi-urban young women in particularly Asian countries, yet this venue as a site for research on the influential and interactive roles of the media, family, and social norms is quite neglected in favor of large corporate sites, a reflection of a Western bias that follows dominant patterns of industrialization (Hsiung 1996).

The few case studies of factory and menial labor in Latin America and Middle East and South Asia have shown that women's work was devalued despite their role as primary breadwinners in the household. At another level of internationalized labor, call centers in particularly China and India are drawn into the discourse of globalization as golden opportunities for tri continent skilled and semi-skilled workers (McMillin 2006). The media, specifically television, performs an important gentrifying role, in cultivating obedient workers for the urban workplace. The call center worker's complicity with an ideology that the "white customer" is always right in a global capitalist economy is an example of the power of ideology to induce consent to starkly unequal labor relations. Television and popular culture, with their caricatures of local accents, idioms, and traditions, "innocuously" disseminate a variety of models of urban desirability, informing workers that the very labor that firmly entrenches them in a racialized, genderized, caste system, is also what liberates them from it, awarding them consuming agency in a market seemingly brimming with choices. Labor and class relations, and the role of the media, particularly cinema and television, in sustaining gendered relations or reconfiguring them in such factory units, constitute intriguing areas for comparative study. As Mohanty posits:

> It is especially on the bodies and lives of women and girls from the Third World/South – the Two Thirds World – that global capitalism writes its scripts, and it is by paying attention to and theorizing the experiences of these communities of women and girls that we demystify capitalism as a system of debilitating sexism and racism and envision anticapitalist resistance. This analysis of the effects of globalization needs to centralize the experiences and struggles of these particular communities of women and girls. (2003, p. 235)

Young (2003) identifies further areas for postcolonial activism: resisting all forms of human and environmental exploitation, interrogating conditions that have been created solely for corporate capitalism, rejecting exploitation accruing from comparative poverty such as sex trade and appropriation of natural resources, and championing basic human rights in terms of the right to security, health, food, education and so on, particularly for gender, ethnic, and class minorities. He summarizes that postcolonialism translates into a transformational politics committed to the eradication of inequality, be it linked to class, ethnicity, or gender differentials that pervade every level of social and cultural life.

The embeddedness of capitalist processes in every part of the world makes it hard to conceptualize spaces through which feminist resistance can emerge since the racialized ideologies of constructs such as masculinity, femininity, and sexuality are integral to the formation of the legitimate consumer, employer, and worker. At the same time, women's bodies and labor provide the terrains upon which global dreams and desires are enacted and ideologies of prosperity and the good life are personified. Mohanty (2003) draws from feminist, political theorist Anna G. Jonasdottir to suggest that first, the activist should recognize that tri continent women have common objective interests as workers where they make the choice to enter such labor, and, second, the workers themselves experience contradictions between their consciousness of exploitation and their desire to continue in such a line of work, making them reluctant to organize for change. Trade unions may be sexist and women's unions (for example, in Korea, China, Sri Lanka, Italy, Malaysia, the Philippines, and India) and church groups (in the United States) provide more meaningful sites for struggle. Significant organizations are the Working Women's Forum (WWF) and the Self-Employed Women's Association (SEWA) in India where the focus is on cooperation, sharing, self-reliance, and education, all within the rubric of collective struggle for change. Transforming the material conditions of daily life first requires a transformation of the consciousness that is anchored to that material life. The analysis of the location of tri continent women in international configurations of labor must be historically situated, drawing in the roots of colonialism and the enduring structures of race, class, capitalism, gender, patriarchy, and sexuality. As subjects of theory, they must be studied with reference to the histories that bind and segregate subject and researcher. Extending Mohanty's suggestions for the feminist to the critical scholar of international media studies, the task at hand is to uncover the workings of power, "to read up the ladder of privilege" (p. 231), so that the scholar can engage from within to transform the ways in which power is used and abused.

The call for resistance against capitalism seems radical especially when ethnographers have shown that consumption allows identity formation (Miller 1994) and that even foreign programming can lead to new forms of assertion and viewer desire. The reason why postcolonial critics urge a more radical stance against capitalism is that in tri continent countries, particularly among developing ones, capitalism is accommodated very differently from how it is in developed, so-called First World countries. In the latter, Abu Lughod (2005) observes that commodities of the middle class such as refrigerators, microwaves, and television sets are available to even those from the lowest rung, barring the homeless and the destitute. In countries such as Egypt, India, and

Indonesia, the distinctions are more pronounced where the poor, the servant class, and even the middle class are more or less excluded from the consumer goods that are utilized by the minority, wealthy elite in these countries.

Also in these societies, while the variety of luxury goods increases on the marketplace and their costs diminish, state support continues to decline, or at best, lumbers along haphazardly. Without a structure that consistently mandates *and enforces* basic standards in health, safety, and wages, to name just a few areas, capitalist expansion cannot be heralded as a glorious era of free choice, of an age where finally the unique needs of the consumer are recognized and met. Both state and private sector are implicated in this situation since both benefit from the undercutting of expensive welfare support and increased market options.

An avenue for activism that is cited over and over is the internet. No doubt critical scholars have questioned its accessibility and freedom for minority groups. They point out that a majority of tri continent populations do not have the luxury of access or the training necessary to use this medium as an effective form of resistance and activism. Yet for the millions around the world that do, the internet has to be revisited for its potential for counter-hegemony. L. Bennett (2003), in his examination of new media technologies which he lists as, "mobile phones, the Internet, streaming technologies, wireless networks, and the high-quality publishing and information-sharing capacities of the World Wide Web" (p. 19), states that all these technologies in some way employ the internet for their function. Bennett cites the websites of Greenpeace and Adbusters and their campaign against Coca-Cola depicting, instead of the mother polar bear enjoying the fizzy drink on an ice floe, a mother bear and her cubs huddling against the environmental effects of Coca-Cola's production process. On a more action-oriented level, activist groups such as those demonstrating at the 1999 WTO summit in Seattle, WA, were able to communicate quickly and mobilize forces through the internet (Indymedia, for example). Other venues where protestors were mobilized to action through the internet are Seoul, London, Paris, Prague, Brisbane, Tel Aviv, New Delhi, Manila, and Mexico City. The convergence of media systems and the sophistication of the lay user lead to a myriad alternate voices to the dominant "truth" projected by mainstream networks. It is true that such alternative voices can express themselves in industrialized contexts. In much of the tri continent, the states' imprint on mainstream media is all too evident, however.

Critical development scholars have also outlined various ways to study and engage in activism. Rodriguez's (2003) study of citizens' media in spreading the messages of the Latin American Catholic Church explicates how such media implement change when connected to progressive social movements.

Rather than obsess over how much access to the media people in a community have, Rodriguez notes that what should be asked is how the media can facilitate the communicative strategies and rituals the community *already* has in place and transmit these beyond local parameters.

Ultimately, studies of audience pleasure, resistance, and subjectivity have to include a political assessment of the limits of consumption rituals. In producing such grounded studies, we encourage students to think of media production and consumption in terms of their implications in various parts of the world; we urge them to question how conservative patriarchal structures are reproduced in the media, at home, and at work; we guide them to examine "freedom discourses" of the marketplace and evaluate critically exactly what the consumer has the right to choose from. In shifting epistemological standpoints, the marginal speaks and is heard, not just spoken for (Spivak, 1988a).

This brings us to the central point of the concluding chapter: the political and social role of the international media researcher. The final chapter addresses the academic constraints that may curtail the depth and extent of analyses on international media institutions and audiences. It also points to the challenges of an activist postcolonial approach where questions of researcher imperialism and outsiderness may paralyse any effort for structural change even before it begins.

Chapter Eight

The Politics of International Media Research

For Karen Hughes, President George W. Bush's Under-Secretary of State for Public Diplomacy, her six-day trip to Cairo, Jeddah, Ankara, and Istanbul during the last week of September 2005, was a bewildering lesson in anti-American sentiment. Aimed at discussing ways to empower women in these Islamic societies and enhancing the image of the United States abroad through photo opportunities and carefully orchestrated media appearances, the trip quickly turned into a series of forums where native women activists protested the US-led war in Iraq as further denigrating the rights of women and children in the Arab world (Kessler 2005). Hughes' surprise at the hostility to her message that the United States was committed to warring for peace and that as a "working mom," she shared their many concerns, is a vivid reminder that the centuries-old processes of capitalist expansion and of colonial condescension are depressingly robust and will endure for centuries to come. Her amazement at forum after forum that, borrowing from Spivak (1988a) and putting it crudely, brown women do not necessarily want to be saved from brown men, least of all by white men and women, is an indication of the incredible pay-off from such a vast ideological divide. Assumptions of brown worlds needing rescue and reform legitimize devastating violence and political policies that spearhead ruthless capitalist expansion. The costs are obvious particularly to subaltern populations who, over the centuries, have faced colonizing forces from radicals within their own nations and imperialists outside. The dominant paradigm of development and modernization is very much alive in national and foreign policies, and minority populations within nations and on foreign soil continue to be spoken for and acted on.

All the more reason why critical international media scholars need to think of themselves as beyond writing machines within a privileged academic structure where the only tangible rewards are tenure and promotion. Theoretical engagement and critical discussions of complex concepts and heated debates on the cultural and social implications of power differentials are useful exercises, but admittedly ironic when conducted primarily in air-conditioned, five star hotels in global cities around the world. The following sections address the academic environment that places high rewards on publishing achievements and limited to no rewards on efforts at social change. Such an environment makes it understandably difficult for the academic scholar, particularly the junior, untenured one, to think and act outside of the daily juggling of teaching, publishing, and university service. These sections identify a few areas for reflection in international media research and writing.

The Eurocentric and political economy biases of the field were discussed in detail in the first two chapters of the book. From an account of these biases, it is obvious that international media studies are skewed toward a representation of media institutions and consumption practices in ex-colonial centers. Also, the political economy of media around the world has received far more attention than its accommodation by audiences.

The preceding chapter has outlined areas in international media research that require further investigation, specifically, countries of the tri continent, and the consuming rituals of subaltern communities within these countries. Such a recommendation to study media phenomenon from the ground up has been accompanied by the strong caution that comparative questions need to drive analyses, not specific communities, place, or media texts. The goal should be not just to overturn positivist assumptions of media and society but to interrogate even non-positivist research that may reproduce the value-free objectivity of Eurocentric dominant paradigms of research. Care should be taken in international media studies not to replicate the biases of North American "area studies" that were undertaken "in the name of scientific objectivity, knowledge acquisition, cross cultural understanding, and other such humanistic ideals which continue to belie the racist underpinnings of the establishment itself" (Chow 1998, p. 6).

This chapter addresses the challenges to the recommendations above through a discussion of the constraints of conducting field-based research, the complexities of representing experiences in the field, the tensions inherent in the postcolonial framework itself, and the debilitating self-consciousness that accompanies the activist postcolonial researcher. The chapter ends with a discussion of the strength of this framework for its multiculturalism and interdisciplinarity, so that international media phenomenon may be observed and theorized.

Negotiating the Complexities of Fieldwork within Academia

The challenges to international media studies are obvious. Quite simply, individual researchers just cannot address the wide range of media networks, programming, and diversity of audience responses across the world. Even when the focus is on a specific community, the variety of experiences and responses, and the multiple social and familial network viewers subscribe to, may all be overwhelming to document within one fieldwork experience. Collaborative research sounds an ideal solution, yet the stark truth is that academic constraints in terms of the tenure clock for the junior scholar, funding limitations, and time-consuming inter-researcher communication may make many hesitant to embark on such qualitative ethnographic research.

More common are collaborations on broad-based quantitative surveys that add to our knowledge of the descriptive parameters of international viewing communities rather than their lived, real contexts. Scholars of both communication and anthropology have documented the academic constraints to field-based research. The limited time available for field research (usually the summer months), the academic clock which requires complete research papers to be conceptualized, designed, executed and written up in the space of a semester or quarter (in the case of the student), and the limited funding available for overseas research lead to any number of articles that base their analyses on international students, self-selecting diasporic communities in university towns, or native populations in the home town of the international scholar. Such articles, for the most part, indicate a sophisticated understanding of the theoretical issues surrounding media globalization and its implications for audiences, yet fall short of making real contributions to theory or methodology.

Paradoxically, critical scholars are bound to an institutionalized process that has specific criteria to reward certain types of research (invariably quantitative and broad based) and quantity of articles produced, making it difficult to indulge in time-consuming, in-depth, qualitative studies that include a critique of the institution itself. Patai addresses the shifting ground critical scholars stand on:

> On the one hand, we are obligated to our academic disciplines and institutions, within which we must succeed if we are to have any impact on the academy (and this in itself involves us in numerous contradictions, as part of our project entails transforming those very disciplines and institutions). On the other hand, if we take feminism seriously, it commits us to a transformative politics. In other

words, most of us do not want to bite the hand that feeds us; but neither do we want to caress it too lovingly. (1991, pp. 138–9)

The result is an investment in an enormous amount of time and energy in defending critical, qualitative studies and particularly the ethnographic method, as legitimate theoretical and methodological enterprises. Fieldwork accounts are almost always accompanied by copious author notes on self-reflexivity, epistemic privilege, power imbalances between researcher and researched, and representation (see C. Katz 1996). Lal (1996) argues that ethnographic fieldwork is regarded with skepticism within the dominant paradigm of sociological research. Such research carries with it an inherent hegemonic structure authenticating computerized survey data and hypotheses-driven research designs. Critical feminist research is viewed with suspicion, creating real barriers for those on the lower rungs of academia such as students and untenured faculty. Such barriers are exacerbated, "particularly in the arena of defining and defending intellectually appropriate research projects that go against the grain of disciplinarity and hegemonic neopositivism" (ibid., p. 189).

Critical feminist and postcolonial revisions of dominant theory, shifting the epistemological standpoints from men and masculinity to issues of women and subalterity is no doubt a noteworthy advancement, yet this shift has not quite translated into revisions in methodology. Research in the field does not adequately locate women as central to fieldwork (Burt and Code 1995). Research instruments are still constructed using the positivist, male-biased survey questionnaire, which positions the researcher as superior from the researched and elicits closed and limited responses. Results continue to be written up in realist style rather than impressionist, conveying the culture of the academic institution rather than the community studied (see Van Maanen 1988). Number-crunching software and quantitative data continue to be privileged, an obstacle to the description of the nuances in culture and experience in the field.

When in the field, researchers are confronted with further academic constraints. Even when embarking on ethnographic research designs, data are not taken seriously unless they include large samples. International media studies, still strongly influenced by methods of the social sciences, continues to place credibility on large representative samples and broad, generalizable conclusions over in-depth qualitative analyses as is evident in the bulk of published articles in top journals in the field. Berik (1996) addresses this constraint in her discussion of her fieldwork experience among 133 female carpet weavers in rural Turkey. Her straddling of the fields of economics and anthropology did not equip her for rigorous qualitative fieldwork but instead demanded of her the quantitative methods prescribed by economics rather than the ethnomethodology of anthropology that she wanted to engage in. Berik's sponsoring research organization, the International Labor Office (ILO) in Geneva, wanted an action oriented, policy-producing research strategy that would not have been possible for her to undertake as a lone researcher. Also, she soon discovered, the formal questionnaire aimed at soliciting quantitative data exacerbated the distance between her and her respondents, causing her to abandon the instrument for informal conversations that resulted in rich qualitative data.

The limitations of the quantitative survey method particularly for Asian communities, have been richly described by various anthropologists (Arrigo 1980; Kung et al. 1984; Sheridan 1984). In many cases, authoritative figures in the field (such as heads of television households, managers and directors of television networks and newspaper offices, in the case of international media research) demand to see the researcher's questionnaire prior to granting an interview. As a recognizable "legitimate" document then, the questionnaire serves to channel responses into researcher-prescribed ones, stemming open-ended conversations that could ensue through less formal points of entry. Such a sociological method that drives much of mainstream positivist international media studies in North American universities finds resonance in media research in other countries as well "where the widespread use of computers has led many researchers to develop an addiction to positivism" (Hsiung 1996, p. 124). Obviously, fieldwork does not have to be conducted within an either/or, quantitative or qualitative framework and can draw from elements of both. Crucial is the research question and the fashioning of interview and observation strategies that tap directly into the question.

Finally, the privileging of theory over empirical research in the academy (C. Katz 1996) also leads to top heavy studies that give much space to theoretical frameworks and much less to descriptions of actual fieldwork and results. The overriding goal seems to be to legitimize fieldwork by anchoring it as solidly as possible to prior theory instead of actively exploring how it could uncover new phenomena or lead to new theoretical directions. Mies (1996) notes that the value-free, objective, and hierarchical researcher over researched relationship; the lack of researcher empathy in the fieldwork experience, and the disengagement of the researcher in the struggles of the researched all re-entrench masculinist paradigms of study, even though women are framed as the topic of analysis.

However, the focus on just experience in the field has its drawbacks as well where feminist scholars, although describing unique experiential frames, may fall back on positivist traditions to generalize the experiences to women in similar social strata across the world. M. Wolf (1996) urges continued courage in engaging in critical research, undertaken with the understanding that power imbalances do exist among researcher, researched, and the academic institution sponsoring the researcher.

Negotiating Power in the Field

Power is a particularly provocative concept in ethnographic research because it is embedded in various relations – between the researcher and the society she or he is researching, within the society itself, between the researcher and her or his data, and so on. Power becomes an important issue because it is tied to the access the researcher has to the data. Ethnographic fieldwork has been extensively critiqued for its colonizing tendencies: its technique and confrontations in the field have been likened by many "post" scholars, as reconstructions of the colonial encounter.

Paredes (1993) provides the foundation for the analysis of power and position negotiated between the ethnographer and the ethnographic subject. He says that the ethnographic encounter offers a site for the manipulation of power by the researcher on the researched and vice versa. It is important to understand therefore that both researcher and researched are complex individuals with their own shifting identities located within a context of multi-layered power structures. Paredes is concerned with border politics, and through his studies on the cultural tensions of the Mexican-Americans in Brownsville, Texas, who lived not only along the border of Texas and Mexico, but also along the border of rural and urban, traditional and modern, and of Mexican American and North American, shows that a cross-disciplinary and transnational perspective is necessary to study such communities. While studying individuals in a specific society, Paredes writes that the researcher must be aware that the people under study have stereotypes about the researcher just as she or he has stereotypes or classifications about them. Also, the ethnographer must be careful not to be too quick to accept those dimensions in the informant's persona that correspond closely with the ethnographer's own beliefs, prejudices, and biases. Although commentaries on ethnographic methodology indicate that the native ethnographer has a greater advantage over the non-native ethnographer in her or his ability to pick up on cultural and linguistic nuances, Paredes says that the important issue is the ethnographic methodology and not the ethnicity of the ethnographer. The ethnographer, however, has to understand first that the community under study is not a homogenous entity, and, second, the ethnographer has to be aware of her or his own subject-position.

The notion that the researcher and the researched are complex individuals with multi-layered identities intersects with feminist theory where neither the researcher nor the researched are essentialized, but are rather regarded through interdisciplinary perspectives as divided and dynamic beings (Lal, 1996; Wolf, 1996; Zavella, 1996). Many feminist ethnographers believe that having insider status, that is, being of the same ethnicity, nationality, and gender as the respondents, alleviates some of the power imbalances between researcher and researched. This is true in many instances as demonstrated in Berik's (1996) camaraderie with the carpet weavers in Turkey, Hsiung's (1996) interaction with Taiwanese female factory workers, Zavella's (1996) fieldwork among fellow Chicana working mothers, Mankekar's (1993) ethnography among middle-class, North Indian television viewers, and McMillin's (2002b) interviews with middle-class cable and television viewers in South India.

B. F. Williams (1996) underscores the importance of knowing a community in varied ways and says that researchers need to do their homework before they enter the field. In so doing, they "must continually try to figure out the power implications of who they are (or better put, how they are being construed and by whom) in relation to what they are doing, asking and observing" (ibid., p. 73). Most important, the researcher and the subjects and their constructions of each other exist within practices of signification and within the overall field of power relations. The researcher is skinfolk but not kinfolk, and is allowed, in this neither-here-nor-there category, to construct a social persona that is not authoritative (as colonizer), but that is benign and well-meaning. When the tri continent researcher goes back to her or his own country to research her or his own society, the nativity of the researcher and her or his position of power over the researched is problematized. The challenge is to come back to the First World and write about one's experience taking care not to reproduce colonizing discourses (Lal 1996). Instead of worrying about the power differentials of research over researched, the researcher would do well to focus on a commitment to what Murphy and Kraidy call a *"critical* ethnography" (2003, p. 15, emphasis in original) that addresses how power emerges and transforms people's lives globally. The ethnographer can and should overcome debilitating concerns about objectifying or essentializing the "Other" because this may result in a further paucity of information about social injustice and the lives of the oppressed.

After returning from the field, the postcolonial researcher struggles with dual modes of representation: one that is turned to the respondents she or he is studying, and the other to the academia where she or he has to write in an authoritative voice on the results obtained in the field. These binaries are based on and are exacerbated by the very methodology of social science research where the researcher with her or his academic credentials, intellect, research questions, and goal of writing up the study for publication, stands apart and above the researched. Crucial is the awareness of multiple locations of the researcher and the researched, and the possibility of hybrid identities between the two. However, hybridity as the new site of epistemic privilege must be resisted (Lal 1996). Instead, the postcolonial intellectual must use her or his dislocation as a starting point for methodology to get out of the dualisms of native–non-native, insider–outsider, and so on and instead question the hyphen between them.

The Politics of Representing Ethnographic Research

The "weakest link in feminist research," Maguire (1987, p. 35) has argued, is the research process itself. Critical scholars, whether from the related feminist, postcolonial or poststructuralist perspectives, write extensively about issues of power. They critique macro institutions and micro cultural experiences as sites where struggles of power and control are played out. In representing their fieldwork they engage in a variety of strategies such as co-authoring with respondents in the field, allowing poly-vocality or presenting respondent voices verbatim in the text, and representation, where respondents have an important role in defining how they are portrayed in the text (D. Wolf 1996). Such strategies alleviate the power differentials between researcher and researched. Yet, Maguire observes, such researchers are reluctant to give up control over exactly what they write up. Their work, even if inclusive of respondent voices, rarely empowers the community studied.

Finnegan (1992) is concerned with the control the researcher has over the text or data. She observes that in writing up the data obtained through the ethnographic encounter, the researcher has to consider such ethical questions as, who owns the data? How far will local voices be recognized? Do local voices prefer to remain anonymous? How should informants be referred to – as subjects, citizens or participants? Who will use the text? How may permission be obtained for recording and filming? Where will intellectual property rights reside? In what language will the text be translated? Does the text contain any derogatory terms? And, how will the researcher align herself or himself in instances of opposing views?

In addressing these issues, the researcher has to carefully consider the style in which the data are represented. It is in writing the text that the authorial self confronts the subject of the study as a captive object – captive through the technologies of research such as tapes, interviews, and word processing.

Writing should be regarded as an extension of fieldwork and should receive greater scrutiny than it has in traditional research conventions where it has been seen as a process separate from the field experience (Lal 1996).

How one writes up the research requires close attention, therefore. The choice among realist, confessional or impressionist styles is essential in that each conveys a different sense of the distance and power the researcher has over the subject. To explain, Van Maanen (1988) describes each of these styles of ethnographic writing. The realist tale is dispassionate and authoritative. It may manifest *experiential authority* where the author hides behind the "authenticity" or neutrality of the text; *typical forms* where the author focuses on mundane details of everyday life; and the *native's point of view* where the author provides a bit of interpretation between quotes from the native. The confessional tale exists as *personalized authority* where the reader shares a certain intimacy with the audience and tries to convince them of her or his human qualities; the *fieldworker's point of view* where the author flits between an insider's passionate perspective and an outsider's dispassionate one; and *naturalness*, where the author tries to convey the impression that the work is uncontaminated and that she or he was part of the society reported on. Finally, the impressionist tale is figurative and highly personalized. It exists as *textual identity* which is a somewhat chronological rolling narrative; as *fragmented knowledge* where cultural knowledge is imparted to the audience in a disjointed way; *characterization* where the author's individuality shines through; and *dramatic control* where the author maintains control to build up tension in the text. Of all these three, the confessional tale is least authoritative while the realist tale is the most authoritative.

Even with careful attention to power differentials in the field and to the connotations associated with different styles of writing, the published research is subject to further scrutiny and criticism. Ironically, the climate of criticism that surrounds a critical scholar serves to subject the latter to various forms of redress, forms that may be constructive but could also be counterproductive as products of residual ideologies of colonialism within academia.

Challenges to Activist Research

A significant challenge to activism is in defining what form it should take and in identifying the appropriate moment of intervention. As Berik (1996) recounts from her experience among 133 female carpet weavers in rural Turkey, her awareness of gross violations of safety, health, and wage standards at the weaving workshops did not propel her to seek action or report registration violations to the Social Insurance Institute. Her reasoning was that intervention by just one researcher was unlikely to accomplish anything. Hsiung (1996) similarly describes her discomfiture at being a part of a satellite factory work environment, forced by her role as participant observer and later worker, to conform to the culture of the place which included overt displays of sexism – from the exploitative work hours for women to the posters of pornographic movies and semi-naked women that adorned the walls. She writes that her outsider status as a US-educated Taiwanese researcher awarded her some immunity from patriarchal norms of the workplace, yet her insider ethnic status made her a target of sexual harassment as well. Hsiung comments:

> The process of getting entry, sustaining access, and resolving tension involves negotiation between the patriarchal/capitalist system, the agents of the system, and the female feminist researcher. The conceptualization of a binary power relationship between female ethnographers and their informants does not leave sufficient room to explore how power structures are constructed and contested through everyday interaction between men and women. (ibid., p. 133)

As in the case of Lal's (1996) study of workers in television assembly factories in North India, when the researched are women, they may be objectified first by the access providers who order them to participate in the interview, and then further by the researcher who, although opposing the hierarchical system, is nevertheless associated with the (usually male) access provider as a person with power. When the ethnographer goes to research a society that is sexist and hierarchical, the researcher's interaction with that society also becomes sexist and hierarchical because the men one is researching have power over the women. They may use the research situation either to regain power over the subverted hierarchy where the foreign-returned female scholar is in the leader's seat or as a means to thwart the researcher's intent of creating non-hierarchical and non-objectifying interactions and relationships.

A study of the role of television in the lives of ancillary factory workers in Bangalore, India, revealed many of the safety violations and managerial sexism discussed in the above anthropological explorations. Again, any sort of activist intervention was not feasible due to the limited time available for the study (the summer months, to be specific), and the fact that recent interventions by a team of doctors and social workers advocating the provision of nutritious food at the workplace at minimal cost to the owners, had been dismissed (McMillin 2003a). Long-term residence and immersion in the field are crucial to any sustained effort, and affiliation with local social activist groups may be one efficient way to gain access to transformative endeavors.

Important also is a renewed focus on women as media consumers and laborers in the global economy. Postcolonial theory's historical focus on acts of resistance has privileged the experiences of male peasants (Visweswaran, 1996). Women's activist interventions in various liberation movements have been small scale, and therefore sidelined because of their perceived lack of import for national change. Yet such small-scale processes are representative of the nature of women's resistance throughout colonial and postcolonial histories and should be addressed cumulatively and historically for their larger emancipatory implications rather than as local acts of resistance. In other words, women's resistance requires a global contextualizing or we continue to regard these as fragmented endeavors, never really amounting to anything, further reinforcing the patriarchal view that such resistance is safe because it keeps women busy and happy outside of the main projects of state and nation.

Critical development communication studies should be given credit for their engagement, more realistically and accurately, with issues of resistance and development, as pointed out in the case studies cited earlier. These case studies rely on historical traditions and draw on indigenous knowledge to endure and create systemic change. Ultimately, despite the stance of some feminist researchers that abandoning fieldwork altogether is better than engaging in the possibility of misrepresenting oppressed populations or of not involving oneself in activism, M. Wolf (1996) urges responsible fieldwork without energy-draining obsession over power discrepancies and insider–outsider politics.

Obviously we need more studies that address the dialectical correspondence between theory and practice, which can be accomplished through a significant engagement with interdisciplinary and transnational scholarship (Kaplan and Grewal 1999).

Criticisms of Critical Research

The circuit of critical studies is not a pleasant one to inhabit. Feminist ethnographers such as Zavella (1996) and critical postcolonialists like Mohanty (2003) and Chow (2002) have written about the attacks on the integrity of research that are generated from within the scholarly community itself. Whether it is the complexity of using labels (such as Spanish, Hispanic, or Chicano in the case of Zavella's fieldwork), of how gender is theorized (in the case of Mohanty's path-breaking analyis of feminism), or the researcher's own ethnic-self (Chow 2002), critical theory and research, after finding their way to publication, are often torn down by fellow inmates. Chow writes scathingly about this tendency among academics, particularly non-Western tri continent scholars. Using Fanon's[1] delineation of the psychic impact of colonization where the colonized sees herself or himself as inferior through the eyes of the colonizer, she writes that the inferiority complex imparted to postcolonials plays out, "not so much [in] the negative emotion directed against those who are deemed superior as a profound self-hatred, [but as a] negative emotion that is, in turn, directed against those who ethnically most resemble oneself" (ibid., p. 187). These are harsh words, no doubt, but startling in their brutal honesty. The culture of criticism is all too evident in how academic journal submissions are treated and the manner in which feedback is communicated, especially when feedback is from researchers in the same theoretical and geographic area of study. Writing and publishing critical international media studies then become an enterprise that requires fortitude and courage.

In particular, the postcolonial framework receives strong attack particularly from postcolonial scholars themselves. Some believe the relatively new interest in postcolonialism is a way for Western scholarship to atone for its sin of imperialist knowledge production. Some others believe it is a space carved out by tri continent scholars in the First World as an opportunist effort to exoticize themselves to build their careers (Ahmad 1992; Appiah 1996; Dirlik 1996). Lopez (2001) counters that such criticism accusing scholars of using the same tropes of victimhood to further their careers in First World academic environments stems from hollow cynicism rather than any substantive base. To frame the critical, tri continent, postcolonial scholar as merely a product of transnational opportunism of which the "comprador intelligentsia" (ibid., p. 9) stand as an essentialized example, handicaps the important advancements such scholars make to critical theory.

For those tenacious critical scholars who persist with or without funding to undertake complex and intricate analyses of media processes in various parts of the world, the very critical framework to which they are anchored also betrays them in creating questions about the imperialist tendencies in their own research. The volumes of articles on self-reflexivity explaining the intent and methodology of the researcher sometimes taking up more space than the actual analysis of the field itself, convey a sense of the depth of introspection that the scholar undergoes at each step of ethnomethodological research. Having clearly identified that the study, ordering, and control of Wallersteinian peripheral cultures are the malevolent arm of colonialists, postcolonial scholars engage in introspective inquiry about their own intent in legitimizing literary resistance and/or postcolonial studies as an academic field. Slemon

(1996) writes that questions such as "Is the 'post-colonial' a synonym for what Wallersteinian world-systems theory calls the periphery in economic relations?" (ibid., p. 72), and

> Is [literary resistance] something actually *there* in the text, or is it produced and reproduced in and through communities of readers and through the mediating structures of their own culturally specific histories?...are crucial ones for a critical industry which at the moment seems to find these two central terms – "post-colonial" and "resistance" – positively shimmering as objects of desire and self-privilege and so easily appropriated to competing, and in fact hostile, modes of critical and literary practice. (ibid., p. 73)

Postcolonial theory, rather than constituting a break in academic theory, represents a new position in a continuing dialogue that precedes the point of entry of the postcolonial scholar and that will continue after she or he leaves (Trouillot 2002). The postcolonial scholar stands upon precarious ground, then, victim of complex academic politics where, in a Western context, writing in English is considered an exotic representative of a whole race, continent, or even the tri continent. On the other hand, as a successful ethnic, the scholar is viewed as suspect, as even a sell-out by fellow postcolonials, just for having made it in that very context (Chow 2002). Lal (1996) explains that the "neither here nor there" status of the postcolonial researcher in the postmodern era of globalization is determined by transnational movements of labor, people, capital, and commodities. Such movements also shape the subjects of empirical study and the nature of the empiricism and theoretical discourse in which they are bound. The scholar is anchored in a matrix of lived material conditions that factor in the formulation of identity, politics, and writing. Finally, the subjects of research may now be located in places and contexts that do not conform to historically or theoretically derived constructions of where they should be.

Tough is the terrain for the postcolonial critic, who has to balance ethical representations of field subjects, seek avenues for activism, write up research according to imperialist-orientalist formats that define the Western academy, and face criticism from fellow critical scholars who are keenly aware of the paradoxes of the situation themselves. The cycle may continue, but what is crucial is the awareness of these competing academic politics so that the researcher is not paralyzed by debilitating self-consciousness, is not tip-toeing around collegial criticism, and is not hesitant to assert interpretations and conclusions of her or his research. Ultimately, while collegial criticism and introspection are healthy up to a point, it takes energy away from real empirical analyses and theory building in this field. As Lather (1991, p. 21) succinctly puts it, "In an era of rampant reflexivity, just getting on with it may be the most radical action one can take."

International Media and the Viability of the Nation-State

To bring us back to the point of entry to this book, central to the discourse of international communication and globalization is the concern for the viability of the nation-state. National government strategies are pitted against that of the corporate global. Local or subnational responses to national and global narratives are examined as strategies of resistance, accommodation or appropriation. Concern over the viability of the nation-state stems from the overt focus on the Anglo-American dominance of international communication. Common questions are: what will happen to the role of the nation-state (Mohammadi, 1997)? And, what will be the future of democracy if the nation-state is erased (Guehenno, 1995)? Such questions implicitly set up dichotomies between the national subject and the consuming subject, and between developmentalist objectives and economic ones. Case studies from tri continent countries have shown that these dichotomies do not exist, that the cultivation of middle-class consumers is very much embedded within the cultivation of them as national citizens, with the localization of products and media messages to suit their specific cultural, ethnic, religious, and class identities. A case in point is Papua New Guinea where the consuming citizen is an important part of the nation-building project. Advertising campaigns position nationhood as synonymous with aggressive consumption, showing that developmentalist and economic goals are not antithetical but crucially inform one another (Foster 1999).

Yet theorists of globalization continue to tout the strategies of transnational corporations to outsource labor and production in different parts of the (primarily developing) world and to create and sustain markets by diminishing government interventions, as evidence of a borderless world (Ohmae 1995). What this discourse ignores is that borders are very much in construction. Markets have borders, products are invested with exchange values rather than sole utility value to create loyal consuming identities. By framing the nation-state as a casualty of globalization, we are distracted from the formidable avatars of centralized power, now located in both governments and their partnering private sectors. For much of the world's population, the state, as a centralized authority, itself divided in its history and identity, still stands as a system of support and social welfare. The discourse of the demise of the nation-state, then, is a corporate one; the notion that globalization and transnational media flows undermine the stability of the nation-state by their very capacity to connect corporations to consumers bypassing national borders, derives from a romantic, liberal market logic. A more accurate way to address the role of the nation-state in an era of globalization is as a manager of complex and competing spheres.

The nation-state as a manager of dissenting publics

In diverse and multicultural societies, the nation-state has to manage multiple groups and curtail the dissent expressed by those on the margins. Chatterjee (1993) suggests that the state has always positioned itself apart and above its subalterns. He writes that:

> Indeed, in setting up its new patriarchy as a hegemonic construct, nationalist discourse not only demarcated its cultural essence as distinct from that of the West but also that of the mass of the people. It has generalized itself among the new middle class, admittedly a widening class and large enough in absolute numbers to be self-reproducing, but is situated at a great distance from the large mass of subordinate classes. (ibid., p. 134)

If we are to accept Chatterjee's summary, we see that the nation-state, particularly in postcolonial countries, has always elevated itself from the masses. Populated by nationalist elites and by powerful "subaltern" political groups, the state continues as a centralized unit arbitrating over, but never truly engaging in, the issues of its people beyond that of the middle and upper classes. Where, then, is the place of subaltern communities in such a configuration? Peasants, farmers, and the poor continue to be wards of the welfare state and many of these have yet to access its entitlements. The stereotype of the simple, ignorant, fatalistic peasant in tri continent countries continues from colonial through postcolonial times. Peasants were an integral part of the freedom struggle in these countries, yet nationalist elites were wary of the peasants themselves, taking care to curtail any internal uprisings. After independence, there was a further separation of the two domains – the nationalist bureaucratic structure and the peasant population that was sent back to the margins, now that it had fulfilled its freedom duties.

Guha (1994) provides an intricate analysis of how peasants in colonial and postcolonial India were set apart so that any resistance from them or demand for rights could be interpreted as an external force, dangerous to the unity and sanctity of the state. In this manner, in the current context of globalization, the state continues to exercise exclusionary politics, allotting external autonomous domains to foreign media and its fans, labeling as irrational, disruptive and threatening, forms of critique arising from these arenas. M. Yang's (1999) commentary on women's rights groups and media activists in transnational China reveals that these are, for the most part, extra-state groups in the sense that they are either part of non-governmental organizations or from outside the nation-state itself. Also, deterritorialized capitalist forces carry on the legacy of patriarchal cultural production, unseating in many ways the projects of feminism undertaken even by state agencies (Jinhua 1999).

Dissenting publics form along various lines of difference, questioning the benefits of state policies for themselves. Chatterjee (1993, p. 217) contends, "[C]ompeting demands may be voiced not only on the basis of permanent interest-group organization but also as mobilizations building upon pre-existing cultural solidarities such as locality, caste, tribe, religious community or ethnic identity." Chow (2002) takes up this point in her discussion of multiculturalism in the United States where resistance and/or representation by ethnic groups are safely relegated to "special interest" status. Such a status is reflected over and over in the media, reinforcing the idea that the unity of the modern state is intact, it just necessarily reacts to interventions from these groups as and when the need arises. The elitist astonishment at uprisings from these externalized groups further legitimizes the positional superiority of the elite. She writes that the displacement of the violence of resistance to another space that doesn't complicate the harmony of the one inhabited by the center, is what perpetuates the violence of exclusion.

The nation-state as projector of unified modernity

Related to the first point explained above, national governments need to portray the unity of the modern sector as crucial and any threat to it is constructed as a threat to the nationalist state itself. This it does through state-controlled media, public relations, and advertising campaigns. Here the media are co-opted into the nationalist effort. In countries where religion is an integral part of the national fabric, religious tropes are woven into patriotic rhetoric, equating the nation family with the divine family as demonstrated in Rajagopal's (1996) discussion of India; popular culture with religious codes as explained in Herrera's (2001) study of the use of religious music by Iranian teenagers; and consumerism with God-fearing citizenship, as carefully delineated by Abu-Lughod (2005) in the case of Egypt. Protectionist media rhetoric and xenophobic national policies may be generated from the center in tandem with aggressive reforms for economic liberalization giving it a Janus-faced character, yet it endures, for these have been strategies it has used ever since independence. The channeling of viewers' pleasures into consumer behavior and the availability of a variety of products on the marketplace decrease oppor-tunities for organized resistance. For many consumers, resistance may not even be desirable.

It is obvious, then, that the nation-state is far from obliterated or even retreating; it becomes a manager of capitalist expansion and consumerism and functions as a welfare state. Cosmopolitanism becomes a nationalist project. The cultivation of the consumer becomes as important for the state govern-ment as it is for marketers. State-sponsored televisual narratives centering on the nobility of the poor now shift to portrayals of the middle-class lifestyle, where consumerism is an integral part of each character's identity. Although developmentalist themes continue (such as the risk of drugs and the depravity of wealth, for example), these are ensconced in urban, middle-class to upper middle-class settings featuring glamorous celebrities, and beautifully furnished sprawling bungalows. Abu-Lughod (2005) argues that although these narra-tives provide moral lessons and promote notions of the law-abiding, religious, and humble citizen, they do so within the frames of conspicuous consumption with few, if any, real consequences for the law breakers. Consumerism, then, is not antithetical to developmentalism, but a crucial component of it.

The nation-state as a broker of the local

Besides its functions of managing dissent and projecting the image of a unified society following a linear trajectory of modernity and process, the nation-state seeks opportunities to proffer the local for global investment. The state–global market alliance may be discussed in terms of the dynamics of relocalization. Robins (1997) discusses this as the politics of place wars where specific spaces are defined as sites of global membership as in the competition of major cities in the world to host the Olympic Games, or to merit the title, "global city" by virtue of their technological advancement (see Sassen 1996). Local traditions, histories and festivals are appropriated in the mission of global marketing, hybridizing the same with global icons to indicate that the glorious past exists side by side and supports the exciting present and promising future. Mega-cities, then (Castells, 1996), become important sites for the study of a recuper-ated history (see Silk 2002), of a reworking of heritage and of a branding of place, to market the local as a fertile site for transnational investment (Corner and Harvey 1991; McMillin 2001).

For example, Silk's (2002) ethnography of the 1998 Kuala Lumpur Com-monwealth Games describes the extensive government efforts to market not just the games, but the city itself, as an arena for global participation. Begin-ning two years before and extending three months after the games, Silk interviewed broadcast personnel, conducted participant observation and immersion in the production process, and follow-up fieldwork (peer debriefing, audit trails, and member checking) after the event. In its advertising campaign, the Malaysian government was able to turn the games into a venue for the marketing of nation and city, laying it open for foreign investment, through the broadcast of images of the sad colonized past juxtaposed with the jubilant, independent and progressive present. The producers of the games became its cultural brokers, showcasing Malaysia as a developed and culturally rich country. While images of vibrant traditions and beautiful landscapes conveyed the idea of a thriving and resource-full community, they could also be interpreted as an ideological and exploitative strategy of the powerful, elite minority who funneled diverse Malaysian identities into a monolithic commercial commodity, ripe for trade and commercial investment.

To cite another example, McMillin's (2001) fieldwork at local, national, and global television networks in Bangalore, India, in 1997, the 50th year of the nation's independence from British rule, uncovered various state-market alliances in how the nation was represented to its people. Advertisements on billboards, in magazines, on television, and on restaurant and shop signs carried the logo of the Indian national flag beside their own logos to assert their allegiance to the nation and their pride in the nation's journey to this milestone. For example, the saffron, white, and green of the Indian national flag were placed beside the red, white, and blue of the Pepsi logo, and MacIntosh computer's multicolored apple bore the legend, "The Colors of Freedom." The ring of confidence around a tube of Colgate toothpaste now encircled the colors of the national flag, and Cadbury's Dairy Milk chocolate had its models posing in India's flag-face. On television, the logos of MTV and Channel [V] contained the colors of the Indian national flag. Pride in the nation provided a context for the expression of pride in city as well. Coca-Cola's slogan, "Always the real thing, Always Coca-Cola" now read "Always Lal Bagh, Always Coca-Cola," or "Always Residency Road, Always Coca-Cola," equating the "real thing" with the real geographical space of landmarks in Bangalore: Lalbagh which is the city's botanical garden, and Residency Road, the city's upscale shopping and residential area. The state then endures, even in the face of competing claims on global cities, in its central managing function, demanding of the global an assertion of the superiority of the national, at least in nationalist events.

Certainly the protective role of the nation-state is called into question when transnational companies engage in substandard practices in countries that have inadequate and insufficient policing mechanisms. The example of pesticides in Coke and Pepsi products at the beginning of this book is a recent illustration of the casual attitude of TNCs in developing countries. The devastating case of the Bhopal tragedy in India in 1984 when thousands died and millions more were poisoned as deadly gases leaked from the Union Carbide production plant while people slept, stands as a stark reminder of the consequences of capitalist opportunity without crucial structural support.

The state also has to tread lightly in its partnerships with the global and the degree of freedom it allows the latter. Resistance from religious fundamentalists and from conservatives within the society itself, tempers exactly how consumerism is promoted. The accommodation of consumerism particularly among the poor, is a complex process. Abu-Lughod (2005), through a vivid account of an Egyptian village family's relationship with its water buffalo, explains that in Mediterranean and South Asian communities, the rural poor are fearful of the "evil eye," the envy of neighbors, if they have more than the latter. The pull of commodities advertised on television is uneasily interpreted and accommodated side by side with a real, time-tested understanding of the value of social commodities such as cattle, land, and home, that are integral components of their lived experiences.

Cultural constraints to crass capitalism notwithstanding, the state participates as an aggressive competitor in privatized markets, not merely as a regulation and policy enforcer. In the case of the media market, the reality is that many tri continent state governments simply cannot afford to keep up with the high cost of television production and the voracious demand for sophisticated programming. Nor can they rely on inexpensive foreign programming as they did in the 1970s and 1980s when primarily US programming was cost-efficient to import. The emergence of private production companies and the siphoning off of actors and creative talent from local film industries (most notably in the cases of India and Egypt) have contributed to the competitive state vs. private media environment. Satellite television in tri continent countries, although a prerogative of the elite in the 1990s and growing in subscription relatively slowly in the 2000s, has caused state-owned networks to think more urgently not just along policy, licensing, and censorship lines, but about their role as strong contenders in the media market as well. Far from being impotent bystanders as foreign and local private networks battle for the hungry consumer, they reinvent traditions and call upon time-tested tropes of nationhood to join the fray with their own media products. The very infrastructure and terrestrial reach of state-owned networks make them a prime target for advertisers who invest far more in these than the private ones that reach only an urban, albeit affluent clientele. Public announcements and pedagogical documentaries continue on the national networks, side by side with game shows, talk shows, dramas and soaps that occupy private networks.

The discussion of some of the roles taken on by the political state leaves us with a crucial question: what becomes of the emotional, nebulous feeling of nation among its citizens? How does nation continue to be imagined in an era of competing networks? Again, the Eurocentric bias of this question is obvious. Any number of ethnographies of subaltern communities in tri continent countries have laid out for us the intricacies in the ways in which community is imagined. The local village, local festivals, the local school and political district may sit, for the average citizen, as far more real communities than the broader nation. Also, the nation is imagined for particularly subaltern communities in various banal ways, through a myriad of social and cultural rituals, not just televisual images. Indigenous forms of entertainment (such as puppetry, street theatre, traditional dances, and oral narrations) recount tales of the nation and portray its diversity and durability – the media then stand as a part of, but not a central feature of, this milieu. How community continues to be imagined, what factors contribute to this imagination, and what forces strain and shift this imagination become interesting areas for further ethnographic exploration.

For the international media scholar who is interested in issues of nationalism and the viability of the nation-state, in an era of globalization, an understanding of the complex strategies of boundary maintenance is crucial. To rely on the ability of global media giants to transcend national boundaries and reach consumers across the world as evidence of the decrease in national sovereignty is misguided and can lead to erroneous assessments of the dynamics of states, communities, and markets. The scholar has to identify how community is constructed by state politics and how it defines good citizens and demarcates between them and the bad ones. The class, caste, religious, and gender structures within that nation are a good starting point for assessing overlapping groups of inclusion and exclusion. The scholar also has to evaluate how the media depict the demarcations of these boundaries and their shifts. Which group is privileged and which is labeled a threat depends on context and the important point here is that the state retains its position as a manager of group politics. Finally, and perhaps most importantly, the scholar has to assess how these politics are consumed, internalized, subverted, or resisted by people, to complete the analysis of the interplay among states, markets, people, and media. Ultimately, it is only by keeping one's feet firmly on the ground and feeling its shifts, anxieties, vulnerabilities, and celebrations, that we can truly build international media theory.

Notes

Preface

1   Not his real name.

Chapter One   Introduction

1   The terms "Third World," "Global South," "Peripheral Countries" and "Developing" or "Underdeveloped" countries have been used to label most countries of the tri continent. Such labels have their roots in transnational politics where nomenclature was essentially a privilege of First World, developed countries. These labels carry tremendous baggage of poverty, backwardness, and underdevelopment and "tri continent" is regarded by recent postcolonial scholarship as a more accurate and appropriate term (see Young 2002).
2   The term "industrialized" is no doubt an ambiguous term in the 2000s since most countries have some degree of industrialization. The term emerges from a 1960s context where fairly clear demarcations could be made between countries that had undergone industrial revolution and those that had not. In this instance, "industrialized" refers to the countries of origin of the leading media corporations of the world such as the United States, Great Britain, Germany, France, and Italy, for example.
3   The terms "global," "national," "transnational," and "local" are not exclusionary concepts. They signify dynamic spaces that are sites of cultural, economic, and political flows. In this project, "local" is used to signify that which is primarily indigenous and which includes audiences and media networks that are native to the country of origin. "National" refers to the country, the political nation-state itself and to state-sponsored media networks. "Global" refers to media networks that reach Western and non-Western countries, while "transnational" refers to pancontinental media networks.
4   Thussu (2000) identifies two broad strains in post-WWII international communication theory: the political economy approach that derived from Karl Marx's

(1818–83) critique of capitalism; and the cultural studies approach from the Birmingham Group that was concerned with the polysemic nature of media texts and their ideological context.

5 Conceptualizations of the subaltern are drawn from the work of Guha (1994) and Spivak (1988a, b) who theorize about the contributions of peasants, agriculturalists, and women, to the construction of nationalism.

Chapter Two   The Fixity of Nation in International Media Studies

1 Falasha means "exiles" or "strangers" in Amharic. Smith speculates that these were probably semi segregated peoples in the house of Israel, cut off from it centuries ago.

2 Although not necessarily Muslim in religion, these peoples chose the ethnic designation "Muslim" in the Yugoslav census in the 1980s to identify with a nationality and religion rather than the region they occupied.

3 Various scholars have documented that Hindu theological principles were used to legitimize religious and economic exploitation. Indian society is caste-based. Although several classes comprise each caste, the caste system is broadly divided into the Brahmins (the priestly or learned class), the Kshatriyas (the warrior class), the Vaisyas (the agricultural class), and the Sudras (the menial class. This class of people usually comprises of scavengers, tanners, and undertakers). While earlier based on occupation, caste is now determined by birth. Social status and the intellectual and physical capacities of an individual are believed to be contained in the blood. The purity of caste is within the blood and can be defiled through contact with people from lower castes. Thus, marriage between castes is considered taboo.

4 Nostalgia then becomes an important component of nation building where members long for a simple semi-nomadic lifestyle as distinct from their current state of urbanization, or a return to a certain territory or both. Organized religion serves to both fortify ethnie and legitimize the obliteration of some in favor of others (as, for example, the imposition of monotheistic salvation religions of the West over polytheistic communities of the East). As a highly centralized mechanism, organized religion uses communication networks to diffuse ethnic symbols and myths that support its existence. Inter-state warfare was crucial in sustaining the position of a well-defined dominant ethnie.

5 Both Anderson and Gellner are modernists in that they regard "nation" as a concept that developed in the eighteenth century and that was guided to maturity through such modern processes as literacy, mass media, and industrialization.

6 Foster (1991) provides similar categories for the development of nationalism and uses three sets of keywords to classify the phases: (1) imagination, invention and memory which refer to how time and space became bounded; (2) classification,

knowledge, and regulation which refer to a phase when technologies of power were set up to control and classify citizens; and (3) commodification, diffusion and consumption which refer to the third phase when citizens and agents subscribed to a particular national ideology.

7 Lerner's target populations were male. He did not specifically address the concerns of women and included a female interviewer who fit very specific criteria. As described in his study, she was not too old, not too young, not too sexy to provoke the men, but chic enough to provoke the women. Although the female interviewer talked to the women of the household, their experiences were not recounted. The experiences of the women were narrated in realistic style (as opposed to the impressionist style in which male experiences were recounted), further distancing the author from his female subjects.

8 Despite his criticisms of the dominant paradigm, Halloran (1997) pushes for a universality of comparison where

> the solution might possibly be in a move towards a universality, which would take into account the diversity of cultural identities...[because]...How can we expect policy-makers, broadcasters and the other media practitioners to take us seriously when a researcher may be found to support almost any point of view or policy? (1997, p. 41)

In his concluding discussion of globalization and the tri continent, Halloran goes back to macro indications of development: transnational media-corporate networks, GDP, trade, use of energy, and military spending – to draw conclusions about the effects of globalization.

9 Scholars such as Canclini (1995) and Appadurai (1996) use autonomy and agency interchangeably, theorizing that the new illusory autonomy in terms of consumption that is made available in modernization is a postmodern ailment.

10 These concerns were not limited to tri continent countries. In the mid-1980s, the French government, in an effort to counter the effects of "Wall to Wall Dallas," sought to create a Latin audiovisual space to unite Latin countries (Brazil, Spain, France, Italy, Mexico, and Portugal) through televisual programming that reflected their cultures rather than that of the United States (see Mattelart et al. 1983).

11 In this vein, Herman and Chomsky (1988) write that certain filters strip the news of critical investigative reports and keep the boundaries of public debate within acceptable limits. The size and ownership of the organization, the dependence of the media on advertising, the reliance of the industry on government information, the flak produced by critics of the media, and social controls such as anticommunism, serve to filter or define what news is presented to the people. The media are basically propaganda tools whose purpose is to defend the social, political, and economic agenda and privileges of the groups that dominate society.

Chapter Three   Connecting Structure and Culture in International Media Studies

1   Thompson (1990) critiques the works of Althusser, Poulantzas, and Gramsci noting that they perceive ideology as a reproduction of the material conditions of social life as well as the reproduction of shared values and beliefs. Through the diffusion of these conditions and values in society, individuals adhere to the social order, and through production and diffusion of a dominant ideology of the state, the long-term interests of the dominant class are maintained. Thompson states that such an approach is based on a core consensual theory while evidence shows that there is a higher degree of dissension and skepticism than is implied by such a consensus theory. Also, the simplistic dominant ideology thesis developed by these theorists imply a "social cement theory of ideology" (p. 91), which, like the core consensus theory, does not have much evidence to support the notion that individuals from all levels of society are tied to the social order through ideology. Finally, in regarding ideology as one of the tasks of the state as postulated by these theorists, what results is "a class-reductionist approach" (evident in both Althusser and Gramsci's work), that does not take into account the historical development of the state. It also excludes the interests of other major classes of interest groups based on sex, age, or ethnic origins.

2   Participatory communication has been questioned for its failure to identify the oppressors as part of the learning process. It assumes the oppressors are out there, watching from the sidelines, waiting to learn of their faults and change as a result. The effectiveness of participatory communications is limited because it does not foresee controls over policy and legislation at all levels by those in positions of power, which might suppress such communication even before it begins.

3   See Young (2001) for a delineation of eight forms of anti-colonial resistance.

4   Examples are African nationalism modeled on Marxism and on socialist and communist reforms in China, Vietnam, and Cuba. Interestingly, although Marxist leftists played an important role in the freedom struggles of India and Pakistan, they were distinct from Nehru's socialist secularism and Jinnah's reformist Islam, respectively, both based more on Italy's bourgeois nationalism.

5   What was significant in tricontinental anti-colonialism as seen in its most staunch proponents such as Guevara in Cuba, Gandhi in India, Fanon in Algeria, and Nkrumah in the Gold Coast, is its internationalism and mission of initiating resistance from the peasants.

6   *Orientalism*'s pitting of the Orient vs. the Orientalist, that is the colonized vs. the colonizers has received criticism for its dichotomic analysis. More textured are C.L.R. James' *The Black Jacobins* (1963) on the nationalist uprisings in Africa and more predominantly, Frantz Fanon's *Black Skins, White Masks* (1952) and *Wretched of the Earth* (1961), which argued for an understanding of the diversity of the oppressed. Fanon's work has also been interrogated for its essentializing analyses of "black" and "white."

7 South African Marxism developed similarly in response to apartheid and has dissipated to a large extent in the post-apartheid context.

8 This collection has been criticized widely for its uncritical grouping of the literatures of such varied nations as India, Sri Lanka, Malyasia, and the United States, without a clear demarcation or at least commentary of the devastatingly different colonial experiences of these countries. The question of power is submerged.

Chapter Four   Reviving the Pure Nation

1 India was producing more films than Great Britain in the 1920s, the Philippines more than 50 films a year by the 1930s, Hong Kong more than 200 films by the 1950s, and Turkey more than 300 films by the 1970s. Burma, Pakistan, South Korea, Thailand, the Philippines, Indonesia, and Bangladesh are other leading film-producing Asian countries.

2 Shohat and Stam (1994) note that the imperial paradigm persists in such relatively recent films as *The Wild Geese* (1978), *King Solomon's Mines* (1985), and the Indiana Jones films, which portray the savagery of Africa. Films such as *A Passage to India* (1984) and *Gandhi* (1982) go to great lengths to soften the British presence in India.

3 Most significant are the Srivijaya empire in AD 600, the Brunei sultanate in AD 1400 the Portuguese in the sixteenth century followed by the Dutch in seventeenth century who also controlled the area's trade through the Dutch East Indian Company, and the British who took over Penang in 1786, Malacca in 1795, Singapore in 1819, and Brunei in 1888 (see McDaniel 1994).

4 A striking example here is Thailand, which, as a monarchic dynasty, had been under Siamese domination before the mid-nineteenth century, with rural populations providing slave labor until the early twentieth century. Colonial rule by the French in the Northeast and British in the South redefined borders and subsequent royal regimes of King Chulalongkorn (1868–1910) and King Vajiravudh (1910–25) were based on the colonial Dutch rule in the East Indies and on British rule in India, Malaya, and Burma. The task of creating a distinct sovereign Thai national identity was the explicit mission of Vajiravudh, taken on by subsequent military regimes (see Hamilton 2002).

5 Hong Kong's media environment was much more free than mainland China or Taiwan in the sense that it had a greater diversity and number of publications, although it was closely monitored by the colonial British government for expressions of anticolonial sentiment. Economic enterprise was encouraged while political activism was curbed so much so that during the period of decolonization (1984–97) under the Sino-British Joint Declaration, the Hong Kong population was faced with the challenge of carving its own identity distinct from that of mainland China or British subjectivity. It was in the 1980s that the Hong Kong

women's movement emerged to implement grassroots activism and assess their trajectory post-1997.

6 South Africa, with its population of approximately 44 million people, consists of a variety of ethnic groups such as the Nguni people (which includes the Zulu, Xhosa and Swazi who account for two-thirds of the population), the Sotho-Tswana (who include the Southern, Northern, and Western Sotho); the Tsonga; the Venda; the Afrikaaners, the English, the Coloreds, and the Indians. Immigrants from other parts of Africa, Europe, and Asia, and from the Khoi and San ethnic groups make up for the rest of the population. Whites account for 10.9 percent with 76.7 percent African, 8.9 percent colored and 2.6 percent as Indian/Asian. Eleven official languages are identified in the nation's 1996 constitution: Afrikaans, English, isiNdebele, isiXhosa, isiZulu, Sepedi, Sesotho, Setswanam siswati, Tshivenda, and Xitsonga. Around 80% of South Africa's population is Christian and other major religions are Hinduism, Islam, and Judaism (Zegeye and Harris 2003).

7 Malaya, including Singapore, Sabah, Sarawah, and Malaysia, gained independence from British rule on August 31, 1957. In 1965, Singapore left Malaya and became an independent state.

8 The Press in Malaysia is controlled under the Printing Presses and Publications Act (1987) and the Broadcasting Act (1988), now called the Multimedia and Telecommunications Act (1998), which provide press permits and broadcasting licenses, respectively.

9 Television in Singapore began in 1963; in 1980, the Singapore Broadcasting Corporation was established to ensure that the latest technology was used for radio and television. It was renamed Media International Singapore (MIS) in 1994 and Media Corporation of Singapore in 1999. Cable television arrived in 1995 with channels in English, Mandarin, Japanese, Bhasa Malaysia/Indonesia, French, Hindi, Tamil, and German. Such transnational production companies as HBO Asia, ESPN Star Sports, Discovery Asia, MTV South East Asia and BBC Worldwide have bases in Singapore. Technological advancement and national programs are intertwined (Lim 2004).

Chapter Five   Competing Networks, Hybrid Identities

1 For example, at the heart of *Sunset at Long Chao* (*Xi Zhao Long Chao Li*), a Shanghai television drama, is the conflict between modernity and traditionalism personified in the story of an elderly Chinese (Zhou He) architect and his America returned son, Zhou Tong with Caucasian American wife, Margie, and son from a previous marriage, Billy, in tow. Margie plans to replace Zhou He's residential creation – Long Chao Li, with a commercial plaza. The confrontations between old and young, traditional and modern, East and West are obvious. Chinese women are symbolically written out of China's transnational journey. Chinese men on the other hand are central agents of this transnationalism, with foreigners

coming to them, awarding them sexual desirability and dominance over females whether Chinese or Caucasian, and over economic spheres (Erwin 1999). Erwin's account of herself playing Margie in *Sunset* is a fascinating analysis of how the White American woman is Sinicized for the greater glorification of the virile, economically, powerful Chinese male.

2   Many of the private regional cable channels have not proved viable. For example, former BJP MP J.K. Jain, owner of Jain TV (Joint American Indian Network) made his money renting out video vans to various parties regardless of his political loyalties. He used funds from non-resident Indians to fuel his network in support of the BJP. However, this station collapsed due to lack of advertising revenue, despite Jain's airing of soft porn on the channel late at night in an attempt to raise audience ratings and keep the station afloat (Swami 1997).

3   Fung (2004, p. 76) calls this "episode insertion" (in the case of Japan's *Hello Kitty Wonderland* in Hong Kong inserted with a Chinese host's voice over), original (indigenously produced), syndication (based on distribution practices and referring to post first-run sales), and finally, free copy (where programs, usually religious ones, are provided by networks free of charge) (Liu and Chen 2004).

Chapter Six   Grounding Theory

1   The French Revolution of 1789 set the paradigm for romanticists not only in France, but in Germany and England as well. Initially greeted with euphoria and hopes that the days of aristocracy and nobility were over, the mood soon changed to disillusionment and depression during the Terror. Shalin notes, "The first decade of the nineteenth century witnessed the romanticists' moving away from cosmopolitanism to patriotism, from republicanism to monarchism, from scientific rationality to Christianity and tradition" (1986, p. 83).

2   Shalin writes that in their vision for a "neither bourgeois nor feudal" (1986, p. 86) society, Karl Marx, William Morris, Gustav Landaver and Georg Lukács may all be considered to be romanticists because they were all committed to liberty and positioned their ideologies above the extreme Right and Left. They focused on individual and social freedom. While this marked their similarity with their predecessors of the Enlightenment, they differed in that they believed a strong government was essential for freedom.

3   Fraser (1995) provides a critique of Habermas's influential *Public Sphere* and says that although Habermas' idea of a public sphere for the production and circulation of discourse is critical for state democracy, he does not develop a post-bourgeois model of the public sphere. Specifically, Habermas' public sphere was premised on the notion that participants (the 19th century bourgeois) with a common vision of public good, would rationally discuss public matters and protect society from private interests. Fraser notes that such a public sphere was deliberately masculine and antithetical to the women-friendly salon cultures that

were thought to be effeminate and artificial. Such a public sphere defined an emerging elite, excluded other liberal, non-bourgeois competing public spheres, and was based on four assumptions: first, participants discussed issues as equals; second, a single public sphere was preferable to a nexus of multiple publics; third, private interests were always opposed to public good; and fourth, a separation between civil society and state was necessary for the function of a democratic public sphere. Fraser counters that public spheres – whether in academic or political environments exclude women and people of color. The task of critical theory is to expose the ways in which so-called public spheres exclude minorities. Second, the notion of a single, overarching public sphere limits participation while a plurality of competing publics (subaltern counter-publics) can better promote varied interests and needs. No doubt some publics will be subordinated to others and it is here, Fraser writes, that we need a critical theory that identifies the mechanisms by which some groups are made subordinate to others. Third, Fraser argues, matters that are considered as private interest, such as domestic abuse, date rape in particular, and oppression against minority groups such as women and immigrants and people of color in general have to find their way into the public sphere because they affect public good. However, by excluding private interests, which are often synonymous with minority interests, the concerns of the marginalized remain unheard. Critical theory should examine the boundaries of private and public and whose interests these ideological demarcations serve. Finally, the separation of civil society and state leads to the formation of what Fraser calls "weak publics" where people indulge in opinion formation but not decision-making because they lack political power. On the other hand, critical theory should show how sovereign parliaments function as public spheres within the state where discourse involves both opinion formation and decision-making leading to strong publics. A post-bourgeois public sphere would include strong and weak publics as well as hybrid forms of these publics. Thus, critical theory should expose the limits of democracy in contemporary capitalist societies.

4   C. Katz (1996) in her fieldwork among Sudanese children in 1981, declared she was married to her partner and that she was Christian, even though she was anti-Zionist and an atheist Jew, in order to be accepted by her respondent community.

5   Couldry (2003) situated his field of observation at the Granada Studios Tour in Manchester where people could observe media production, and at protest sites where people became involved in a mediated event without really intending to.

Chapter Seven   Reconfiguring the Global in International Media Studies

1   In her analysis of Ann Hui films in Hong Kong, Lin Ho (1999) writes that Hong Kong's modernity, technology, and commercialism followed that of the British

colonial administration leading to a sense of in-betweenness, with the colonial character imprinted on Chinese culture and tradition. Hui's films of the Hong Kong New Wave cinema, demonstrate this in-between sensibility, assuming "the mantle of cultural workers chiseling and mining at the edges of Hong Kong's modernity, locating fissures where they existed and bringing them into public view" (ibid., p. 164). Hui's films in the 1970s although rife with stereotypical representations of women, nevertheless portrayed their realities in their incapacitation "by a patriarchal culture of labor, and the complicity of Chinese patriarchy with colonial rule and economy" (ibid., p. 165).

Chapter Eight   The Politics of International Media Research

1   Larsen (2000) writes in his commentary on Fanon, "the immediate realities of the Cold War including northern ('socialist' and otherwise) labor's *de facto* abandonment of nations such as Algeria to the racist brutalities of French colonialism, appear to Fanon to disprove the universalist claims of Marxism, to unmask it even, as theory inevitably vulnerable to a West-centered stigmatism" (2004, p. 36).

References

Abrahamian, E. (1999) *Tortured Confessions: Prisons and Public Recantations in Modern Iran*, University of California Press, Berkeley, CA.

Abu-Lughod, L. (1997) "The interpretation of culture(s) after television," *Representation*, vol. 59, pp. 109–33.

Abu-Lughod, L. (2002) "Egyptian melodrama: technology of the modern subject?" in F. D. Ginsburg, L. Abu-Lughod, and B. Larkin (eds) *Media Worlds*, University of California Press, Berkeley, CA.

Abu-Lughod, L. (2005) *Dramas of Nationhood: The Politics of Television in Egypt*, University of Chicago Press, Chicago.

Acosta-Alzuru, C. (2005) "Home is where my heart is: Reflections on doing research in my native country," *Popular Communication*, vol. 3, no. 3, pp. 181–93.

Adler, I. (1993) "Press–government relations in Mexico: A study of freedom of the Mexican press and press criticism of government institutions," *Studies in Latin American Popular Culture*, vol. 12, pp. 1–30.

Adorno, T. W. (1969) "Scientific experiences of a European scholar in America," in D. Fleming and B. Bailyn (eds) *The Intellectual Migration: Europe and America, 1930–1960*, Cambridge University Press, Cambridge.

Adorno, T. W. (1991) *The Culture Industry*, Routledge, London.

Ahluwahlia, P. (2003) "The struggle for African identity: Thabo Mbeki's African Renaissance," in A. Zegeye and R. L. Harris (eds) *Media, Identity and the Public Sphere in Post-Apartheid South Africa*, Brill, Leiden and Boston.

Ahmad, A. (1992) *In Theory: Classes, Nations, Literatures*, Verso, London.

Ahmad, A. (1995) "The politics of literary postcoloniality," *Race and Class*, vol. 36, no. 3, pp. 1–20.

Aidoo, A. A. (1991) "That capacious topic: gender politics," in P. Mariani (ed.) *Critical Fictions*, Bay Press, Seattle.

Aksoy, A. and Robins, K. (1992) "Hollywood for the 21st century: Global competition for critical mass in image markets," *Cambridge Journal of Economics*, vol. 16, no. 1, pp. 1–22.

Algan, E. (2003) "The problem of textuality in ethnographic media research: Lessons learned in southeast Turkey," in P. D. Murphy and M. W. Kraidy (eds) *Global Media Studies: Ethnographic Perspectives*, Routledge, New York and London.

Althusser, L. (1971) *Lenin and Philosophy and Other Essays*, New Left Books, London.

Amin, H. (1996) "Egypt and the Arab world in the satellite age," in J. Sinclair, E. Jacka, and S. Cunningham (eds) *New Patterns in Global Television: Peripheral Vision*, Oxford University Press, New York.

Amin, S. (1974) *Accumulation on a World Scale: A Critique of the Theory of Development*, Monthly Review Press, New York.

Amit, V. (2000) "Introduction: Constructing the field," in V. Amit (ed.) *Constructing the Field*, Routledge, New York.

Anderson, B. (1991) *Imagined Communities: Reflections on the Origin and Spread of Nationalism*, Verso, London.

Ang, I. (1985) *Watching Dallas: Soap Opera and the Melodramatic Imagination*, Methuen, London and New York.

Ang, I. (1991) *Desperately Seeking the Audience*, Routledge, New York and London.

Ang, I. (1996) *Living Room Wars: Rethinking Media Audiences for a Postmodern World*, Routledge, London and New York.

Appadurai, A. (ed.) (1986) *The Social Life of Things: Commodities in Cultural Perspective*, Cambridge University Press, Cambridge.

Appadurai, A. (1990) "Disjuncture and difference in the global economy," in M. Featherstone (ed.) *Global Culture: Nationalism, Globalization and Modernity*, Sage, London and New Delhi.

Appadurai, A. (1996) *Modernity at Large: Cultural Dimensions of Globalization*, University of Minnesota, Minneapolis, MN.

Appiah, K. A. (1996) "Is the post in postmodernism the post in postcolonial?" in P. Mongia (ed.) *Contemporary Postcolonial Theory: A Reader*, Oxford University Press, Oxford.

Archer, M. (1990) "Theory, culture and post-industrial society," in M. Featherstone (ed.) *Global Culture: Nationalism, Globalization and Modernity*, Sage, London and New Delhi.

Arnason, J. P. (1990) "Nationalism, globalization and modernity," in M. Featherstone (ed.) *Global Culture: Nationalism, Globalization and Modernity*, Sage, London and New Delhi.

Arrigo, L. G. (1980) "The industrial work force of young women in Taiwan," *Bulletin of Concerned Asian Scholars*, vol. 12, pp. 25–34.

Ballentine, C. (1993) *Marabi Nights: Early South African Jazz and Vaudeville*, Ravan Press, Johannesburg.

Ball-Rokeach, S. J. and DeFleur, M. L. (1976) "A dependency model of mass-media effects," *Communication Research*, vol. 15, no. 2, pp. 311–18.

Bandura, A. (1977) *Social Learning Theory*, Prentice Hall, Englewood Cliffs, NJ.

References

Baran, P. (1957) *The Political Economy of Growth*, Monthly Review Press, New York.

Baudrillard, J. (1983) *Simulations*, Semiotext(e), New York.

Bauman, Z. (1998) *Globalization: The Human Consequences*, Columbia University Press, New York.

Bausinger, H. (1984) "Media, technology and daily life," *Media, Culture and Society*, vol. 6, pp. 343–51.

Bendix, R. (1970) *Embattled Reason: Essays on Social Knowledge*, Oxford University Press, New York.

Bennett, L. (2003) "New media power: The internet and global activism," in N. Couldry and J. Curran (eds) *Contesting Media Power: Alternative Media in a Networked World*, Rowman and Littlefield, Lanham, MD.

Bennett, T. (2001) "Texts in history: The determinations of readings and their texts," in J. L. Machor and P. Goldstein (eds) *Reception Theory: From Literary Theory to Cultural Studies*, Routledge, New York and London.

Bereciartu, G. J. (1994) *Decline of the Nation-State*, University of Nevada Press, Reno.

Bergeson, A. (1990) "Turning world-system theory on its head," in M. Featherstone (ed.) *Global Culture: Nationalism, Globalization and Modernity*, Sage, London and New Delhi.

Berik, G. (1996) "Understanding the gender system in rural Turkey: Fieldwork dilemmas of conformity and intervention," in D. L. Wolf (ed.) *Feminist Dilemmas in Fieldwork*, Westview Press, Oxford.

Bernal, M. (1995) "Race, class, and gender in the formation of Aryan models of Greek origins," in V. Y. Mudimbe (ed.) *South Atlantic Quarterly*, special issue, *Nations, Identities, Cultures*, vol. 94, no. 4, pp. 987–1008.

Berry, C., Hamilton, A., and Jayamanne, L. (1994) *The Filmmaker and the Prostitute: Dennis O'Rourke's "The Good Woman of Bangkok,"* Power Institute, Sydney.

Bhabha, H. K. (1990) *Nation and Narration*, Routledge, London and New York.

Bhabha, H. K. (1994) *The Location of Culture*, Routledge, New York.

Bhandare, N. (1997) "Pulling the plug," *India Today*, no. 22, pp. 72–3.

Bhandare, N. and Joshi, N. (1997) "Too little, too late," *India Today*, no. 22, p. 9.

Bird, E. (2003) *The Audience in Everyday Life*, Routledge, London.

Blumler, J. G. and Katz, E. (eds) (1974) *The Uses of Mass Communications: Current Perspectives on Gratification Research*, Sage, Beverly Hills, CA.

Blumler, J. G., Guerevitch, M., and Katz, E. (1985) "Reaching out: A future for gratifications research," in K.E. Rosengren, L. A. Wenner, and P. Palmgreen (eds) *Media Gratifications Research: Current Perspectives*, Sage, Beverly Hills, CA.

Bobo, J. (1995) *Black Women as Cultural Readers*, Columbia University Press, New York.

Boyd-Barrett, O. (1997) "International communication and globalization: Contradictions and directions," in A. Mohammadi (ed.) *International Communication and Globalization*, Sage, London, Thousand Oaks, CA, and New Delhi.

233

Boyd-Barrett, O. and Rantanen, T. (eds) (1998) *The Globalization of News*, Sage, London.

Boyne, R. (1990) "Culture and the world-system," in M. Featherstone (ed.) *Global Culture: Nationalism, Globalization and Modernity*, Sage, London and New Delhi.

Brent, W. (1998) "CCTV to test DTH, ramps up programming," *Variety*, vol. 42, May, pp. 4–10, 42.

Breuilly, J. (1994) *Nationalism and the State*, University of Chicago Press, Chicago.

Brown, M. (1997) "Yesterday, the world," *The Guardian*, June 16, sect. 2, pp. 8–9.

Brown, W. J. and Singhal, A. (1990) "Ethical dilemmas of prosocial television," *Communication Quarterly*, vol. 38, pp. 206–19.

Brundson, C. (1981) "*Crossroads*: Notes on soap opera," *Screen*, vol. 22, no. 4, pp. 32–7.

Buarque de Almeida, H. B. (2003) "On the border: Reflections on ethnography and gender," in P. D. Murphy and M. W. Kraidy (eds) *Global Media Studies: Ethnographic Perspectives*, Routledge, New York and London.

Burch, E. (2002) "Media literacry, cultural proximity and TV aesthetics: Why Indian soap operas work in Nepal and the Hindu diaspora," *Media, Culture, and Society*, vol. 24, pp. 571–9.

Burt, S. and Code, L. (1995) *Changing Methods: Feminists Transforming Practice*, Broadview Press, Peterborough.

Burton, A. (ed.) (2003) *After the Imperial Turn: Thinking with and through the Nation*, Duke University Press, Durham, NC.

Butler, J. (1997) *The Psychic Life of Power: Theories in Subjection*, Stanford University Press, Stanford, CA.

Callaway, H. (1992) "Ethnography and experience: Gender implications in fieldwork and texts," in J. Okely and H. Callaway (eds) *Anthropology and Autobiography*, Routledge, New York.

Canclini, N. G. (1995) *Hybrid Cultures: Strategies for Entering and Leaving Modernity*, University of Minnesota Press, Minneapolis, MN.

Canclini, N. G. (1997) "Hybrid cultures and communicative strategies," *Media Development*, vol. 44, no. 1, pp. 22–9.

Capino, J. B. (2003) "Soothsayers, politicians, lesbian scribes: The Philippine movie talk show," in L. Parks and S. Kumar (eds) *Planet TV: A Global Television Reader*, New York University Press, New York.

Caputo, V. (2000) "At 'home' and 'away': Reconfiguring the field for late twentieth-century anthropology," in V. Amit (ed.) *Constructing the Field*, Routledge, New York.

Castells, M. (1996) *The Rise of the Network Society*, Blackwell, Oxford.

Castells, M. (2001) *The Internet Galaxy*, Oxford University Press, Oxford.

Chadha, K. and Kavoori, P. (2000) "Media imperialism revisited: Some findings from the Asian case," *Media, Culture and Society*, vol. 22, no. 2, pp. 415–32.

Chakrabarty, D. (1989) *Rethinking Working-Class History: Bengal, 1890–1940*, Princeton University Press, Princeton, NJ.

Chakravarti, U. (1989) "Whatever happened to the Vedic *Dasi*? Orientalism, nationalism, and a script for the past," in K. Sangari and S. Vaid (eds) *Recasting Women: Essays in Colonial History*, Kali for Women, New Delhi.

Chakravarty, S. (1998) *National Identity in Indian Popular Cinema 1947–1987*, Oxford University Press, New Delhi.

Chan, J. M. (1994) "National responses and accessibility to STAR TV in Asia," *Journal of Communication*, vol. 44, no. 3, pp. 112–31.

Chan, J. M. (1996) "Television in Greater China: Structure, exports and market formation," in J. Sinclair, E. Jacka, and S. Cunningham (eds) *New Patterns in Global Television: Peripheral Vision*, Oxford University Press, New York.

Chatterjee, P. (1993) *The Nation and its Fragments*, Princeton University Press, Princeton, NJ.

Chatterji, P. C. (1991) *Broadcasting in India*, Sage, New Delhi.

Chen, H. and Chan, J. M. (1998) "Bird-caged press freedom in China," in J. Y. S. Chang (ed.) *China in the Post-Deng Era*, The Chinese University Press, Hong Kong.

Chow, R. (1996) "Where have all the natives gone?" in P. Mongia (ed.) *Contemporary Postcolonial Theory: A Reader*, Oxford University Press, Oxford.

Chow, R. (1998) *Ethics After Idealism*, Indiana University Press, Bloomington, IN.

Chow, R. (2000) "King Kong in Hong Kong: Watching the 'handover' from the USA," in H. Schwarz and S. Ray (eds) *A Companion to Postcolonial Studies*, Blackwell Publishers, Malden, MA.

Chow, R. (2002) *The Protestant Ethnic and the Spirit of Capitalism*, Columbia University Press, New York.

Clark, L. S. (2005) "Globalizing popular communication audience research: Looking to our sister fields for new directions," *Popular Communication*, vol. 3, no. 3, pp. 153–66.

Clifford, J. (1988) *The Predicament of Culture: Twentieth Century Ethnography, Literature and Art*, University of California Press, Berkeley, CA.

Clifford, J. (1992) "Traveling cultures," in L. Grossberg, C. Nelson, and P. A. Treichler (eds) *Cultural Studies*, Routledge, New York.

Clua, A. (2003) "Where is audience ethnography's fieldwork?" in P. D. Murphy and M. W. Kraidy (eds) *Global Media Studies: Ethnographic Perspectives*, Routledge, New York and London.

Code, L. (1995) "How do we know? Questions of method in feminist practice," in S. Burt and L. Code (eds) *Changing Methods: Feminists Transforming Practice*, Broadview Press, Peterborough.

Cohen, H. (1998) "Local consumption of global television: Satellite television in East Java," in S. R. Melkote, P. Shields, and B. C. Agarwal (eds) *International Satellite Broadcasting in South Asia*, University Press of America, Lanham, MD.

Corner, J. and Harvey, S. (1991) "Mediating tradition and modernity: The heritage/ enterprise couplet," in J. Corner and S. Harvey (eds) *Enterprise and Heritage: Crosscurrents of National Culture*, Routledge, London.

Corner, J. (1998) *Critical Ideas in Television Studies*, Oxford University Press, New York.

Corner, J., Schlesinger, P., and Silverstone, R. (eds) (1997) *International Media Research: A Critical Survey*, Routledge, New York.

Couldry, N. (2003) "Passing ethnographies: Rethinking the sites of agency and reflexivity in a mediated world," in P. D. Murphy and M. W. Kraidy (eds) *Global Media Studies: Ethnographic Perspectives*, Routledge, New York and London.

Couldry, N. and Curran, J. (2003) "The paradox of media power," in N. Couldry and J. Curran (eds) *Contesting Media Power: Alternative Media in a Networked World*, Rowman and Littlefield, Lanhma, MD.

Cunningham, S. and Sinclair, J. (eds) (2000) *Floating Lives: The Media and Asian Diasporas*, University of Queensland Press, St. Lucia, Queensland.

Curran, J. (1990) "The new revisionism in mass communication research: A reappraisal," *European Journal of Communication,* vol. 5, no. 2/3, pp. 135–64.

Curran, J. (2003) "Global journalism: A case study of the internet," in N. Couldry and J. Curran (eds) *Contesting Media Power: Alternative Media in a Networked World*, Rowman and Littlefield, Lanhma, MD.

Curran, J. and Park, M. J. (2000) "Beyond globalization theory," in J. Curran and M-J. Park (eds) *De-westernizing Media Studies*, Routledge, London and New York.

Curtin, M. (1999) "Feminine desire in the age of satellite television," *Journal of Communication*, vol. 49, no. 2, pp. 55–70.

Curtin, M. (2002) "Cultural geographies of global TV," paper presented at the annual meeting, International Communication Association Conference, Seoul, Korea, July 15–19.

Curtin, M. (2003) "Television and trustworthiness in Hong Kong," in L. Parks and S. Kumar (eds) *Planet TV: A Global Television Reader*, New York University Press, New York.

Dahlgren, P. (1988) "What's the meaning of this? Viewers' plural sense-making of TV news," *Media, Culture, and Society*, vol. 10, pp. 285–301.

Dahlgren, P. (1997) "Cultural studies as a research perspective: Themes and tensions," in J. Corner, P. Schlesinger, and R. Silverstone (eds) *International Media Research: A Critical Survey*, Routledge, London and New York.

Darling-Wolf, F. (2003) "Negotiation and position: On the need and difficulty of developing 'thicker descriptions,'" in P. D. Murphy and M. W. Kraidy (eds) *Global Media Studies: Ethnographic Perspectives*, Routledge, New York and London.

Dayan, D. and Katz, E. (1992) *Media Events: The Live Broadcasting of History*, Harvard University Press, Cambridge, MA.

De la Garde, R. (1994) "Cultural development: State of the question and prospects for Quebec," *Canadian Journal of Communications*, vol. 19, pp. 447–75.

Derrida, J. (1976) *Of Grammatology*, Johns Hopkins University Press, Baltimore, MD.

Devendra, K. (1994) *Changing Status of Women in India*, Vikas Publishing House Pvt. Ltd, New Delhi.

DH News Service (2003a) "High cadmium levels found in Coke sludge," *The Deccan Herald*, 6 Aug., p. 7.

DH News Service (2003b) "Mixed reaction to report on soft drinks," *The Deccan Herald*, 7 Aug., p. B.

DH News Service (2003c) "Oppn demands ban on sale of Coca-Cola, Pepsico drinks," *The Deccan Herald*, 7 Aug., p. 4.

DH News Service (2003d) "Pepsi, Coke banned in parliament," *The Deccan Herald*, 7 Aug., p. 1.

DH News Service. (2003e) "Now, pesticides in Coke, Pepsi," *The Deccan Herald*, 7, Aug., p. 1.

Dhanraj, D. (1994) "A critical focus," in A. Joseph and K. Sharma (eds) *Whose News: The Media and Women's Issues*, Sage, New Delhi.

Dickey, S. (1993) *Cinema and the Urban Poor in South India*, Cambridge University Press, Cambridge.

Dilley, R. (2004) "Global connections, local ruptures: The case of Islam in Senegal," in W. Van Binsbergen and R. Van Dijk (eds) *Situating Globality: African Agency in the Appropriation of Global Culture*, Brill, Boston and Leiden.

Dirlik, A. (1996) "The postcolonial aura: Third World criticism in the age of global capitalism," in P. Mongia (ed.) *Contemporary Postcolonial Theory*, Oxford University Press, New Delhi.

Dirlik, A. (2002) "The romance of Africa: Three narratives by African-American women," in E. Mudimbe-Boyi (ed.) *Beyond Dichotomies: Histories, Identitities, Cultures, and the Challenge of Globalization*, State University of New York Press, Albany, NY.

Donadey, A. (2001) *Recasting Postcolonialism: Women Writing Between Worlds*, Heinemann, Portsmouth, NH.

Doordarshan Audience Research Unit (1996) Nutech Pholithographers, New Delhi.

Dornfeld, B. (1998) *Producing Public Television, Producing Public Culture*, Princeton University Press, Princeton, NJ.

Downing, J. (1996) *Internationalizing Media Theory: Transition, Power, Culture: Reflections on Media in Russia, Poland and Hungary, 1980–1995*, Sage, London.

Downing, J. (2003) "Where we should go next and why we probably won't: An entirely idiosyncratic, utopian, and unashamedly peppery map for the future," in A. Valdivia (ed.) *A Companion to Media Studies*, Blackwell Publishing, Oxford.

Drotner, K. (1993) "Media ethnography: An(other) story," *Nordicom Review*, vol. 2, pp. 1–14.

Drotner, K. (2000a) "Less is more: Media ethnography and its limits," in I. Hagen and J. Wasko (eds) *Consuming Audiences? Production and Reception in Media Research*, Hampton Press, Cresskill, NJ.

Drotner, K. (2000b) "Difference and diversity: trends in young Danes' media uses," *Media, Culture and Society*, vol. 22, no. 2, pp. 149–66.

Dupagne, M. and Waterman, D. (1999) "Determinants of US television fiction imports in Western Europe," *Journal of Broadcasting and Electronic Media*, vol. 42, no. 2, pp. 208–19.

Dyer-Bennem, S. Y. (1994) "Cultural distinctions in communication patterns of African-American women," in P. Riaño (ed.) *Women in Grassroots Communication: Furthering Social Change*, Sage, Thousand Oaks, CA.

Economic Times (1994) "Murdoch buys balance 36 pc stake of Star TV," July.

Ellis, J. (1982) *Visible Fictions*, Routledge and Kegan Paul, London.

Enloe, C. (1989) *Bananas, Beaches, and Bases: Making Feminist Sense of International Politics*, University of California Press, Berkeley, CA.

Erwin, K. (1999) "White women, male desires: A televisual fantasy of the transnational Chinese family," in M. Yang (ed.) *Spaces of Their Own: Women's Public Sphere in Transnational China*, University of Minnesota Press, Minneapolis, MN.

Escosteguy, A. C. (2001) "Cultural studies: A Latin American narrative," *Media, Culture and Society*, vol. 23, pp. 861–73.

Eze, E. C. (2002) "Mankind's proverbial imagination: Critical perspectives on human universals as a global challenge," in E. Mudimbe-Boyi (ed.) *Beyond Dichotomies: Histories, Identitities, Cultures, and the Challenge of Globalization*, State University of New York Press, Albany, NY.

Fair, J. (2003) "*Francophonie* and the national airwaves: A history of television in Senegal," in L. Parks and S. Kumar (eds) *Planet TV: A Global Television Reader*, New York University Press, New York.

Fanon, F. ([1952] 1986) *Black Skin, White Masks*, trans. C. L. Markmann, Pluto, London.

Fanon, F. ([1961] 1965) *The Wretched of the Earth*, trans. H. Chevalier, Monthly Review Press, New York.

Featherstone, M. (ed.) (1990) *Global Culture*, Sage, London.

Featherstone, M. (1995) *Undoing Culture: Globalization, Postmodernism and Identity*, Sage, London, Thousand Oaks, CA, New Delhi.

Ferguson, M. (1993) "The mythology about globalization," *European Journal of Communications*, vol. 7, no. 1, pp. 69–93.

Fernandes, L. (2000) "Nationalizing 'the global': Media images, cultural politics and the middle class in India," *Media, Culture and Society*, vol. 22, pp. 611–28.

Finnegan, R. (1992) *Oral Traditions and Verbal Arts: A Guide to Research Practices*, Routledge, London and New York.

Fish, S. (2001) "Yet one more," in J. L. Machor and P. Goldstein (eds) *Reception Theory: From Literary Theory to Cultural Studies*, Routledge, New York and London.

References

Fiske, J. (1989) *Understanding Popular Culture*. Unwin Hyman, London.

Fiske, J. (2001) "Madonna," in J. L. Machor and P. Goldstein (eds) *Reception Theory: From Literary Theory to Cultural Studies*, Routledge, New York and London.

Fiske, J. (2003) "Think globally, act locally," in L. Parks and S. Kumar (eds) *Planet TV: A Global Television Reader*, New York University Press, New York.

Forbes, G. (1996) *Women in Modern India*, vol. 4 of *The New Cambridge History of India*, 2, Cambridge University Press, Cambridge.

Fortner, R. S. (1993) *International Communication*, Wadsworth, Belmont, CA.

Foster, R. (1999) "The commercial construction of new nations," *Journal of Material Culture*, vol. 4, pp. 263–82.

Foster, R. J. (1991) "Making national cultures in the global ecumene," *Annual Review of Anthropology*, vol. 20, pp. 235–60.

Foucault, M. (1977) *Discipline and Punish*, Pantheon, New York.

Foucault, M. (1980) *Power/Knowledge*, Pantheon, New York.

Fox, E. (1997) "Media and culture in Latin America," in J. Corner, P. Schlesinger, and R. Silverstone (eds) *International Media Research: A Critical Survey*, Routledge, London and New York.

Frank, A. G. (1969) *Capitalism and Underdevelopment in Latin America: Historical Studies of Chile and Brazil*, Monthly Review Press, New York.

Frank, A. G. (1984) *Critique and Anti-critique: Essays on Dependence and Reformism*, Macmillan, London.

Fraser, N. (1995) "Politics, culture, and the public sphere: Towards a postmodern conception," in L. Nicholson and S. Seidman (eds) *Social Postmodernism*, Cambridge University Press, Cambridge.

Friedman, T. (2005) *The World is Flat: A Brief History of the Twenty-First Century*, Farrar, Straus and Giroux, New York.

Fung, A. (2004) "Coping, cloning and copying: Hong Kong in the global television format business," in A. Moran and M. Keane (eds) *Television across Asia: Television Industries, Programme Formats and Globalization*, Routledge Curzon, London and New York.

Galtung, J. (1980) *The True Worlds: A Transnational Perspective*, Free Press, New York.

Ganti, T. (2002) "'And yet my heart is still Indian': The Bombay film industry and the (H)Indianization of Hollywood," in F. D. Ginsburg, L. Abu-Lughod, and B. Larkin (eds) *Media Worlds*, University of California Press, Berkeley, CA.

Garnham, N. (1995) "Political economy and cultural studies: Reconciliation or divorce?" *Critical Studies in Mass Communication*, vol. 12, pp. 62–71.

Gellner, E. (1983) *Nations and Nationalism*, Cornell University Press, Ithaca, NY.

Gerbner, G. and Gross, L. (1976) "Living with television: The violence profile," *Journal of Communication*, vol. 26, no. 2, pp. 173–99.

Giddens, A. (1990) *The Consequences of Modernity*, Polity Press, London.

Gillespie, M. (1995) *Television, Ethnicity and Cultural Change*, Routledge, London.

Ginsburg, F. D., Abu-Lughod, L., and Larkin, B. (eds) (2002) *Media Worlds: Anthropology on New Terrain*, University of California Press, Berkeley, CA.

Gitlin, T. (1978) "Media sociology: The dominant paradigm," *Theory and Society*, vol. 6, pp. 205–53.

Goetz, A. M. (1988) "Feminism and the limits of the claim to know: Contradictions in the feminist approach to women in development," *Millenium: Journal of International Studies*, vol. 17, no. 3, pp. 477–96.

Gramsci, A. (1957) *The Modern Prince, and Other Writings*, trans. L. Marks, International Publishers, New York.

Gramsci, A. (1971) *Selections from the Prison Notebooks*, eds Q. Hoare and G. Nowell-Smith, Lawrence and Wishart, London.

Grossberg, L. (1984) "Another boring day in paradise: Rock and roll and the empowerment of everyday life," *Popular Music*, vol. 4, pp. 225–57.

Grossberg, L. (1988) "Wandering audiences, nomadic critics," *Cultural Studies*, vol. 2, no. 3, pp. 377–90.

Guehenno, J-M. (1995) *The End of the Nation State*, University of Minnesota Press, Minneapolis, MN.

Guerevitch, M., Bennett, T., Curran, J., and Woollacott, J. (eds) (1982) *Culture, Society, and the Media*, Routledge, London.

Guha, R. (1994) "The prose of counter-insurgency," in N. B. Dirks, G. Eley, and S. B. Ortner (eds) *Culture, Power, History*, Princeton University Press, Princeton, NJ.

Gupta, A. and Ferguson, J. (1997) "Discipline and practice: 'The Field' as site, method, and location in anthropology," in A. Gupta and J. Ferguson (eds) *Anthropological Locations*, University of California Press, Berkeley, CA.

Habermas, J. (1989) *The Structural Transformation of the Public Sphere*, trans. T. Burger with F. Lawrence, MIT Press, Cambridge, MA.

Hall, S. (1980) "Cultural studies: Two paradigms," *Media, Culture and Society*, vol. 2, no. 1, pp. 57–72.

Hall, S. (1981) "Encoding/decoding," in S. Hall, D. Hobson, A. Lowe, and P. Willis (eds) *Culture, Media, Language*, Hutchinson, London.

Hall, S. (1997) "The centrality of culture: Notes on the cultural revolutions of our time," in K. Thompson (ed.) *Media and Cultural Regulation*, Sage, London.

Hall, S. and Jefferson, T. (eds) (1976) *Resistance Through Rituals: Youth Subcultures in Post-War Britain*, Hutchinson, London.

Hallin, D. C. (1994) *We Keep America on Top of the World: Television Journalism and the Public Sphere*, Routledge, New York.

Halloran, J. (1997) "International communication research: Opportunities and obstacles," in A. Mohammadi (ed.) *International Communication and Globalization*, Sage, London, Thousand Oaks, CA, and New Delhi.

Hamelink, C. (1983) *Cultural Autonomy in Global Communications*, Longman, New York.

References

Hamelink, C. (1997) "International communication: Global market and morality," in A. Mohammadi (ed.) *International Communication and Globalization*, Sage, London, Thousand Oaks, CA, and New Delhi.

Hamilton, A. (2002) "The national picture: Thai media and cultural identity," in F. D. Ginsburg, L. Abu-Lughod, and B. Larkin (eds) *Media Worlds*, University of California Press, Berkeley, CA.

Hannerz, U. (1989) "Notes on the global ecumene," *Public Culture*, vol. 1, no. 2, pp. 66–75.

Hannerz, U. (1996) *Transnational Connections: Culture, People, Places*, Routledge, London and New York.

Harindranath, R. (2003) "Reviving 'cultural imperialism': International audiences, global capitalism, and the transnational elite," in L. Parks and S. Kumar (eds) *Planet TV: A Global Television Reader*, New York University Press, New York.

Harris, D. (1992) *From Class Struggle to the Politics of Pleasure*, Routledge, London.

Hartsock, N. (1987/1990) "Foucault on power: A theory for women," in C. Lemert (ed.) *Social Theory: The Multicultural and Classic Readings*, Westview Press, Boulder, CO.

Harvey, D. (1989) *The Condition of Postmodernity*. Basil Blackwell, Oxford.

Hastrup, K. and Hervik, P. (eds) (1994) *Social Experience and Anthropological Knowledge*, Routledge, London.

Hay, J. (1996) "Afterword," in J. Hay, L. Grossberg, and E. Wartella (eds) *The Audience and Its Landscape*, Westview Press, Boulder, CO.

Hebdige, D. (1979) *Subculture: The Meaning of Style*, Routledge, London and New York.

Hebdige, D. (1988) *Hiding in the Light: On Images and Things*, Comedia, London.

Hegde, R. S. and Shome, R. (2002) "Postcolonial scholarship – Productions and directions: An interview with Gayathri Chakravorty Spivak," *Communication Theory*, vol. 12, no. 3, pp. 271–86.

Herman, E. S. and Chomsky, N. (1988) *Manufacturing Consent: The Political Economy of the Mass Media*, Pantheon Books, New York.

Herman E. S. and McChesney, R. (2003) "The rise of the global media," in L. Parks and S. Kumar (eds) *Planet TV: A Global Television Reader*, New York University Press, New York.

Herrera, L. (2001) "Accommodating disco and Quran: Lay female pedagogies and the education of metropolitan Muslims," in A. Salvatore (ed.) *Muslim Traditions and Modern Techniques of Power*, Yearbook of the Sociology of Islam, Munster.

Hills, J. (1986) *Deregulation: Telecoms, Competition and Control in the United States, Japan and Britain*, Frances Pinter, London.

Himpele, J. D. (2002) "Arrival scenes: Complicity and media ethnography in the Bolivian public sphere," in F. D. Ginsburg, L. Abu-Lughod, and B. Larkin (eds) *Media Worlds*, University of California Press, Berkeley, CA.

Hirst, P. and Thompson, G. (1995) *Globalization in Question: The International Economy and the Possibilities of Governance*, Polity, Cambridge.

Hobart, M. (2002) "Live or dead? Televising theater in Bali," in F. D. Ginsburg, L. Abu-Lughod, and B. Larkin (eds) *Medai Worlds*, University of California Press, Berkeley, CA.

Hobsbawm, E. (1990) *Nations and Nationalism Since 1780: Program, Myth and Reality*, Cambridge University Press, Cambridge.

Hoggart, R. (1957) *The Uses of Literacy*, Penguin, Harmondsworth.

Horkheimer, M. and Adorno, T. (1972) *Dialectic of Enlightenment*, Herder and Herder, New York.

Horkheimer, M. and Adorno, T. (1989) *Dialectic of Enlightenment*, 2nd edn, trans. J. Cumming, Continuum, New York.

Hoselitz, B. F. (1960) *Sociological Factors in Economic Development*, Free Press, Glencoe, IL.

Hoskins, C. and Mirus, R. (1988) "Reasons for the US dominance of the international trade in television programs," *Media, Culture and Society*, vol. 10, pp. 499–515.

Hout, W. (1993) *Capitalism and the Third World*, Edward Elgar, Cheltenham.

Hovland, C., Janis, I., and Kelley, H. H. (1953) *Communication and Persuasion*, Yale University Press, New Haven, CT.

Hsiung, P-C. (1996) "Between bosses and workers: The dilemma of a keen observer and a vocal feminist," in D. L. Wolf (ed.) *Feminist Dilemmas in Fieldwork*, Westview Press, Oxford.

Iwabuchi, K. (2004) "Feeling glocal: Japan in the global television format business," in A. Moran and M. Keane (eds) *Television across Asia: Television Industries, Programme Formats and Globalization*, Routledge Curzon, London and New York.

Jackson, P. (1999) "The enchanting spirit of Thai capitalism: The cult of Luang Phor Khoon and the postmodernisation of Thai Buddhism," *Southeast Asian Research*, vol. 7, pp. 5–60.

Jacobs, S. (2003) "How good is the South African media for democracy? Mapping the South African public sphere after Apartheid," in A. Zegeye and R. L. Harris (eds) *Media, Identity and the Public Sphere in Post-Apartheid South Africa*, Brill, Leiden and Boston.

James, C. L. R. (1963) *The Black Jacobins*, Vintage Books, New York.

Jameson, F. (1991) *Postmodernism, or the Cultural Logic of Late Capitalism*, Verso, London.

Jameson, F. and Miyoshi, M. (eds) (1998) *The Cultures of Globalization*, Duke University Press, Durham, NC.

JanMohamed, A. R. and Lloyd, D. (1990) *The Nature and Context of Minority Discourse*, Oxford University Press, New York.

Jauss, H. R. (2001) "The identity of the poetic text in the changing horizon of understanding," in J. L. Machor and P. Goldstein (eds) *Reception Theory: From Literary Theory to Cultural Studies*, Routledge, New York and London.

Jensen, K. B. (1991) "Reception analysis: Mass communication as the social production of meaning," pp. 135–48, in K.B. Jensen and N. Jankowski (eds) *A Handbook of Qualitative Methodologies for Mass Communication Research*, Routledge, London.

References

Jhally, S. and Lewis, J. (1992) *Enlightened Racism: The Cosby Show, Audiences, and the Myth of the American Dream*, Westview Press, Boulder, CO.

Jinhua, D. (1999) "Rewriting Chinese women: Gender production and cultural space in the eighties and nineties," in M. Yang (ed.) *Spaces of Their Own: Women's Public Sphere in Transnational China*, University of Minnesota Press, Minneapolis, MN.

Kandiyoti, D. (1994) "Identity and its discontents: Women and nation," in P. Williams and L. Chrisman (eds) *Colonial Discourse and Post-colonial Theory: A Reader*, Columbia University Press, New York.

Kaplan, C. and Grewal, I. (1999) "Transnational feminist cultural studies: Beyond the Marxism/poststructuralism/feminism divides," in *Between Woman and Nation: Nationalism, Transnational Feminisms, and the State*, Duke University Press, London.

Karve, I. (1993) "The kinship map of India," in P. Uberoi (ed.) *Family, Kinship and Marriage in India*, Oxford University Press, New Delhi.

Katrak, K. H. (1992) "Indian nationalism, Ghandhian 'satyagraha,' and representations of female sexuality," in A. Parker, M. Russo, D. Summer, and P. Yaeger (eds) *Nationalisms and Sexualities*, Routledge, New York.

Katz, C. (1996) "The expeditions of conjurers: Ethnography, power and pretense," in D. L. Wolf (ed.) *Feminist Dilemmas in Fieldwork*, Westview Press, Oxford.

Katz, E., Haas, H. and Gurevitch, M. (1997) "20 years of television in Israel: Are there long-run effects on values, social connectedness, and cultural practices?" *Journal of Communication*, vol. 47, no. 2, pp. 3–20.

Katz, E. and Lazarsfeld, P. F. (1955) *Personal Influence: The Part Played by People in the Flow of Mass Communication*, Free Press, Glencoe, IL.

Kawaja, J. (1994) "Process video: Self-reference and social change," in P. Riaño (ed.) *Women in Grassroots Communication*, Sage, Thousand Oaks, CA.

Keane, M. (2004a) "Asia: New growth areas," in A. Moran and M. Keane (eds) *Television across Asia: Television Industries, Programme Formats and Globalization*, Routledge Curzon, London and New York.

Keane, M. (2004b) "A revolution in television and a great leap forward for innovation? China in the global television format business," in A. Moran and M. Keane (eds) *Television across Asia: Television Industries, Programme Formats and Globalization*, Routledge Curzon, London and New York.

Kessler, G. (2005) "Turks challenge Hughes on Iraq," *The Washington Post*, 29 Sept. [Online], p. A16. Available: washingtonpost.com [accessed 1 Oct. 2005].

Khiabany, G. (2003) "De-Westernizing media theory, or reverse Orientalism: 'Islamic communication' as theorized by Hamid Mowlana," *Media, Culture and Society*, vol. 25, pp. 415–22.

Kottak, C. P. (1990) *Prime Time Society: An Anthropological Analysis of Television and Culture*, Wadsworth, Belmont, CA.

Kraidy, M. M. (2002) "Hybridity in cultural globalization," *Communication Theory*, vol. 12, no. 3, pp. 316–39.

References

Kraidy, M. M. (2003) "Globalization *avant la lettre?* Cultural hybridity and media power in Lebanon," in P. D. Murphy and M. W. Kraidy (eds) *Global Media Studies: Ethnographic Perspectives*, Routledge, New York and London.

Krishnan, P. and Dighe, A. (1990) *Affirmation and Denial: Construction of Femininity on Indian Television*, Sage, New Delhi and London.

Kumar, K. (1998) "History of television in India: A political economy perspective," in S. R. Melkote, P. Shields, and B. Agarwal (eds) *International Satellite Broadcasting in South Asia*, University Press of America, New York.

Kumar, R. (1993) *The History of Doing*, Kali for Women, New Delhi.

Kung, L., Arrigo, L. G., and Salaff, J. W. (1984) "Doing fieldwork," in M. Sheridan and J. W. Salaff (eds) *Lives: Chinese Working Women*, Indiana University Press, Bloomington, IN.

Kust, M. J. (1964) *Foreign Enterprise in India: Laws and Policies*, University of North Carolina Press, Chapel Hill, NC.

Lal, J. (1996) "Situating locations: The politics of self, identity and 'Other' in living and writing the text," in D. L. Wolf (ed.) *Feminist Dilemmas in Fieldwork*, Westview Press, Oxford.

La Pastina, A. C. (2003) " 'Now that you're going home, are you going to write about the natives you studied?': Telenovela reception, adultery and the dilemmas of ethnographic practice," in P. D. Murphy and M. W. Kraidy (eds) *Global Media Studies: Ethnographic Perspectives*, Routledge, New York and London.

Larsen, N. (2000) "Imperialism, colonialism, postcolonialism," in H. Schwarz and S. Ray (eds) *A Companion to Postcolonial Studies,* Blackwell Publishers, Malden, MA.

Lash, S. and Urry, J. (1987) *The End of Organized Capitalism*, Polity Press, Cambridge.

Lasswell, H. (1926) *Propaganda Technique in the World War*, MIT Press, Cambridge, MA.

Lather, P. (1991) *Getting Smart: Feminist Research and Pedagogy with/in the Postmodern*, Routledge, Chapman and Hall, New York.

Lazarsfeld, P. F. and Merton, R. K. (1948) "Mass communication, popular taste and social action," in L. Bryson (ed.) *The Communication of Ideas*, Harper and Brothers, New York.

Lee, C-C. (2000) "State, capital, and media: The case of Taiwan," in J. Curran and M-J. Park (eds) *De-westernizing Media Studies*, Routledge, London and New York.

Lee, D-H. (2004) "A local mode of programme adaptation: South Korea in the global television format business," in A. Moran and M. Keane (eds) *Television across Asia: Television Industries, Programme Formats and Globalization*, Routledge Curzon, London and New York.

Lee, F. L. F. (2004) "Constructing perfect women: The portrayal of female officials in Hong Kong newspapers," *Media, Culture and Society*, vol. 26, no. 2, pp. 207–25.

Lerner, D. (1958) *The Passing of Traditional Society: Modernizing of the Middle East*, Free Press, Glencoe, IL.

Liebert, R. and Sprafkin, J. (1988) *The Early Window: Effects of Television on Children and Youth*, Pergamon, New York.

Liebes, T. and Katz, E. (1990) *The Export of Meaning: Cross Cultural Readings of Dallas*, Oxford University Press, New York.

Lim, T. (2004) "Let the contests begin! 'Singapore slings' into action: Singapore in the global television format business," in A. Moran and M. Keane (eds) *Television across Asia: Television Industries, Programme Formats and Globalization*, Routledge Curzon, London and New York.

Lin Ho, E. Y. (1999) "Women on the edges of Hong Kong modernity: The films of Ann Hui," in M. Yang (ed.) *Spaces of Their Own: Women's Public Sphere in Transnational China*, University of Minnesota Press, Minneapolis, MN.

Ling, S. (2003) "The alternative media in Malaysia: Their potential and limitations," in N. Couldry and J. Curran (eds) *Contesting Media Power: Alternative Media in a Networked World*, Rowman and Littlefield, Lanham, MD.

Lippmann, W. (1922) *Public Opinion*, Harcourt Brace Jovanovich, New York.

Lippmann, W. (1925) *The Phantom of Public*, Harcourt Brace Jovanovich, New York.

Liu, Y-L. and Chen, Y-H. (2004) "Cloning, adaptation, import and originality: Taiwan in the global television format business," in A. Moran and M. Keane (eds) *Television across Asia: Television Industries, Programme Formats and Globalization*, RoutledgeCurzon, London and New York.

Livingstone, S. (1997) "The work of Elihu Katz: Conceptualizing media effects in context," in J. Corner, P. Schlesinger, and R. Silverstone (eds) *International Media Research: A Critical Survey*, Routledge, London and New York.

Lofgren, O. (1989) "The nationalization of culture," *Ethnologia Europea*, vol. 19, pp. 5–23.

Loomba, A. (1994) "Overworlding the 'Third World,'" in P. Williams and L. Chrisman (eds) *Colonial Discourse and Post-Colonial Theory: A Reader*, Columbia University Press, New York.

López, A. J. (2001) *Posts and Pasts: A Theory of Postcolonialism*, State University of New York Press, Albany.

Lush, D. (1998) "The role of the African media in the promotion of democracy and human rights," in S. Kayizzi-Mungerwa, A. O. Olukoshi, and L. Wohglemuth (eds) *Towards a Partnership with Africa: Challenges and Opportunities*, Nordiska Afrikainstituet, Uppsala.

Lyotard, J-F. (1984) *The Postmodern Condition: A Report on Knowledge*, trans. G. Bennington and B. Massumi, University of Minnesota Press, Minneapolis, MN.

Ma, K. E. (1999) *Culture, Politics, and Television in Hong Kong*, Routledge, London.

Ma, K. E. (2000) "Re-thinking media studies: The case of China," in J. Curran and M-J. Park (eds) *De-westernizing Media Studies*, Routledge, London and New York.

Machor, J. L and Godlstein, P. (2001) "Introduction," in J. L. Machor and P. Goldstein (eds) *Reception Theory: From Literary Theory to Cultural Studies*, Routledge, New York and London.

Maguire, P. (1987) "Doing participatory research: Feminist approach," *Perspectives 5*, no. 3, pp. 35–7.

Mailloux, S. (2001) "Interpretation and rhetorical hermeneutics," in J. L. Machor and P. Goldstein (eds) *Reception Theory: From Literary Theory to Cultural Studies*, Routledge, New York and London.

Malkki, L. H. (1997) "News and culture: Transitory phenomena and the fieldwork tradition," in A. Gupta and J. Ferguson (eds) *Anthropological Locations: Boundaries and Grounds of a Field Science*, University of California Press, Berkeley, CA.

Mandel, R. (2002) "A Marshall Plan of the mind: The political economy of a Kazakh soap opera," in F. D. Ginsburg, L. Abu-Lughod, and B. Larkin (eds) *Media Worlds*, University of California Press, Berkeley, CA.

Mankekar, P. (1993) "National texts and gendered lives: An ethnography of television viewers in a North Indian city," *American Ethnologist*, vol. 20, pp. 543–63.

Mankekar, P. (1999) *Screening Culture, Viewing Politics*, Duke University Press, Durham, NC.

Mankekar, P. (2002) "Epic contests: Television and religious identity in India," in F. D. Ginsburg, L. Abu-Lughod, and B. Larkin (eds) *Media Worlds*, University of California Press, Berkeley, CA.

Mann, S. and Cheng, Y. (eds) (2001) *Under Confucian Eyes*, University of California Press, Berkeley, CA.

Manuel, P., Bilby, K., and Largey, M. (1995) *Caribbean Currents: Caribbean Music from Rumba to Reggae*, Temple University Press, Philadelphia, PA.

Marcus, D. L. (1999) "Indonesia revolt was net driven," in E. Aspinall, G. Klinken, and H. van Feith (eds) *The Last Days of President Suharto*, Monash Asia Institute, Monash, Australia.

Marcus, G. E. (1992) "Past, present and emergent identities: Requirements for ethnographies of late twentieth-century modernity worldwide," in S. Lash and J. Friedman (eds) *Modernity and Identity*, Basil Blackwell, Oxford.

Marcus, G. E. (1998) *Ethnography through Thick and Thin*, Princeton University Press, Princeton, NJ.

Marcus, G. E. and Fischer, M. M. J. (1986) *Anthropology as Cultural Critique*, University of Chicago Press, Chicago.

Marks, L. (2000) *The Skin of the Film: Intercultural Cinema, Embodiment, and the Senses*, Duke University Press, Durham, NC.

Masmoudi, M. (1990) "The new world information order," in L. J. Martin and R. E. Hiebert (eds) *Current Issues in International Communication*, Longman, New York and London.

Massey, D. (1997) "A global sense of place," in A. Gray and J. McGuigan (eds) *Studying Culture: An Introductory Reader*, Arnold, London.

Mattelart, A. (1979) *Transnational Corporations and the Control of Culture*, Harvester Press, Brighton.

Mattelart, A. (1983) *Transnationals and the Third World: The Struggle for Culture*, Bergin and Garvey, South Hadley, MA.

Mattelart, A. (1994) *Mapping World Communication*, University of Minnesota Press, Minneapolis, MN.

Mattelart, A. (2003) "Realpolitik and utopias of universal bonds: For a critique of technoglobalism," trans. S. Hassa, in A. Valdivia (ed.) *A Companion to Media Studies*, Blackwell Publishing, Oxford.

Mattelart, A., Delcourt, X., and Mattelart, M. (1983) *International Image Markets: In Search of an Alternative Perspective*, trans. D. Buxton, Comedia, London.

McChesney, R. (1998) "Media convergence and globalisation," in D. K. Thussu (ed.) *Electronic Empires: Global Media and Local Resistance*, Arnold, London.

McClelland, D. C. (1966) "The impulse to modernization," in *Modernization: The Dynamics of Growth*, Basic Books, New York.

McClintock, A. (1995) *Imperial Leather: Race, Gender, and Sexuality in the Colonial Conquest*, Routledge, New York.

McDaniel, D. O. (1994) *Broadcasting in the Malay World: Radio, Television, and Video in Brunei, Indonesia, Malaysia, and Singapore*, Ablex Publishing Corporation, Norwood, NJ.

McDaniel, D. O. (2002) *Electronic Tigers of Souheast Asia: The Politics of Media, Technology, and National Development*, Iowa State University Press, Ames, IA.

McLagan, M. (1996) "Computing for Tibet: Virtual politics in the post-Cold War era," in G. Marcus (ed.) *Connected: Engagements with Media*, University Press of Chicago, Chicago.

McLeod, J., Kosciki, G., and Pan, Z. (1991) "On understanding and misunderstanding media effects," in J. Curran and M. Gurevitch (eds) *Mass Media and Society*, Edward Arnold, London.

McMillin, D. C. (2001) "Localizing the global: Television and hybrid programming in India," *International Journal of Cultural Studies*, vol. 4, no. 1, pp. 45–68.

McMillin, D. C. (2002a) "Ideologies of gender on television in India," *Indian Journal of Gender Studies*, vol. 9, no. 1, pp. 1–26.

McMillin, D.C. (2002b) "Choosing commercial television's identities in India: A reception analysis," *Continuum: Journal of Media and Cultural Studies*, vol. 16, no. 1, pp. 135–48.

McMillin, D. C. (2003a) "Television, gender, and labor in the global city," *Journal of Communication*, vol. 53, no. 3, pp. 496–511.

McMillin, D. C. (2003b) "Marriages are made on television: Globalization and national identity in India," in S. Kumar and L. Parks (eds) *Planet TV: A Global Television Studies Reader*, New York University Press, New York.

McMillin, D. C. (2004) "Television's response to the 'women's question' in India," in K. Prasad (ed.) *Communication and Empowerment of Women: Strategies and Policy Insights from India*, vol. 1, The Women's Press, New Delhi.

McMillin, D. C. (2005) "Teen crossings: Emerging cyberpublics in India," in S. Mazarella (ed.) *Girl Wide Web: Girls, the Internet, and the Negotiation of Identity*, Peter Lang Publishers, New York.

McMillin, D. C. (2006) "Outsourcing identities: Call centers and cultural transformation in India," *Economic and Political Weekly*, vol. 41, no. 3, pp. 235–41.

McMillin, D. C. (forthcoming) "Youth culture, gender, and television in India," *TelevIZIon*, Internationales Zentralinstitut für das Jugend- und Bildungsfernsehen.

McPhail, T. L. (2002) *Global Communication: Theories, Stakeholders, and Trends*, Allyn and Bacon, Boston.

McRobbie, A. (1982) "The politics of feminist research: Between talk, text and action," *Feminist Review*, vol. 12, pp. 46–57.

McRobbie, A. (1994) *Postmodernism and Popular Culture*, Routledge, New York and London.

Melkote, S. R. (1991) *Communication for Development in the Third World: Theory and Practice*, Sage, Newbury Park, CA.

Melkote, S. R., Sanjay, B. P., and Ahmed, S. A. (1998) "Use of STAR TV and Doordarshan in India: An audience-centered case-study of Chennai City," in S. R. Melkote, P. Shields, and B. C. Agarwal (eds) *International Satellite Broadcasting in South Asia*, University Press of America, Lanham, MD.

Mennell, S. (1990) "The globalization of human society as a very long-term social process: Elias's theory," in M. Featherstone (ed.) *Global Culture: Nationalism, Globalization and Modernity*, Sage, London and New Delhi.

Mensah-Kutin, R. (1994) "The WEDNET initiative: A sharing experience between researchers and rural women," in P. Riaño (ed.) *Women in Grassroots Communication: Furthering Social Change*, Sage, Thousand Oaks, CA.

Meyer, A. G. (1985) "Feminism, socialism and nationalism in Eastern Europe," in S. L. Wolchik and A. G. Meyer (eds) *Women, State, and Party in Eastern Europe*, Duke University Press, Durham, NC.

Meyrowitz, J. (1985) *No Sense of Place: The Impact of Electronic Media on Social Behavior*, Oxford University Press, New York.

Mies, M. (1983) "Towards a methodology for feminist research," in G. Bowles and R. Klein (eds) *Theories of Women's Studies*, Routledge and Kegan Paul, London.

Mies, M. (1996) "Liberating women, liberating knowledge: Reflections on two decades of feminist action research," *Atlantis*, vol. 21, no. 1, pp. 10–24.

Mignolo, W. D. and Schiwy, F. (2002) "Beyond dichotomies: Translation/transculturation and the colonial difference," in E. Mudimbe-Boyi (ed.) *Beyond Dichotomies: Histories, Identities, Cultures, and the Challenge of Globalization*, State University of New York Press, Albany, NY.

Miller, D. (1994) *Modernity: An Ethnographic Approach*, Berg Publishers, Oxford.

Miller, M. and Darling, J. (1997) "The eye of the tiger: Emilio Azcarraga and the Televisa Empire," in W. A. Orme, Jr (ed.) *A Culture of Collusion: An Inside Look at the Mexican Press*, Lynne Reiner, Boulder, CO.

Minh-ha, T. (1987) "Not you/like you: Post-colonial women and the interlocking questions of identity and difference," *Inscriptions*, vol. 3, no. 4.

Minh-ha, T. (1989) *Woman, Native, Other: Writing Postcoloniality and Feminism*, Indiana University Press, Bloomington, IN.

Mitra, A. (1993) *Television and Popular Culture in India*, Sage, New Delhi.

Mitra, A. (2004) "Voices of the marginalized on the internet: Examples from a website for women of South Asia," *Journal of Communication*, pp. 492–510.

Mlama, P. (1994) "Reinforcing existing indigenous communication skills: The use of dance in Tanzania," in P. Riaño (ed.) *Women in Grassroots Communication: Furthering Social Change*, Sage, Thousand Oaks, CA.

Modleski, T. (1982) *Loving with a Vengeance: Mass Produced Fantasies for Women*, Methuen, London.

Modleski, T. (1986) "Introduction," in T. Modleski (ed.) *Studies in Entertainment: Critical Approaches to Mass Culture*, Indiana University Press, Bloomington, IN.

Mohammadi, A. (1997) "Development communication and the globalization process in the developing world," in A. Mohammadi (ed.) *International Communication and Globalization*, Sage, London, Thousand Oaks, CA, and New Delhi.

Mohanty, C. T. (1987) "Feminist encounters: Locating the politics of experience," *Copyright*, vol. 1, pp. 30–44.

Mohanty, C. T. (2003) *Feminism Without Borders: Decolonizing Theory, Practicing Solidarity*, Duke University Press, Durham, NC.

Mongia, P. (1996) "Introduction," in P. Mongia (ed.) *Contemporary Postcolonial Theory: A Reader*, Oxford University Press, Oxford.

Moran, A. (1998) *Copycat TV: Globalisation, Program Formats and Cultural Identity*, University of Luton Press, Luton.

Moran, A. (2004) "Television formats in the world/the world of television formats," in A. Moran and M. Keane (eds) *Television across Asia: Television Industries, Programme Formats and Globalization*, Routledge Curzon, London and New York.

Moran, A. and Keane, M. (2004) "Joining the circle," in A. Moran and M. Keane (eds) *Television across Asia: Television Industries, Programme Formats and Globalization*, Routledge Curzon, London and New York.

Morley, D. (1980) *The "Nationwide" Audience*, BFI, London.

Morley, D. (1986) *Family Television: Cultural Power and Domestic Leisure*, Comedia/Routledge, London.

Morley, D. (1992) *Television, Audiences and Cultural Studies*, Routledge, London and New York.

Morley, D. (1994) "Postmodernism: The highest stage of cultural imperialism," in M. Perryman (ed.) *Altered States: Postmodernism, Politics, Culture*, Lawrence and Wishart, London.

Morley, D. (1996) "The geography of television: Ethnography, communications, and community," in J. Hay, L. Grossberg, and E. Wartella (eds) *The Audience and Its Landscape*, Westview Press, Boulder, CO.

Morley, D. (2003) "Where the global meets the local: Notes from the sitting room," in L. Parks and S. Kumar (eds) *Planet TV: A Global Television Reader*, New York University Press, New York.

Morley, D. and Robins, K. (1995) *Spaces of Identity: Global Media, Electronic Landscapes and Cultural Boundaries*, Routledge, New York.

Morley, D. and Silverstone, R. (1990) "Domestic communications: Technologies and meanings," *Media, Culture and Society*, vol. 12, no. 1, pp. 31–55.

Mowlana, H. (1996) *Global Communication in Transition: The End of Diversity?* Sage, Thousand Oaks, CA.

Mudibme-Boyi, E. (2002) *Beyond Dichotomies: Histories, Identitities, Cultures, and the Challenge of Globalization*, State University of New York, Albany, NY.

Mukherjee, A. P. (1996) "Interrogating postcolonialism: Some uneasy conjectures," in H. Trivedi and M. Mukherjee (eds) *Interrogating Post-Colonialism: Theory, Text and Context*, Rashtrapathi Nivas, Shimla.

Muñoz, S. (1994) "Notes for reflection: Popular women and uses of mass media," in P. Riaño (ed.) *Women in Grassroots Communication: Furthering Social Change*, Sage, Thousand Oaks, CA.

Murdock, G. (1995) "Across the great divide: Cultural analysis and the condition of democracy," *Critical Studies in Mass Communication*, vol. 12, pp. 89–100.

Murdock, G. (1997) "Thin descriptions: Questions of method in cultural analysis," in J. McGuigan (ed.) *Cultural Methodologies*, Sage, London.

Murdock, G. and Golding, P. (1977) "Capitalism, communications and class relations," in J. Curran, M. Gurevitch and J. Woollacott (eds) *Mass Communications and Society*, Edward Arnold, London.

Murphy, P. (1999) "Doing audience ethnography: A narrative account of establish-ing ethnographic identity and locating interpretive communities in fieldwork," *Qualitative Inquiry*, vol. 5, no. 4, pp. 479–504.

Murphy, P. (2003) "Chasing echoes: Cultural reconversion, self-representation and mediascapes in Mexico," in P. D. Murphy and M. W. Kraidy (eds) *Global Media Studies: Ethnographic Perspectives*, Routledge, New York and London.

Murphy, P. (2005) "Fielding the study of reception: Notes on 'negotiation' for global media studies," *Popular Communication*, vol. 3, no. 3, pp. 167–80.

Murphy, P. and Kraidy, M. (2003) "Towards an ethnographic approach to global media studies," in P. D. Murphy and M. W. Kraidy (eds) *Global Media Studies: Ethnographic Perspectives*, Routledge, New York and London.

Nairn, T. (1977) *The Break-up of Britain*, New Left Books, London.

Nelson, B. and Chowdhury, N. (eds) (1994) *Women in Politics World-wide*, Yale University Press, New Haven, CT.

Ngolet, F. (2000) "Ideological manipulations and political longevity: The power of Omar Bongo in Gabon since 1967," *African Studies Review*, vol 43, no. 2, pp. 55–71.

Nightingale, V. (1986) "What's happening to audience research?," *Media Information Australia*, vol. 39, pp. 21–2.

Nightingale, V. (1990) "Women as audiences," in *Television and Women's Culture: The Politics of the Popular*, Sage, London.

Nightingale, V. (1993) "What's 'ethnographic' about ethnographic audience research?" in J. Frow and M. Morris (eds) *Australian Cultural Studies*, University of Illinois Press, Urbana Champagne, IL.

Nightingale, V. (1996) *Studying Audiences: The Shock of the Real*, Routledge, New York.

Nyamnjoh, F. B. (2004) "Global and local trends in media ownership and control: Implications for cultural creativity in Africa," in W. Van Binsbergen and R. Van Dijk (eds) *Situating Globality: African Agency in the Appropriation of Global Culture*, Brill, Boston and Leiden.

Ohmae, K. (1995) *The End of the Nation State: The Rise and Fall of Regional Economies*, Harper Collins, London.

Okely, J. (1992) "Anthropology and autobiography: Participatory experience and embodied knowledge," in J. Okely and H. Callaway (eds) *Anthropology and Autobiography* Routledge, New York.

Oloyede, B. (1996) *Press Freedom in Nigeria: A Critical Analysis of Salient Issues*, Kunle Alayande Printing and Publishing Company, Abeokuta.

Olson, S. R. (1999) *Hollywood Planet: Global Media and the Competitive Advantage of Narrative Transparency*, Lawrence Erlbaum Associates, Mahwah, NJ.

Ong, A. (1987) *Spirits of Resistance and Capitalist Discipline: Factory Women in Malaysia*, State University of New York Press, Albany, NY.

Paik, H. and Comstock, G. (1994) "The effects of television violence on anti-social behavior: A meta-analysis," *Communication Research*, vol. 21, pp. 516–46.

Papa, M. J., Singhal, A., Law, S., Pant, S., Sood, S., Rogers, E. M., and Shefner-Rogers, C. L. (2000) "Entertainment-education and social change: An analysis of parasocial interaction, social learning, collective efficacy, and paradoxical communication," *Journal of Communication*, Autumn, pp. 31–55.

Paredes, A. (1993) "Folk medicine and the intercultural jest," in R. Bauman (ed.) *Folklore and Culture on the Texas-American Border*, Unversity of Texas, Center of Mexican-American Studies, Texas.

Park, M-J., Kim, C-N., and Sohn, B-W. (2000) "Modernization, globalization, and the powerful state: The Korean media," in J. Curran and M-J. Park (eds) *De-westernizing Media Studies*, Routledge, London and New York.

Parry, B. (1996) "Resistance theory/theorizing resistance, or two cheers for nativism," in P. Mongia (ed.) *Contemporary Postcolonial Theory*, Oxford University Press, New Delhi.

Patai, D. (1991) "Sick and tired of scholars' nouveau solipsism," *Chronicle of Higher Education*, vol 40, no. 25, p. A52.

Peterson, V. (ed.) (1992) *Gendered States: Feminist (Re)Visions of International Relations Theory*, Lynne Reiner, Boulder, CO.

Pieterse, J. N. and Parekh, B. (eds) (1995) *The Decolonization of Imagination: Culture, Knowledge and Power*, Zed Books, London and New Jersey.

Pityana, N. B. (2000) "South Africa's inquiry into racism in the media: The role of national institutions in the promotion and protection of human rights," *African Affairs*, vol. 99, no. 397, pp. 525–32.

Prakash, G. (1990) "Writing post-orientalist histories of the Third World: Perspectives from Indian historiography," *Comparative Studies in Society and History*, vol. 32, no. 2, pp. 383–408.

Pratt, M. L. (2002) "Beyond dichotomies: Communicative action and cultural hegemony," in E. Mudimbe-Boyi (ed.) *Beyond Dichotomies: Histories, Identitities, Cultures, and the Challenge of Globalization*, State University of New York Press, Albany, NY.

Press, A. and Cole, E. R. (1999) *Speaking of Abortion: Television and Authority in the Lives of Women*, University of Chicago Press, Chicago.

Press, A. (1991) *Women Watching Television: Gender, Class, and Generation in the American Television Experience*, University of Pennsylvania Press, Philadelphia, PA.

Price, M. E. (1995) *Television, the Public Sphere and National Identity*, Oxford University Press, Oxford.

Protz, M. (1994) "Understanding women's grassroots experiences in producing and manipulating media," in P. Riaño (ed.) *Women in Grassroots Communication: Furthering Social Change*, Sage, Thousand Oaks, CA.

Pye, L. (1963) *Communication and Political Development*, Princeton University Press, Princeton, NJ.

Radway, J. (1984) *Reading the Romance*, University of North Carolina Press: Chapel Hill, NC.

Radway, J. (2001) "Readers and their romances," in J. L. Machor and P. Goldstein (eds) *Reception Theory: From Literary Theory to Cultural Studies*, Routledge, New York and London.

Rajagopal, A. (1996) "Mediating modernity: Theorizing reception on a non-western society," *The Communication Review*, vol. 1, p. 4, pp. 441–69.

Rajagopal, A. (2001) *Politics after Television: Hindu Nationalism and the Reshaping of the Public in India*, Cambridge University Press, Cambridge.

Rao, L. (1987) "Medium and the message: An Indian experience," in N. Jayaweera and S. Amunugama (eds) *Rethinking Development Communication*, AMIC, Singapore.

Reddy, P. (1995) "Opposition MPs want Star TV to close shop," *The Hindu*, 5 May, p. 2.

Renan, E. ([1947] 1990) "Qu'est-ce qu'une nation?/What is a nation?" In H. K. Bhabha (ed.) *Nation and Narration*, Routledge, New York and London.

Riaño, P. (ed.) (1994) *Women in Grassroots Communication*, Sage, Thousand Oaks, CA.

Robertson, R. (1990) "Mapping the global condition: Globalization as the central concept," in M. Featherstone (ed.) *Global Culture: Nationalism, Globalization and Modernity*, Sage, London and New Delhi.

Robins, K. (1997) "What in the world is going on?" in P. Du Gay (ed.) *Production of Culture/Cultures of Production*, Sage, London.

Rodriguez, C. (1994) "A process of identity deconstruction: Latin American women producing video stories," in P. Riaño (ed.) *Women in Grassroots Communication*, Sage, Thousand Oaks, CA.

Rodriguez, C. (2003) "The bishop and his star: Citizen's communication in Southern Chile," in N. Couldry and J. Curran (eds) *Contesting Media Power: Alternative Media in a Networked World*, Rowman and Littlefield Publishers, Inc., Lanham, MD.

Rofel, L. (1999) "Museum as women's space: Displays of gender in post-Mao China," in M. Yang (ed.) *Spaces of Their Own: Women's Public Sphere in Transnational China*, University of Minnesota Press, Minneapolis, MN.

Rogers, E. (1962) *Diffusion of Innovations*, Free Press, New York.

Rogers, E. and Shoemaker, F. F. (1971) *Communication of Innovations: A Cross-cultural Approach*, Free Press, New York.

Rogers, E. and Svenning, L. (1969) *Modernisation among Peasants: The Impact of Communication*, Holt, Rinehart, and Winston, New York.

Rønning, H. and Kupe, T. (2000) "The dual legacy of democracy and authoritarianism: The media and the state in Zimbabwe," in J. Curran and M-J. Park (eds) *De-westernizing Media Studies*, Routledge, London and New York.

Roome, D. M. (1999) "Global versus local: 'Audience-as-public' in South African situation comedy," *International Journal of Cultural Studies*, vol. 2, no. 3, pp. 307–28.

Ruiz, C. (1994) "Losing fear: Video and radio productions of native Aymara women in Bolivia," in P. Riaño (ed.) *Women in Grassroots Communication*, Sage, Thousand Oaks, CA.

Ryanto, T. (1998) "Homegrown hits on TV," *Variety* 30 Nov.–6 Dec., no. 30.

Said, E. (1978) *Orientalism*, Vintage Books, New York.

Samarajiwa, R. (1987) "The murky beginnings of the communication and development field," in N. Jayaweera and S. Amunugama (eds) *Rethinking Development Communication*, The Asian Mass Communication and Information Center, Singapore.

Sangari, K. and Vaid, S. (eds) (1989) *Recasting Women: Essays in Colonial History*, Kali for Women, New Delhi.

Sardar, Z. (1993) "Paper, printing and compact discs: The making and unmaking of Islamic culture," *Media, Culture and Society*, vol. 15, no. 1, pp. 43–59.

Sassen, S. (1996) "Whose city is it? Globalization and the formation of new claims," *Public Culture*, vol. 8, pp. 205–23.

Saussure, F. de (1966) "Arbitrary social values and the linguistic sign," in C. Bally and A. Sechehaye (eds) *Course in General Linguistics*, McGraw-Hill, New York.

Schiller, H. I. (1969) *Mass Communications and American Empire*, Augustus M. Kelley, New York.

Schiller, H. I. (1976) *Communication and Cultural Domination*, International Arts and Sciences Press, White Plains, NY.

Schiller, H. I. (1989) *Culture Inc.: The Corporate Takeover of Public Expression*, Oxford University Press: New York.

Schiller, H. I. (1996) *Information Inequality: The Deepening Social Crisis in America*, Routledge, New York.

Schiller, H. I. (1998) "Striving for communication dominance: A half-century review," in D. K. Thussu (ed.) *Electronic Empires: Global Media and Local Resistance*, Arnold, London and New York.

Schiller, H. I. (2000) "The social context of research and theory," in *Consuming Audiences? I.* Hagen and J. Wasko (eds) *Production and Reception in Media Research*, Hampton Press, Cresskill, NJ.

Schramm, W. (1964) *Mass Media and National Development: The Role of Information in the Developing Countries*, Stanford University Press, Standford, CA.

Schrøder, K. C. (1994) "Audience semiotics, interpretive communities and the 'ethnographic turn' in media research," *Media, Culture and Society*, vol. 16, pp. 337–47.

Schudson, M. (1996) "The sociology of news production revisited," in J. Curran and M. Gurevitch (eds) *Mass Media and Society*, Arnold, London.

Schwarz, H. (2000) "Mission impossible: Introducing postcolonial studies in the US academy," in H. Schwarz and S. Ray (eds) *A Companion to Postcolonial Studies*, Blackwell Publishers, Malden, MA.

Servaes, J., Jacobson, T. L., and White, S. A. (eds) (1996) *Participatory Communication for Social Change*, Sage, Thousand Oaks, CA.

Seton-Watson, H. (1977) *Nations and States: An Enquiry into the Origins of Nations and the Politics of Nationalism*, Westview Press, Boulder, CO.

Shalin, D. N. (1986) "Romanticism and the rise of sociological hermeneutics," *Social Research*, vol. 53, no. 1, pp. 77–123.

Sheridan, M. (1984) "The life history method," in M. Sheridan and J. W. Salaff (eds) *Lives: Chinese Working Women*, Indiana University Press, Bloomington, IN.

Shih, S. (1999) "Gender and a geopolitics of desire: The seduction of mainland women in Taiwan and Hong Kong media," in M. Yang (ed.) *Spaces of Their Own: Women's Public Sphere in Transnational China*, University of Minnesota Press, Minneapolis, MN.

Shohat, E. and Stam, R. (1994) *Unthinking Eurocentrism: Multiculturalism and the Media*, Routledge, New York.

Shohat, E. (1996) "Notes on the postcolonial," in P. Mongia (ed.) *Contemporary Postcolonial Theory*, Oxford University Press, New Delhi.

Shome, R. and Hegde, R. S. (2002) "Postcolonial approaches to communication: Charting the terrain, engaging the intersections," *Communication Theory*, vol. 12, no. 3, pp. 249–70.

Siebert F., Peterson, T., and Schramm, W. (1956) *Four Theories of the Press*, University of Illinois Press, Urbana, IL.

Silk, M. (2002) "'Bangsa Malaysia': Global sport, the city and the mediated refurbishment of local identities," *Media, Culture and Society*, vol. 24, pp. 775–94.

Simpson, C. (1994) *Science of Coercion: Communication Research and Psychological Warfare*, BFI Publishing, London.

Sinclair, J. (1990) "Neither West nor Third World: The Mexican television industry within the NWICO debate," *Media, Culture and Society*, vol. 12, no. 3, pp. 343–60.

Sinclair, J. (1998) "Culture as a 'market force': Corporate strategies in Asian skies," in S. R. Melkote, P. Shields, and B. C. Agarwal (eds) *International Satellite Broadcasting in South Asia*, University Press of America, Lanham, MD.

Sinclair, J., Jacka, E., and Cunningham, S. (1996) "Peripheral vision," in J. Sinclair, E. Jacka, and S. Cunningham (eds) *New Patterns in Global Television: Peripheral Vision*, Oxford University Press, New York.

Singhal, A. and Rogers, E. (1999) *Entertainment-Education: A Communication Strategy for Social Change*, L. Erlbaum Associates, Mahwah, NJ.

Skuse, A. (2002) "Vagueness, familiarity and social realism: Making meaning of radio soap opera in South-east Afghanistan," *Media, Culture and Society*, vol. 24, no. 3, pp. 409–27.

Slemon, S. (1996) "Unsettling the empire: Resistance theory for the Second World," in P. Mongia (ed.) *Contemporary Postcolonial Theory*, Oxford University Press, New Delhi.

Smart, B. (1993) *Postmodernity*, Routledge, London.

Smith, A. (1986) *The Ethnic Origins of Nations*, Blackwell, Oxford.

Sokolov, R. (1991) *Why We Eat What We Eat: How the Encounter Between the New World and the Old Changed the Way Everyone on the Planet Eats*, Touchstone, New York.

Soyinka, W. (1994) "Culture, memory, and development," in I. Serageldin and J. Taboroff (eds) *Culture and Development in Africa*, The World Bank, Washington, DC.

Sparks, C. (1998) *Communism, Capitalism, and the Mass Media*, Sage, London.

Spitulnik, D. (2002) "Mobile machines and fluid audiences: Rethinking reception through Zambian radio culture," in F. D. Ginsburg, L. Abu-Lughod, and B. Larkin (eds) *Medai Worlds*, University of California Press, Berkeley, CA.

Spivak, G. C. (1987) *In Other Worlds: Essays in Cultural Politics*, Methuen, New York.

Spivak, G. C. (1988a) "Can the subaltern speak?," in C. Lemert (ed.) *Social Theory: The Multicultural and Classic Readings*, Westview Press, Boulder, CO.

Spivak, G. C. (1988b) "Subaltern studies: Deconstructing historiography," in R. Guha and G. C. Spivak (eds) *Selected Subaltern Studies*, Oxford University Press, New York.

Spivak, G. C. (1996) "Poststructuralism, marginality, postcoloniality and value," in P. Mongia (ed.) *Contemporary Postcolonial Theory*, Oxford University Press, Oxford.

Sreberny, A. (2000) "Television, gender, and democratization in the Middle East," in J. Curran and M-J. Park (eds) *De-westernizing Media Studies*, Routledge, London and New York.

Sreberny-Mohammadi, A. (1997) "The many faces of cultural imperialism," in P. Golding and P. Harris (eds) *Beyond Cultural Imperialism*, Sage, London.

Sreberny-Mohammadi, A. and Mohammadi, A. (1994) *Small Media, Big Revolution: Communication, Culture, and the Iranian Revolution*. University of Minneapolic Press: Minneapolis, MN.

Srinivas, L. (2002) "The active audience: Spectatorship, social relations and the experience of cinema in India," *Media, Culture and Society*, vol. 24, no. 2, pp. 155–73.

Staff (1998) "Suharto approves Indonesia Broadcasting Bill," *Asia Pulse*, 6 Oct., p. 4.

Star TV Annual Report (1996) *Vision into Reality*, Star TV.

Steeves, L.H. (1993) "Creating imagined communities: Development communication and the challenge of feminism," *Journal of Communication*, vol. 43, no. 3, pp. 218–29.

Stevenson, R. L. (1994) *Global Communication in the Twenty-First Century*, Longman, New York and London.

Stewart, S. (1993) *On Longing: Narratives of the Miniature, the Gigantic, the Souvenir, the Collection*, Duke University Press, Durham, NC.

Straubhaar, J. D. (1991) "Beyond media imperialism: Asymmetrical interdependence and cultural proximity," *Critical Studies in Mass Communication*, vol. 8, pp. 39–59.

Strauss, C. L. (1963) *Structural Anthropology*, Basic Books, New York.

Strelitz, L. (2003) "Where the global meets the local: South African youth and their experience of global media," in P. D. Murphy and M. W. Kraidy (eds) *Global Media Studies: Ethnographic Perspectives*, Routledge, New York and London.

Strelitz, L. (2004) "Against cultural essentialism: Media reception among South African youth," *Media, Culture and Society*, vol. 26, no. 5, pp. 625–41.

Sudhir, P. (1993) "Colonialism and the vocabularies of dominance," in T. Niranjana, P. Sudhir, and V. Dhareshwar (eds) *Interrogating Modernity: Culture and Colonialism in India*, Seagull, Calcutta.

Suleri, S. (1996) "Woman skin deep: Feminism and the postcolonial condition," in P. Mongia (ed.) *Contemporary Postcolonial Theory: A Reader*, Oxford University Press, Oxford.

Sunder Rajan, R. (1993) "The subject of *Sati*," in T. Niranjana, P. Sudhir, and V. Dhareshwar (eds) *Interrogating Modernity: Culture and Colonialism in India*, Seagull, Calcutta.

Suroor, H. (1995) "Prime time still for DD," *The Times of India*, 15 March, p. 7.

Sutton, C. (ed.) (1995) *Feminism, Nationalism, and Militarism*, Association for Feminist Anthropology/American Anthropological Association, Arlington, VA.

Sutton, R. A. (2003) "Local, global, or national? Popular music on Indonesian television," in L. Parks and S. Kumar (eds) *Planet TV: A Global Television Reader*, New York University Press, New York.

Swami, P. (1997) "A TV debate: Questions of broadcast policy," *Frontline*, vol. 14, no. 3, pp. 10–12.

Tanner, E. (2001) "Chilean conversations: Internet forum participants debate August Pinochet's detention," *Journal of Communication*, vol. 51, no. 2, pp. 383–403.

Tehranian, M. (1999) *Global Communication and World Politics: Domination, Development and Discourse*, Lynne Reiner, London.

Tehranian, M. and Tehranian, K. K. (1997) "Taming modernity: Towards a new paradigm," in A. Mohammadi (ed.) *International Communication and Globalization*, Sage, London, Thousand Oaks, CA, and New Delhi.

Tharu, S. and Niranjana, T. (1996) "Problems for a contemporary theory of gender," in S. Amin and D. Chakrabarthy (eds) *Subaltern Studies IX: Writings on South Asian History and Society*, Oxford University Press, New Delhi.

Thom, A. (1990) "Tribes within nations," in H. K. Bhabha (ed.) *Nation and Narration*, Routledge, New York and London.

Thomas, A. O. and Kumar, K. J. (2004) "Copied from without and cloned from within: India in the global television format business," in A. Moran and M. Keane (eds) *Television across Asia: Television Industries, Programme Formats and Globalization*, RoutledgeCurzon, London and New York.

Thompson, E. P. (1963) *The Making of the English Working Class*, Vintage, New York.

Thompson, J. B. (1990) *Ideology and Modern Culture*, Stanford University Press, Stanford, CA.

Thussu, D.K. (1998) "Localising the global – Zee TV in India," in D. K. Thussu (ed.) *Electronic Empires: Global Media and Local Resistance*, Arnold, London and New York.

Thussu, D. K. (2000) *International Communication: Continuity and Change*, Arnold, London.

The Times of India (Bangalore), "Midnight session not for TNC ad gimmicks: Elders," 14 August 1997, pp. 7, 11.

Tomaselli, G. T, and Teer-Tomaselli, R. (2003) "New nation: Anachronistic Catholicism and liberation theology," in N. Couldry and J. Curran (eds) *Contesting Media Power: Alternative Media in a Networked World*, Rowman and Littlefield Publishers, Inc., Lanham, MD.

Tomlinson, J. (1991) *Cultural Imperialism*, Johns Hopkins University Press, Baltimore, MD.

Tomlinson, J. (1997) "Cultural globalization and cultural imperialism," in A. Mohammadi (ed.) *International Communication and Globalization*, Sage, London, Thousand Oaks, CA, and New Delhi.

Tomlinson, J. (2003) "Media imperialism," in L. Parks and S. Kumar (eds) *Planet TV: A Global Television Reader*, New York University Press, New York.

Trivedi, H. (1996) "India and post-colonial discourse," in H. Trivedi and M. Mukherjee (eds) *Interrogating Post-Colonialism: Theory, Text and Context*, Rashtrapathi Nivas, Shimla.

Trouillot, M-R. (2002) "Modernity and periphery: Toward a global and relational analysis," in E. Mudimbe-Boyi (ed.) *Beyond Dichotomies: Histories, Identitities, Cultures, and the Challenge of Globalization*, State University of New York Press, Albany, NY.

Tufte, T. (2000) "The popular forms of hope: About the force of fiction among TV audiences in Brazil," in I. Hagen and J. Wasko (eds) *Consuming Audiences? Production and Reception in Media Research*, Hampton Press, Cresskill, NJ.

Tunstall, J. and Machin, D. (1999) *The Anglo American Media Connection*, Oxford University Press, New York.

Turner, B. S. (1990) "The two faces of sociology: Global or national?" in M. Featherstone (ed.) *Global Culture: Nationalism, Globalization and Modernity*, Sage, London and New Delhi.

Turner, G. (1990) *British Cultural Studies*, Unwin Hyman, London.

Turner, T. (2002) "Representation, politics, and cultural imagination in indigenous video: General points and Kayapo examples," in F. D. Ginsburg, L. Abu-Lughod, and B. Larkin (eds) *Media Worlds*, University of California Press, Berkeley, CA.

Unnikrishnan, N. and Bajpai, S. (1996) *The Impact of Television Advertising on Children*, Sage, New Delhi.

Van Binsbergen, W., Van Dijk, R. and Gewald, J-B. (2004) "Situating globality: African agency in the appropriation of global culture," in W. Van Binsbergen and R. Van Dijk (eds) *Situating Globality: African Agency in the Appropriation of Global Culture*, Brill, Boston and Leiden.

Van der Veer, P. (1997) *Religious Nationalism: Hindus and Muslims in India*, University of California Press, Berkeley, CA.

Van Dijk, R. (2004) "'Beyond the rivers of Ethiopia,': Pentecostal pan-Africanism and Ghanian identities in the transnational domain," in W. Van Binsbergen and R. Van Dijk (eds) *Situating Globality: African Agency in the Appropriation of Global Culture*, Brill, Boston and Leiden.

Van Maanen, J. (1988) *Tales of the Field: On Writing Ethnography*, University of Chicago Press, Chicago.

Van Zoonen, L. (1994) *Feminist Media Studies*. Sage, London and New Delhi.

Verdery, K. (1994) "From parent-state to family patriarchs: Gender and nation in contemporary Eastern Europe," *East European Politics and Societies*, vol. 8, no. 2.

Vijaykumar, T. (1996) "Post-colonialism or postcolonialism? Re-locating the hyphen," in H. Trivedi and M. Mukherjee (eds) *Interrogating Post-Colonialism: Theory, Text and Context*, Rashtrapathi Nivas, Shimla.

Vickers, J. (2002) "Methodologies for scholarship about women," in V. Dhruvarajan and J. Vickers (eds) *Gender, Race, and Nation: A Global Perspective*, University of Toronto Press, Toronto.

Vickers, J. and Dhruvarajan, V. (2002) "Gender, race, and nation," in V. Dhruvarajan and J. Vickers, (eds) *Gender, Race, and Nation: A Global Perspective*, University of Toronto Press, Toronto.

Vilanilam, J. (1989. "Television advertising and the Indian poor," *Media, Culture and Society*, vol. 11, pp. 485–97.

Visweswaran, K. (1996) "Small speeches, subaltern gender: nationalist ideology and its historiography," in S. Amin and D. Chakrabarthy (eds) *Subaltern Studies IX: Writings on South Asian History and Society*, Oxford University Press, New Delhi.

Waisbord, S. (2000) "Media in South America: Between the rock of the state and the hard place of the market," in J. Curran and M-J. Park (eds) *De-westernizing Media Studies*, Routledge, London and New York.

Wallerstein, I. (1974) *The Modern World-System: Capitalist Agriculture and the Origins of the World-Capitalist Economy in the Sixteenth Century*, 2 vols, Academic Press, New York.

Wallerstein, I. (1982) "Crisis as transition," in S. Amin et al. (eds) *Dynamics of Global Crisis*, Monthly Review Press, New York.

Wallerstein, I. (1986) "Walter Rodney: The historian spokesman for historical forces," *American Ethnologist*, vol. 12, no. 2, pp. 330–6.

Wallerstein, I. (1990a) "Culture as the ideological battleground of the modern world-system," in M. Featherstone (ed.) *Global Culture: Nationalism, Globalization and Modernity*, Sage, London and New Delhi.

Wallerstein, I. (1990b) "Culture is the world-system: A reply to Boyne," in M. Featherstone (ed.) *Global Culture: Nationalism, Globalization and Modernity*, Sage, London and New Delhi.

Wang, G. (1993) "Satellite television and the future of broadcast television in the Asia-Pacific," *Media Asia*, vol. 20, no. 3, pp. 140–8.

Waterman, D. and Rogers, E. M. (1994) "The economics of television program production and trade in Far East Asia," *Journal of Communication*, vol. 44, no. 3, pp. 89–111.

Weiss, L. (1998) "Globalization and the myth of the powerless state," *New Left Review*, vol. 225, pp. 3–26.

Wilkin, P. (2001) *The Political Economy of Global Communication*, Pluto Press, London.

Williams, B. F. (1996) "Skinfolk, not kinfolk: Comparative reflections on the identity of participant-observation in two field situations," in D. Wolf (ed.) *Feminist Dilemmas in Fieldwork*, Westview, Boulder, CO.

Williams, R. (1958) *Culture and Society, 1780–1950*, Columbia University Press, New York.

Williams, R. (1974) *Television, Technology and Cultural Form*, Collins, London.

Wilson, T. (2001) "On playfully becoming the 'Other': Watching *Oprah Winfrey* on Malaysian television," *International Journal of Cultural Studies*, vol. 4, no. 1, pp. 89–110.

Wolcott, H. F. (1999) *Ethnography: A Way of Seeing*, AltaMira Press, Walnut Creek, CA.

Wolf, D. (1996) "Situating feminist dilemmas in fieldwork," in D. Wolf (ed.) *Feminist Dilemmas in Fieldwork*, Westview, Boulder, CO.

Wolf, M. (1996) "Aterword: Musings from an old gray wolf," in D. Wolf (ed.) *Feminist Dilemmas in Fieldwork*, Westview, Boulder, CO.

Worsley, P. (1990) "Models of the modern world-system," in M. Featherstone (ed.) *Global Culture: Nationalism, Globalization and Modernity*, Sage, London and New Delhi.

Yang, G. (2003) "The Internet and the rise of a transnational Chinese cultural sphere," *Media, Culture and Society*, vol. 25, pp. 469–90.

Yang, M. (1996) "Sacrifice and sexuality: Female media icons and the changing relationship between domestic and public/state spheres in China," paper presented at the annual meeting, American Anthropological Association, San Francisco, California.

Yang, M. (1999) "From gender erasure to gender difference: State feminism, consumer sexuality, and women's public sphere in China," in M. Yang (ed.) *Spaces of Their Own: Women's Public Sphere in Transnational China*, University of Minnesota Press, Minneapolis, MN.

Yang, M. (2002) "Mass media and transnational subjectivity in Shanghai: Notes on (re)cosmopolitanism in a Chinese metropolis," in F. D. Ginsburg, L. Abu-Lughod, and B. Larkin (eds) *Media Worlds*, University of California Press, Berkeley, CA.

Young, R. J. C. (2001) *Postcolonialism: An Historical Introduction*, Blackwell Publishers, Oxford.

Young, R. J. C. (2002) "Reincarnating immigrant biography: On migration and trans-migration," in E. Mudimbe-Boyi (ed.) *Beyond Dichotomies: Histories, Identitities, Cultures, and the Challenge of Globalization*, State University of New York Press, Albany, NY.

Young, R. J. C. (2003) *Postcolonialism: A Very Short Introduction*, Oxford University Press, New York.

Zaharom. N. (2000) "Globalized theories and national controls: The state, the market, and the Malaysian media," in J. Curran and M-J. Park (eds) *De-westernizing Media Studies*, Routledge, London and New York.

Zakaria, F. (2006) "India rising," *Newsweek*, 6 March, pp. 34–42.

Zavella, P. (1996) "Feminist insider dilemmas: Constructing ethnic identity with Chicana informants," in D. Wolf (ed.) *Feminist Dilemmas in Fieldwork*, Westview Press, Boulder, CO.

Zegeye, A. and Harris, R. L. (2003) "Introduction," in A. Zegeye and R. L. Harris (eds) *Media, Identity and the Public Sphere in Post-Apartheid South Africa*, Brill, Leiden and Boston.

Zhao, Y. (2003) "Falun Gong, identity, and the struggle over meaning inside and outside China," in N. Couldry and J. Curran (eds) *Contesting Media Power: Alternative Media in a Networked World*, Rowman and Littlefield, Lanham, MD.

Zhong, Y. (2002) "Debating with muzzled mouths: A case analysis of how control works in a Chinese television debate used for educating youths," *Media, Culture and Society*, vol. 24, no. 1, pp. 27–47.

Zinn, B. M. et al. (2000) *Gender through the Prism of Difference*, Allyn and Bacon, Toronto. Zutshi, S. (1993) "Women, nation, and the outsider in contemporary Hindi Cinema," in T. Niranjana, P. Sudhir, and V. Dhareshwar eds *Interrogating Modernity: Culture and Colonialism in India*, Seagull, Calcutta.

Index